CREATING NEW SCHOOLS

How Small Schools Are Changing
American Education

CREATING NEW SCHOOLS

How Small Schools Are Changing American Education

EVANS CLINCHY, EDITOR

Teachers College, Columbia University
New York and London

Published by Teachers College Press, 1234 Amsterdam Avenue, New York, NY 10027
Copyright © 2000 by Teachers College Press

Chapter 1, The Educationally Challenged American School District © 1998 *Phi Delta Kappan*. Reprinted by permission of the publisher.

Chapter 2, A Journey Toward Autonomy © 1999 *Phi Delta Kappan*. Reprinted by permission of the publisher.

Chapter 4, The State's Role in Shaping a Progressive Education © 1998 *Phi Delta Kappan*. Reprinted by permission of the publisher.

Chapter 12, Can the Odds Be Changed? © 1999 *Phi Delta Kappan*. Reprinted by permission of the publisher.

Library of Congress Cataloging-in-Publication Data

Creating new schools : how small schools are changing American education / Evans Clinchy, editor.
    p. cm.
   Includes bibliographical references and index.
   ISBN 0-8077-3877-8 (cloth) — ISBN 0-8077-3876-X (paper)
    1. School improvement programs—United States. 2. Small schools—United States. I. Clinchy, Evans.
   LB2822.82.C76 2000
   371.01—dc21   99-048170

ISBN 0-8077-3876-X (paper)
ISBN 0-8077-3877-8 (cloth)

Printed on acid-free paper
Manufactured in the United States of America

07 06 05 04 03 02 01 00   8 7 6 5 4 3 2 1

This book is dedicated to five great school superintendents:

William H. Ohrenberger,
Former Superintendent of the Boston Public Schools

Patrick J. Mogan,
Former Superintendent of the Lowell, Massachusetts Public
Schools

George N. Tsapatsaris,
Present Superintendent of the Lowell, Massachusetts Public
Schools

Seymour Fliegel,
Former Deputy Superintendent in New York City's Community
School District Four in East Harlem

and
Harold B. Gores
Former Superintendent of the Newton, Massachusetts Public
Schools and President of Educational Facilities Laboratories Inc.

Contents

Editor's Note

This book is the second in a trilogy of edited books that explore some of the major educational reform issues currently facing our American system of public education.

The first book in the trilogy—*Transforming Public Education: A New Course for America's Future*—was published in 1997 by Teachers College Press and sets forth in general terms a new educational mission and a new organizational structure for this country's public schools.

This second book, *Creating New Schools: How Small Schools Are Changing American Education*, deals in considerable detail with the creation in two of our major urban systems—those of New York City and Boston—of what we might hope to see as the wave of the future: a broad diversity of new, small, strictly public, relatively autonomous schools that can be chosen by parents, students, and a school system's professional staff. Some of these new schools might be public state "charter" schools created independent of any local school district. But the bulk of them are—and should be—created *within* our local districts. These schools, indeed, can and perhaps should be seen as the forerunners of an entirely new and much more democratic American public school system in which *every* school becomes an autonomous school of parent and professional choice.

The creation of these schools, however, is requiring massive changes in the way our local districts are organized and operated. Indeed, these changes add up to a new organizational structure: a new *kind* of public school system. It is this new system that the contributors to this book spell out in some detail.

The third book in this trilogy, entitled *Reforming American Education From the Bottom to the Top* (Heinemann, 1999), deals with the constrictive, authoritarian, and therefore anti-innovative and antidemocratic role played by our institutions of higher education in the attempts to reform the elementary and secondary schools of this country. Indeed, it is possible to argue, as this book does, that true reform and innovation are not going to happen in our elementary and secondary schools unless and until there is an equivalent reform in our colleges and universities. A special editorial section based on this book appeared in *Phi Delta Kappan* in December 1996.

Acknowledgments

The editor would like gratefully to acknowledge the support and encouragement over the years of the editors of *Phi Delta Kappan*: Stanley Elam, Robert Cole and especially Pauline Gough, Bruce Smith, Lise Koben and Terri Hampton. In the case of this book and the two other books in the trilogy, most of the chapters have appeared in that journal either as part of special editorial sections or as individual articles. In short, none of these books would have seen the light of day had not these editors been possessed of their extraordinary editorial brilliance and wisdom.

CHAPTER 1

Introduction: The Educationally Challenged American School District

Evans Clinchy

Pity the poor American school district, trapped between a massive rock and at least one small but growing hard place.

The massive rock is the powerful national educational agenda that was launched in 1983 with the publication of the U.S. Department of Education's widely heralded *A Nation at Risk* report. That document, based largely on national and international test-score data, famously accused the nation's system of public education of being awash in "a tide of mediocrity," therefore posing a severe threat to the present and future economic health of American society. The authoritarian, top-down national education agenda derived from that report is aimed at instituting new national "world-class" academic standards and a system of national tests in all of the nation's schools. This national agenda was codified into national law with the Clinton administration's Goals 2000 legislative program and is currently being implemented throughout the country as state legislatures and state education officials are mandating the program's "world-class" academic standards and "high-stakes" tests for all schools and all students at all grade levels.

The small but growing hard place that also faces our local school districts, however, is a countermovement emerging not from the top down but from the bottom up. Rather than advocating uniform, rigidly imposed, and mandated national or state "standards," national and statewide testing of all students, and therefore pressures for all schools to be roughly the same, the advocates of this movement believe that no single set of imposed academic standards, no set of national or statewide tests, no single, uniform curriculum, no single vision of what a "school" should be could possibly adequately serve the enormous diversity of this country's parents and students. Indeed, that diversity is not only racial, ethnic, social, and geo-

1

graphic but also philosophical—there is simply no agreement among all parents, all teachers, all school administrators, all educational researchers, and all educational thinkers and philosophers about what the "best" or even a "good" education for all students is or could be.

THE GOALS 2000 AGENDA

To deal with the Goals 2000 agenda first, the instigators of the *Nation at Risk* report were and still are legitimately concerned with the sorry history in all too many school districts—and especially urban school districts—of students graduating from high school unable to read or write at minimal levels, of teachers who lack the skills, concern, or drive to reach their students, of the racial pattern of special-education placements and the practice and results of rigid tracking. They wished to issue a national "wake-up" call insisting upon high academic standards for all students, a call that might force weak schools to dramatically improve their performance.

The report therefore went on to advocate a major effort on the part of all local school districts, all state governments, and the federal education establishment to dramatically raise the academic standards and academic achievement-test scores of *all* American students.

This enormous task, the report said, should be pursued by establishing that new set of national "world-class" academic standards in all of the "core" academic disciplines: English, mathematics, science, history, economics, geography, civics, government, foreign languages, and the arts. These new "higher" standards should be accompanied by equally rigorous national (and international) "high-stakes" tests to make sure that all students are meeting these standards. The "high stakes" here are that the results of these tests will be used to determine whether a student can be promoted to the next grade or graduated from high school (thus ending "social promotion" as advocated in President Clinton's 1999 State of the Union address). Those results will also be used to determine whether individual schools are performing up to standard and whether schools thus labeled "failing" will be closed down, "reconstituted," or both.

This powerful standards-based agenda is proposing to raise those academic achievement levels and the scores on standardized tests of all American students by spelling out in considerable detail "what every student in this country should know and be able to do at each grade level" and therefore what all schools and all teachers should teach at each of those grade levels in each of those traditional "core" academic subjects. This agenda also aims at increasing the number of students who obtain high scores on the Scholastic Assessment Test (SAT) and the College Board examinations, thus meeting the academic requirements of the college admissions process so that more students can be admitted either to 2-year community colleges or to 4-year public and private colleges and universities.

This *Nation at Risk*/Goals 2000 agenda for our elementary and secondary schools is currently being adopted in one form or another by every state board and state department of education all across the country, largely with funds supplied by the federal Goals 2000 program and private foundations. Most of those state authorities are adapting to their own purposes the "voluntary" national academic standards and national tests and are in almost every case then mandating them through compulsory state curricular and "high-stakes" testing directives onto local school districts and thence onto every local school. At least one state, Massachusetts, is also imposing directives spelling out the number of *minutes* during the school day teachers should spend as "structured learning time" on each traditional academic subject, even if time must therefore be reduced for recess, lunch, the arts, and physical education.

THE GREAT NATION AT RISK MYTH

The reputed "failure" of the public schools described in *A Nation at Risk*, Goals 2000, and all subsequent and similar criticisms based upon national and international test results, however, has been shown to be largely a myth based on questionable interpretations of the test data (see Berliner & Biddle, 1996).

A more "correct" reading of the test data, these researchers have maintained, suggests that American students actually score quite well on such tests when their scores are compared with those of comparable students in other industrial nations.

This does not demonstrate, of course, that the public schools of this or any other advanced industrial country are doing the job they might or should be doing. Indeed, the range of possibly legitimate criticisms of what is going on in this country's schools is broad and often well founded in deeply disturbing fact.

A SIMULTANEOUS MOVEMENT

However, we are witnessing the emergence of a quite different response to this perceived educational crisis even as this authoritarian, "top-down" Goals 2000 agenda is being put into place. A smaller but growing "bottom-up" movement is aiming at radically democratizing our public school systems through decentralizing the decision-making power in our local school districts down to the level of newly created, small, relatively autonomous but strictly public schools.

This is a movement that began in the 1960s with the creation of two kinds of "alternative" public schools. One set was modeled on the "open," "integrated-day" infant and primary schools in Great Britain. These were both public and private schools in no small measure based upon the ideas of Maria Montessori and John Dewey, and they fostered the "progressive education" movement that flourished briefly in this country during the 1920s and 30s.

The second kind of "alternative" schools were the semiautonomous "magnet" schools created all across the country in the late 1960s and the 1970s, a result of the necessity to desegregate our local systems. That magnet-school movement, in many ways similar to and overlapping the progressive movement, was founded upon four basic educational assumptions. One was the already mentioned belief that the enormous intellectual, social, racial, ethnic, and cultural diversity of the American student population—and especially the urban student population—makes it educationally unwise to insist that all students be required to undergo a single, preestablished, predetermined, and highly academic educational process.

The second assumption was, again, recognition that simply no agreement exists among parents, teachers, school administrators, school board members, educational theorists, and academic scholars on any one, single, best, and only way to educate all children and young people.

The third assumption was the belief that a basic rule that should govern the education of the young is that in any truly democratic society and therefore in any truly democratic system of public education it cannot be the task of any federal government, any state government, or any local school board to impose, as we have all too often done in the past and are now once again doing, a single one and only way of educating on all children and all students and therefore to impose as well a single one and only curriculum and a single one and only set of academic "standards" on all principals, all teachers, all parents.

The fourth assumption was based on the discovery that the desegregation of our local school systems when carried out by court-mandated "forced busing" was creating enormous resistance and was rapidly becoming a national disaster. The experience of riots in Boston when such forced-busing remedies were ordered in 1974 and 1975 served to convince many people, including the federal courts, that this was not a wise policy, either educationally or socially.

A much more productive course, the alternative-and magnet-school advocates believed, was to create a broad diversity of different kinds of schools, different approaches to schooling ranging from very traditional to very untraditional, innovative programs. These were schools consciously designed to match and begin to serve the enormous diversity of the country's students, especially those in the inner city. Those magnet schools were (and often still are) granted a degree of curricular autonomy and were based upon both parent and professional *choice*. Parental choice of these magnet schools, with such choices carefully controlled to produce an integrated student body, allowed desegregation to be accomplished peacefully and at the same time produced significant educational innovation and improvement. These schools, therefore, have led not only to the idea of system-wide *in*-district, strictly *public* school choice but also to the notion of *inter*-district, strictly public school choice.

The current form of the magnet school/decentralization movement—the movement toward creating those new, smaller, autonomous schools—is perhaps best illustrated by the changes that are currently under way in the school systems of two East Coast cities, New York and Boston.

In New York, the movement was spearheaded in the 1970s in East Harlem's Community School District Four by Anthony Alvarado, community district superintendent, and Seymour Fliegel, deputy superintendent, at that time. Another major influence was Deborah Meier, founder of the district's famed Central Park East schools and later also the founder of the Center for Collaborative Education (CCE), an independent organization devoted to assisting teachers and parents throughout the city to establish the new, small, autonomous schools.

A recent study conducted by researchers from the State University of New York at Stony Brook has indicated that the provision of such schools of choice in District Four has led to improved achievement by students in *all* of the district's schools, not just the choice schools.

The broader movement that has grown out of the District Four initiative is now supported not only by the central board of education administration but by the CCE along with other independent institutions such as Theodore Sizer's Coalition of Essential Schools (CES) and an organization similar to CCE called New Visions for Public Schools. It is supported also by the local teachers union, the United Federation of Teachers. The movement has so far created over 100 new, small, theoretically autonomous elementary and secondary schools, with many more now in the planning stages. Some of these new schools have been created by breaking down large schools into smaller, self-contained, autonomous sub-schools. A recent study conducted by the Institute for Education and Social Policy at New York University appears to show that although these schools may cost a bit more per pupil, they are more cost effective in the long run because they have fewer drop-outs and graduate more students in the normal 4-year period (see Ann Cook's Chapter 7 and Beth Lief's Chapter 8).

In Boston, the movement has created 11 small, relatively autonomous "pilot" schools that are currently in operation with 4 more in the planning stages. The 11 operating pilot schools are all assisted by an independent Center for Collaborative Education–Metro Boston (modeled on the New York CCE) and again by the CES, the Boston School Committee, the school system's central administration, and, most notably, the Boston Teachers Union, which was in large measure responsible for their creation (see Robert Pearlman's Chapter 3, and Chapter 2, by Linda Nathan and Larry Myatt).

Not only are all of these schools, like their counterparts in New York, small (ranging from 75 to a maximum of 350 students) so that students, parents, and staff can all get to know each other, but also they represent a wide diversity of different approaches to schooling and are intimately connected to both their parent bodies and civic, business, cultural, and community groups throughout the city.

In Boston this movement has had a long and semi-illustrious history. Those of us ancient enough to remember the educational turmoil of the 1960s, including the alternative-school movement, will recall Boston's first radical experimental venture into this field: the school system's Office of Program Development and its Model Demonstration Sub-system created in 1965 under the courageous leadership of then Superintendent William H. Ohrenberger. I served as the designer and first director of the office, the sub-system, and the school system's Educational Planning Center from 1965 to 1969. The model sub-system consisted of three schools: the Boardman Elementary (which in 1969 became the voluntarily integrated William Monroe Trotter School, one of the first, if not *the* first, such magnet school in the country), the Lewis Junior High (which eventually became the Phillis Wheatley Middle School), and the Pierce High School (which eventually became the Muriel Snowden High School for International Studies).

These "experimental" sub-system schools were all located in the largely African American Roxbury section of the city and thus had entirely African American student bodies. Each of the schools—and the sub-system as a whole—had complete philosophical, curricular, and fiscal autonomy. We could select our teaching staffs from anywhere in the Boston system, and our schools were supported not only by the usual per-pupil funding of all Boston schools but by additional federal money supplied by what is now called Chapter I. The "experiment" we were set up to conduct was the introduction into Boston at all three schools of that open, integrated-day, progressive type of schooling that was being practiced in the British infant and primary schools.

When desegregation came to Boston in 1975, these three schools became the system's (and, like the Trotter, were among the country's) first magnet schools, schools that both minority and majority parents could *choose* because they wanted a particular type of education for their children. It was thus the country's magnet schools that first introduced the twin ideas of curricular autonomy and both parental and professional choice into the contemporary American system of public education.

Unfortunately over the years, those three Boston sub-system/magnet schools—and many others like them throughout the country—gradually lost the autonomy necessary to conduct their experiments and therefore the ability to explore new and more educationally productive ways of educating children. Boston's controlled-choice desegregation plan still allows for parental choice, but in the case of the three sub-system magnets, the school-level autonomy necessary to their carrying out their distinctive educational mission was increasingly nibbled away at by the authoritarian central bureaucracy, which exerted constant pressure on them to revert to the established "norms" of traditional schooling.

And the reason for this failure was also simple: Although the original magnets were created in order (we hoped) to change and improve public education in Boston dramatically, the rigid, hierarchical structure of the central school system bureaucracy remained essentially unchanged, able to respond only with the greatest difficulty to any and all demands for meaningful decentralization and school-level autonomy on the part of individual schools.

THE BIRTH OF THE FACTORY SCHOOL SYSTEM

That typical American top-down, highly centralized school bureaucracy model was put in place roughly 100 years ago not only in Boston and New York but throughout the country as a result of the perceived success of the "scientific industrial management" model introduced into our businesses and industries around the turn of the century by Frederick W. Taylor and his "efficiency expert" associates. "Efficiency" and "low cost" (and the attempt to shield schools from the intrusions of hack politicians intent on giving their relatives and girlfriends jobs in the system) were the order of the day.

As Elwood P. Cubberley, a respected reformer of the day, put it back in 1916:

> Our schools are, in a sense, factories in which the raw products (children) are to be shaped and fashioned into products to meet the various demands of life. The specifications for manufacturing come from the demands of the

twentieth century civilization, and it is the business of the school to build its
pupils to the specifications laid down. This demands good tools, specialized
machinery, continuous measurement of production to see if it is according to
specification, the elimination of waste in manufacture, and a large variety in
the output. (Callahan, 1972, p. 152)

This "factory" approach to organizing and operating a public school
system meant that all members of the system had to be treated as interchangeable cogs in the educational production machine. Everything—and
everyone—in the system had to be standardized: What all teachers were
supposed to teach and how they were supposed to teach it in each of the
standard academic subjects at each grade level (the specifications for manu-
facturing) were spelled out in detail. Standardized achievement tests (the
continuous measurement of production to see if it is according to specification) were devised and administered for all students to make sure they
were learning what they were supposed to learn (thus making sure that
pupils are being built to the specifications laid down). The presently existing maze of authoritarian supervisory bureaucratic rules and regulations
were instituted to make sure that no teacher and no school deviated from
the established task of shaping and fashioning students "into products to
meet the various demands of life" (Callahan, 1972, p. 152).

One perhaps inevitable result of the imposition of this industrial "factory" system was that teachers and administrators did precisely what their
compatriots in industry did, which was to form adversarial unions designed to give some degree of job protection and security to the system's
"workers," although the unions were almost always limited to negotiating about wages, hours, and working conditions. This led to a further set
of limitations on the autonomy and freedom of the schools to innovate, as
the unions strictly enforced uniform rules and regulations about what teachers could and could not do in the schools, almost always including the crip-
pling provision that all teacher vacancies must be filled according to an
applicant's seniority in the system rather than that teacher's fitness for
teaching in a particular school.

The now advocated contemporary form of this system is based not
upon the old industrial factory but upon the sleek, modern, downsized,
technologically advanced global corporation. Whereas the older system
spoke of children as "raw products" and principals and teachers as "fore-
men" and "factory hands," the new model speaks of human beings as
"human resource capital" for the new "information age" economic system.
The new system is concerned with producing human beings who are able
to work well together in the corporate domain, people who are able to solve
problems as they arise and learn new skills as the technology they use be-

comes more complex and competitive, thus enabling the system's products to contribute better to the all-commanding "bottom line" of corporate profit. The language may have become more sophisticated and up-to-date, but the autocratic, antidemocratic ideology of corporate domination and control is essentially unchanged.

Given this authoritarian organizational structure, it is not surprising that most educational "reforms" and "innovations" have over the past 100 or so years met with either subtle or outright hostility and eventually a refusal on the part of the central bureaucracy to allow drastic changes ever to survive in anything like their original, intended forms. This was true of the progressive education reforms of Dewey and his followers in the 1920s, 30s, and 60s, the "curriculum reform" movement of the 1950s and 60s, and the reforms, such as magnet schools, introduced as a result of the civil rights movement and the necessity to desegregate our schools in the 1960s, 70s, and 80s. It has been equally true in recent years of such reforms as those being implemented by the once much heralded New American Schools Development Corporation.

In short, our established system of public education is a system that by its origins and design finds it virtually impossible even to entertain, much less support and sustain, innovation and diversity. It is what one of the great modern educational reformers, Seymour Sarason, has termed an "unrescuable system."

HOWEVER, THE MOVEMENT CONTINUES

Despite the difficulties experienced by the magnet-school/decentralization reformers, the national oppositional ground swell against the traditional authoritarian school system has continued and grown, creating increasing pressures in favor of breaking up and liberally decentralizing—and in some cases simply end-running—those inflexible centralized districts.

Indeed, in addition to the in-district pilot- or alternative-school movement, this still radical idea of professional autonomy and parental choice has created two national movements specifically designed as end-runs. The first of these is the push for *vouchers* that would provide parents with public funds and allow them to send their children to either the public *or private* school of their choice. The other end-run is the movement to create *charter* schools, public schools responsible not to a local school district but to the state.

Vouchers are still embroiled in a controversy over whether it is both legal and wise to allow public money to go to the support of private and, particularly, religious schools. But the charter-school movement is very much alive and spreading throughout just about every state in the union. Indeed, it was the advent in 1993 of charter-school legislation in Massachusetts that compelled the Boston school system to once again entertain the idea of allowing a handful of schools enough autonomy that they could at least appear to be innovative, exciting, in-district challenges to the charter schools. Such competition from charter schools was not welcomed by then Superintendent Lois Harrison-Jones, but with leadership provided by the Boston Teachers Union, the school committee voted to allow six charters to be developed either as new, small schools to be created by people in the system or as reconstituted existing schools, or pilots (again, see the chapters by Pearlman, and by Nathan and Myatt).

In a recent move, the Massachusetts legislature has authorized, in addition to more charters, the creation of 13 state "Horace Mann" schools, that is, in-district charter schools modeled on Boston's pilots that must be approved by the local district and the local union but that are supposed to have the same degree of autonomy granted to the state's charter schools. Several of Boston's pilots are applying for this status (see Dan French's Chapter 4).

ARE THESE TWO NATIONAL MOVEMENTS COMPATIBLE?

These two large national movements—the *Nation at Risk* agenda and the small, autonomous schools decentralization movement—clearly share a deep and honest desire to dramatically improve our system of public education. However, the two movements have also clearly started from quite different philosophical and educational assumptions and therefore have quite different results in mind.

The *Nation at Risk*/Goals 2000 agenda is still at heart a movement based upon the establishment and broad implementation at the state and local levels of some form of those nationally approved, uniform "high" or "world-class" academic standards at all grade levels and a system of national (and comparative international), standardized academic testing. President Clinton has been an especially vigorous advocate of the latter.

The decentralization movement, on the other hand, though ardently devoted to "high learning expectations" and "intellectual rigor," nevertheless believes that the decision-making power as to what will be studied and how it will be studied should be based not on predetermined, uniform standards imposed at the national or state levels but upon high intellectual expectations and curricular standards developed by the staffs and parent bodies of the individual schools. Such programs may often use national and state standards, if these are deemed appropriate to the school's mission, as "frameworks" but not as compulsory, mandated guidelines. The New Visions schools in New York, for instance, stress the need for a rigorous academic curriculum and believe that there can be high standards that enable small schools to work in different ways toward common goals.

Many of the people in the small, autonomous schools movement see the *Nation at Risk* agenda not as a reform strategy but as an educational agenda that simply reinforces the traditional, established, essentially centralized, and thus still basically authoritarian, top-down American educational structure we have had in this country for the past 100 years. It is an agenda, they believe, that rather than espousing fundamental reform instead promotes the continuation of the existing orthodox academic disciplines, the traditional school grade-structures, and the traditional "information and skill transmission" mode of teaching. It thereby continues and strengthens the curricular and organizational straitjacket of our existing school systems, effectively choking off attempts at achieving genuine educational diversity and therefore genuine innovation and reform.

THUS THIS BOOK

The aim of this book is to explore this presently insufficiently examined conflict between these two different and opposing educational agendas. It is a conflict—the dilemma of the rock and the hard place—that is already manifesting itself as a *very* real and troubling circumstance for every local school district in this country and therefore for all parents and all professional staff working in our local public schools.

This conflict between our traditional hierarchical authoritarianism and the democratic diversity represented by the devolution of decision-making power down to the level of the individual school is at present all too often being handled either by papering over the fundamental differences between these two agendas and pretending that somehow the problem will solve itself and disappear or by saying that the new, small schools have the "autonomy" to meet the new mandated standards and their accompanying tests in their own particular educational fashion. Autonomy is thus all too often limited to the relatively superficial aspects of schooling, such as discipline codes, test preparation, school uniforms, the purchase of educational materials, and so on, while leaving the core of education—educational philosophy and curriculum, testing, teaching methodology, staffing, real fiscal power, and so forth—in the hands of the external federal, state, and local school authorities.

In the case of the charter schools in Massachusetts and other states, for instance, there are still serious questions as to whether these schools really do have autonomy from state regulations. In the case of the small, theoretically autonomous pilot or in-district charter schools in New York and Boston, there are likewise serious questions as to whether they are now receiving or will in the future actually receive from their school systems *and* from their states the freedom and the nurturance they need in order to survive and grow to maturity. And perhaps most importantly, it is unknown whether they will be allowed to multiply; that is, whether there will be a true devolution of decision-making power in these systems down to the level of *all* schools in the system. In other words and in the final analysis, the greatest question is whether the concept of small, autonomous schools—both charter and in-district—will be extended throughout these systems and throughout the states so that *every* public school in a school system, and by extension every school in every state in the country, will eventually become a truly autonomous school created by parents and the school system's professional staff, a school that can then be freely chosen by parents and teachers. Any and all such parental and staff choices must, of course, be controlled by admissions and staff-selection guidelines ensuring that poor and minority students and minority staff have equal access to all schools.

What we are proposing to do in this book is to listen carefully to the voices of some of the people who have been, and still are, actually engaged in the enterprise of creating and operating the new, small schools in both New York and Boston. We have asked these people to tell us about and, if possible, describe in some detail such matters as the process by which these schools became "small, autonomous," in-district charter or pilot schools, the nature and extent of their "autonomy," any and all difficulties and triumphs they are currently experiencing with their supervising state and district authorities, what they see as the future prospects of their schools and any and all other schools seeking genuine educational reform in their cities, and the role that their local unions are playing (or are failing to play) in the creation and operation of their schools.

We would in particular, like them to tell us precisely how *autonomy* is defined by their state and school-system bureaucracies and therefore how much and what kinds of autonomy they really do have. For example, are they able to define and then implement their own educational philosophy, even though that philosophy may differ radically from the orthodox, highly academic, "information transmission" philosophy we have had in this country for the past approximately 100 years? As instances, would the "autonomy" granted to such schools allow for the creation and operation of a true Montessori school, or a genuine "open-education," integrated-day, or full-fledged "micro-society" school, or an authentic CES-model high school? Are they as practitioners able to introduce and use an interdisciplinary curriculum that is *not* based upon the traditional "core" academic subject-matter compartments, and can they thus adapt to their own purposes any and all national and state academic "standards" based upon those compartments, and if necessary ignore them? Are they able then to develop their own assessment systems to match their unusual curricula and refuse, for instance, to administer local, state, or national standardized academic achievement tests?

Further, are they able to select their own staff without reference to seniority or centralized placement lists, and can they organize teacher time and work schedules in ways that possibly violate traditional union work rules? Do they have fiscal autonomy such as a lump-sum budget based upon a set of graduated per-pupil costs and, if so, what areas does such fiscal autonomy cover?

We would like them especially to deal with the always perplexing issues of "accountability": the ways in which they and their supervising authorities are attempting to determine whether they are succeeding or failing and what can and should be done about schools that are manifestly failing.

We would then like several of our authors to explore the question of what they see as the necessary changes in the structure of our local and state school systems if their own schools and others like them are to succeed (see in particular Chapter 12 by Deborah Meier and Chapter 13 by Seymour Sarason). In the end, all of us who have contributed to this volume are dedicated to discovering what might shape a truly democratic American public school system in the unpredictable new millennium.

REFERENCES

Berliner, D. C., & Biddle, B. J. (1996). *The manufactured crisis: Myths, fraud, and the attack on America's public schools.* New York: Addison-Wesley.

Callahan, R. E. (1972). *Education and the cult of efficiency.* Chicago: University of Chicago Press.

PART I

Voices from the Front Lines: Boston

EDITOR'S NOTE

The superintendent of schools in Boston, Dr. Thomas W. Payzant, was invited to contribute a chapter to this section of the book, thus giving a "view from the top" as a complementary chapter to Deputy Chancellor Judith Rizzo's chapter on the new, small schools in New York City. Dr. Payzant declined, citing the pressures of work. He also declined to name another person in his central administration to contribute such a chapter.

However, in a joint publication by the Boston Public Schools and the Center for Collaborative Education–Metro Boston entitled "Commitment to Innovation: The Boston Public Schools in Action: A Guide to Boston's Pilot Schools," Dr. Payzant contributed the following "Message From the Superintendent of the Boston Public Schools":

> I am pleased to welcome parents, students, and friends of the Boston Public Schools, to Boston's unique and exciting new centers for educational innovation, known as the Pilot Schools. These schools have been created to explore new approaches to teaching and learning, where students, faculty and administrators are encouraged to test new educational strategies and to share best practices with other schools throughout the city.
>
> Pilot Schools in Boston have a special status as one of the few groups of "in-district charter schools" in the United States that have the support of the local teachers union as an equal partner in their creation. A product of the contract between the Boston Teachers Union and the Boston Public Schools, Pilot Schools have in many cases been designed and are governed by parents, teachers and administrators to provide high quality educational experiences for every student and to develop strong connections between school and community.

CHAPTER 2

A Journey Toward Autonomy

Linda Nathan and Larry Myatt

Fenway is now entering its 16th year as a small public high school in the Boston Public Schools (BPS), its 9th year as a member of the Coalition of Essential Schools (CES), and its 4th year as one of Boston's pilot schools.

When the Boston Teachers Union and the Boston School Committee signed a landmark contract in 1994 that created pilot schools, Fenway made the decision to return a previously awarded state charter in order to become a pilot school. As proposed, Boston's pilot schools were to be comparable to charter schools in terms of the autonomy offered to school leaders, and the idea offered great promise and hope for our school community. This article explores Fenway's progress in its second year as a pilot school in pursuit of the autonomy we felt was required to be a successful school and concludes with a brief discussion of the "lessons learned" as we enter year 3 and the challenges we still face.

FENWAY'S MISSION AND HISTORY

Since Fenway's inception in 1983, the school's dual mission has been to create a dynamic community of learners and to challenge traditional school structures and policies in order to increase student engagement and achievement. Although we started slowly (in 1985, the year of Fenway's first graduating class, only three students took the SAT), we were soon involved in a number of "experiments," spurred by our interest in community collaboration and authentic learning and provoked by the mediocrity of most of our public schools as exposed in Theodore Sizer's *Horace's Compromise* (1984). Within 5 years of our founding, we had piloted an interdisciplinary American studies curriculum, long teaching blocks, an advisory program, performance assessment, and had assembled an ad hoc board of advisors.

We were focused on raising money and finding time for an intense conversation about teaching and learning, and the organized abandonment of inherited policies, structures, and incentives that we knew simply did not work and that, in fact, were turning students off: for example, reading "condensed" history from textbooks, filling out worksheets in math, diagramming sentences, and doing true-false and multiple-choice assessments.

Following our formal acceptance and involvement in the CES movement in 1989, our slow but steady improvement continued through the early 1990s. Collaboration with partners such as Children's Hospital, CVS Pharmacies, the Museum of Science, and others, predated what is now known as the "school-to-career" movement, bringing us an expanded sense of the classroom, opportunities to learn from other people and organizations, and higher standards. In 1992 we were presented with one of twenty U.S. Department of Labor "Lift America" awards for our pre-professional programs with Children's Hospital of Boston as well as two other regional awards from the private sector.

By this time, we had also created an "essential curriculum" focusing on three areas, integrated humanities, integrated math, and science. Class times were long and flexible, we had begun to formalize our portfolios in each content area, and an advisory format provided students with a social and academic support group. We had also formalized our board of advisors, welcoming the support of many committed and influential collaborators. Still, our attempts to raise the stakes even higher were limited by the seat time and point structure that came with Carnegie Units, and our general lack of autonomy in governance and budget issues. We were also fatigued from years of union grievances and central-office resistance to Fenway's progressive curriculum, assessment, and organizational ideas. When the Massachusetts legislature passed an Education Reform Act in 1994, the landscape changed dramatically. Part of that act was the authorization to create 25 charter schools. Fenway was quick to apply for this new status, and within a few months we received one of the first charters granted.

Within months of our receipt of a charter, however, the BPS, in a rare alignment of the teachers union, the school committee and superintendent, and the mayor, secured a teachers' contract that created "in-district" charters to be known as "pilot schools." This decision was interpreted in a number of ways—a union response to privatization efforts that were appearing at an alarming rate in other cities; an attempt by a very traditional superintendent to show movement toward more progressive ideas; and an effort by the new mayor to show his support for improving the schools. Regardless of the interpretation, our job was to divine what the day-to-day reality would be for our school.

Many of our parents, faced with the choice of "going charter" or staying in-district, felt that the pilot status might be a safer choice. Some of them had been involved in the recent failure of small, independent school start-ups, and they likened charters to "boutique" private schools. Others were concerned that a legislative act could suddenly wipe out charter funding, or that we might not be able to attract a diverse student population. Even though there was great skepticism about the school system's ability to keep the promise of pilots, the fickle nature of the legislature and questions about its commitment to education reform also contributed to indecision.

Pilot-school status seemed to present a monetary advantage, since personnel costs were computed as an average rather than an actual cost. In pilots as well as charters, the money follows the child. Charters must operate with the actual dollar allocation. So, if the district cost of educating a child is calculated at $7,400, that is exactly what the charter school will receive. Charter schools then have total autonomy to set teachers' salaries. There is no obligation to adhere to any union or district pay scales based on the number of years of experience or level of educational attainment.

However, the lines of fiscal purity are more blurred with pilot schools. Because the district (because of size and scale) can absorb the costs of less expensive or more expensive teachers, pilot schools use average teacher salaries to construct their budgets. In a school like Fenway where 50% of the faculty have 10 years or more of service as well as advanced degrees and therefore cost well over the district average, this is a tremendous monetary advantage to the school. In addition, because the school's budget won't suffer, there is an incentive to encourage newer teachers to pursue further education. These teachers will then get paid more, but it will not cost the school because their salary is computed on an average cost. When teachers are relatively new and inexperienced (read that as "inexpensive"), the charter system of budgeting may work, but because there is no way to raise revenues in charter schools through tuition, how will teachers' earning power be encouraged to increase?

When Fenway became a charter school, many veteran faculty worried that in a charter school there might be a budget shortfall if the school retained its mostly veteran educators with advanced degrees (and paid them and other less experienced teachers on a par with Boston salaries). Monetarily, in a pilot school that used average salaries for budget purposes, no incentive existed to hire younger, less experienced teachers. Pilot schools could always hire the best qualified personnel regardless of cost.

After much deliberation, Fenway's parents, faculty, administration, and board voted to return the state charter in favor of in-district, pilot-school status. Our belief, in 1995, was that Fenway could contribute to and benefit more from systemic reform pushed from the "inside" rather than the "outside." Courted by school committee officials and the mayor, Fenway made the decision to stay in-district. So, emboldened with what might have been called a Pollyannaish view that Fenway could lead by example, and convinced that faculty expertise and morale were critical, the school began its first year as a pilot in 1995.

Momentum picked up almost immediately. Our new staff were hand-picked via a portfolio and interview process, complete with micro-teaching demonstrations. Our board, with the help of pro bono attorneys, began the process of developing a Memorandum of Agreement with the superintendent and the school committee that would assure us longevity and operating conditions as promised under pilotship. Content teams were able to proceed full steam ahead on implementing our curriculum, with our own standards to be honed with the help of a range of collaborators and contributors, not imposed by some remote source with little knowledge of our school and its ethos. We began networking with the other pilot schools in Boston, entering for the first time into an authentic conversation about teaching and learning.

And we initiated our long-awaited CES-inspired plan to graduate students by portfolio and exhibition, which, as we like to say, changed everything. Only 2 years after initiating this plan, in recognition of Fenway's consistent efforts to restructure in order to improve student achievement, the school was named one of ten "New American High Schools" by the U.S. Department of Education. This prestigious award recognized the school's ability to create high standards of academic excellence and prepare students for both college and the workplace, and it propelled us into a position of leadership in education circles.

What were the conditions that allowed us to move forward in our pursuit of excellence? On the basis of our experience and abundant research, we had determined our optimal size, 250 to 300. We also knew that beyond size and scale were four different kinds of autonomy that were crucial for us if we were to offer a rich learning environment for students and adults in the school: curriculum and assessment, budget, governance, and personnel. We knew that the design of our academic program should be shaped by the intellectual powers of the students, not by course titles or the random accumulation of facts and credits via "subjects," and, furthermore, that decisions about our course of studies and our standards should be shaped by us, as leaders, and by our staff, parents, and advisors and not by remote authorities and "mandates."

We knew that we in the school should decide what amount of money would be allocated to personnel, instructional materials, professional development, and so forth, as well as when and how we wanted to procure services and materials. We knew that we wanted to search for and hire the best faculty imaginable, teachers who knew and were committed to our particular values, community, and mission. Finally, we knew that we needed the guidance and power of a governance structure that knew us intimately and appreciated our needs and persuasions and that served us by choice and with determination because of what our school represented.

THE MAJOR SUCCESSES AS A PILOT SCHOOL DURING THE FIRT TWO YEARS

During the 1996–97 academic year, our dropout rates were very low and promotion rates high. Graduates were admitted to a wide variety of colleges, many with full scholarships. Two students were admitted with full scholarships to Wheaton College—both of these young people want to be teachers and return to a school like Fenway to work; two students were admitted to Boston University, with full scholarships; two students, again with significant financial aid, were admitted to Boston College; for the second year in a row, as a result of Fenway's collaboration with CVS pharmacies, a student was admitted to the prestigious Massachusetts College of Pharmacy. Other students in Fenway's prepharmacy program are going to Wentworth, Franklin Institute, and Tuskegee. The list of college acceptances is impressive. College retention rates are increasing as well.

In order to achieve these results, the school focused considerable attention on its work with curriculum and assessment. Curriculum teams in humanities, math, and science met intensively during the academic year and summer to critically examine and improve curriculum content as well as techniques for assessing student mastery of skills in each discipline. To assist with this endeavor, content experts, particularly those from colleges and universities, were consulted. Standards from national and local curriculum frameworks helped focus the central question for each team: Is what we are teaching good enough and how do we know? And a second, closely related, question followed naturally: Is students' work good enough and how do we know? Answering the "how do we know" part of the question requires tireless examination of student work and a willingness to hold it up to the critical eyes of "outsiders" from other schools, institutions in the community, business partners, university experts, and so on.

No one at Fenway just settles for a score on a standardized test to tell teachers and students how they are doing. That type of cursory look at student work may suffice for some parents and school systems but has never been enough for the constituents of the Fenway community. Fenway teachers and students must be able to describe articulately what a graduate should know and be able to do. Both teachers and students learn, through the use of exemplary student work, student exhibitions of mastery, portfolios, and so forth. The process of graduation by portfolio and exhibition allows every student to work closely with a graduation committee that views and judges student work and determines whether the student has earned a diploma. This is similar to the process in which graduate school students present oral defenses to their doctoral committees.

Although the presentation of portfolios and exhibitions to graduation committees is time-consuming, it has proven to be an excellent indicator of student preparedness. The stakes are high—the diploma is meaningful—and students do not shy away from the rigors of demonstrating their competence. This process is helping Fenway students achieve increasingly high standards. It is also helping teachers to critically appraise their own work as well as the work of their colleagues. Most importantly, by clearly describing what we expect a 12th grader to know and be able to do, Fenway faculty are able to "work backwards" and determine what must be taught in grades 9 through 11. In a traditional school, a teacher may teach just from a text and test only on the content covered therein. At Fenway, there is no single text and there are many mirrors held up to check on whether the work is good enough. This is a complex process that requires dedication to working together over time as well as a willingness to accept critical feedback and grow and change with that feedback.

Much of our time and energy at Fenway has been focused on developing our own set of standards. We do not agree with the standards-based approach, because we feel that in large part it misses the point of why things are not working and locks us into traditional structures and relationships. The question of standards at Fenway must be considered both internally (What is good work? How good is good enough? What are our exemplars of good work across grade levels, content, styles, etc.?) and externally (How does our students' work compare with authentic work being done in other schools? Are there authentic standards to compare? Are we allowing sufficient input from the outside on our graduation committees, from parents, experts, collaborators? Is our documentation sufficient?).

Many other schools accept external and remote standards, such as test scores (SATs, APs, state tests), and combine them with internal standards with questionable meaning (GPAs) to reassure their communities of their schools' excellence. They are working in a paradigm that says the "excellence pie" is limited, the bell curve is alive and well, and high achievement is for some, not for all, by the very nature of the academic meritocracy. At Fenway we seldom talk in these terms. Although in our triangulated assessment format, standardized tests must be taken, reported, and analyzed, these results offer us little of consequence. They give us a poor return on our energy expenditure, and they can be hurtful and demoralizing to many students. There is very little measuring of students against the same standard referenced to a notion of vertical IQ. We realize our obligation to develop our own exemplars—persuasive essays, math exhibitions, lab experiments—that we can use both to show students what the standards are and to check with and against the perceptions of our collaborators and critical friends. A long-held dream is to develop an exhibitions collection containing both hard copy and videotape of our Fenway exemplars to counteract the too common perception that only test scores can be "hard" data.

In order to create a community focused on developing high expectations for all students, professional-development activities must also be focused and reflect the school's goals. To that end, the faculty decided on two key initiatives that would guide their work: (a) understanding their own and their students' diversity and multicultural backgrounds and (b) learning how to teach more effectively in a heterogeneous classroom that includes special-needs and "regular" students. To accomplish these goals, we have brought in highly trained diversity consultants to help us improve our understanding of issues of race, class, and gender bias among ourselves. We felt that we needed to connect as diverse adults before we began this difficult work with students. We have also hired a special-education consultant to work with mentor teachers and their mentees to document classroom practices and begin to identify and understand those practices that promote learning for all students. Both these professional-development goals are in many ways lifelong goals, but by making them central to our faculty meetings, we hope that we will all grow as educators.

A third major initiative undertaken during the 1996–97 school year was the introduction of our second strategic planning process. A team of teachers, students, parents, and board members reviewed our goals, as described in our 1994 plan, and drafted a revised set to guide us through the next few years. During the 1997–98 school year, this group continued to hone the goals and develop the means to achieve them. Although often a slow and arduous process, strategic planning has been a hallmark of Fenway since its inception. Not only does the process involve many constituents in the life of the school; it also forces the school to stay focused—to avoid taking "too many cookies from the cookie jar," or undertaking too much, as one of our board members cautioned.

During 1998, a fourth area of success was the growth and strengthening of the pilot-school network. Fenway's directors meet monthly with the seven other pilot-school directors. Although the meetings sometimes include the frustration of having to deal with central-office issues (inability to control job descriptions and titles, difficulty in having job announcements posted in a timely fashion, or concerns about not using central office's curriculum materials), they more often focus on more substantive issues, such as the use of portfolios to develop a system of teacher evaluation, analysis of a student project, or the development of an accountability framework that will help pilot schools critically review each other's process along defined goals. These meetings are never long enough, always raise more questions than answers, and help create a feeling of solidarity among the directors that education can be transformative and that all students can learn and achieve at high standards.

These pilot-school directors' meetings are convened by a not-for-profit organization called the Center for Collaborative Education–Metro Boston (or CCE). This organization serves as the regional center for the Coalition of Essential Schools (CES). Although not all pilot schools are members of the coalition, they have all embraced CCE's principles (which are very similar to those of CES). We founded the center in 1995 in the hope that it would provide an avenue for like-minded educators to join together in pursuit of educational change. For more than a decade Fenway had existed as a lonely island of progressive practices, but with the formation of the center, various schools could work on issues of policy, practice, and advocacy with some leadership. As a not-for-profit, independent organization, we also hoped the center would provide some dissonance and positive tension that would have an impact on the BPS. Given that department's propensity to operate from one crisis to another, we wanted an independent group that could consistently hold up examples and visions of what the schools might be.

Although we had many successes in the 1997–98 school year and navigated some difficult waters in reconstituting a relationship with our central office, many questions remain about the district's commitment and ability to restructure itself in order to serve the schools, rather than vice versa. Many tensions and test cases in the 1997–98 school year raised serious issues about pilot schools' autonomy.

INS/OUTS WITH THE DISTRICT

Although we have made definite progress with the four kinds of autonomy we need to run the most successful school possible, there are still daily "tests" to our fortitude, creativity, and good humor. Budgeting and purchasing as well as curriculum, assessment, and "standards" continue to be areas where the school's definition of *autonomy* and the district's do not equate.

As a pilot school we can designate funds to certain line items and switch funds from one line item to another (except for personnel). In 1997, we had a small grant to send a teacher to an out-of-state conference. We had the money available, designated for the purpose of travel and professional development; however, we did not realize that we had to submit forms in triplicate requesting permission from the superintendent to travel. Without that prior permission, we found our requests for reimbursement for travel expenses continually rejected. Even though autonomy of budget, in our minds, signifies autonomy to designate staff members to present at conferences, this does not appear to be a belief shared by those in the central office. In our minds the notion that a superintendent must sign travel requests for more than 6,000 employees does not demonstrate a belief in school-based autonomy.

A smaller, yet equally irritating, incident occurred with the need to pay a vendor for routine services provided to the school. Much of our strategic planning meetings over the course of 1997 were held at Children's Hospital, a longtime collaborator of Fenway's. A hospital staff member arranged for coffee and donuts for these meetings and then billed the school, per our arrangement, for reimbursement. However, when we submitted the bill to the central budget office, we were told that the Children's Hospital was not on the approved vendor list for the BPS, that it would take at least 30 more days to get them on the approved list, and that it would take another 2 to 3 weeks to reimburse the hospital.

The idea of pilot-school status meant to us that deciding just how we spent money would be a school-based decision. Within the guidelines of the laws of public financing, the administration of the school (with board oversight and approval where necessary) would determine specifics about allowable reimbursements, consulting contracts, travel, and a host of other routine procedures and details. In actuality, the BPS's business office has not yet developed such a protocol for pilot schools. No separate method has been established to enable the business office to allow schools to operate as a small business would, without cumbersome and compliance-oriented bureaucratic constraints, spending money as any small business would.

In addition, Fenway and other pilot schools have experienced endless red tape with the Office of Personnel and Human Resources. Although the staff is always pleasant and friendly, there is no shared understanding that pilot schools actually do have the authority to issue contracts or letters of agreement with employees. Thus pilot-school teachers continue to receive letters of reasonable assurance as well as layoff notices for provisional teachers from the central office. This, of course, serves only to undermine the authority of Fenway's directors and confuse teachers. "Who really hires me?" a teacher wants to know after signing a letter of reasonable assurance from the central office. "Why did I sign a Fenway 'Employee Contract at Will' document and then another document at central office?" a confused faculty member asks. Although Fenway's directors have repeatedly explained to the Office of Personnel and Human Resources, the central office's liaison with pilot schools, and to the superintendent that these systems need to be worked out, this kind of practice remains commonplace.

Just as we thought that the teachers union, after harassing us for years, seemed finally on our "side," we were informed that they considered pilot-school teachers and counselors subject to "bumping" on the basis of seniority. That is to say, they contended that a biology teacher is a biology teacher, regardless of the school and its context. When we loudly protested, we were told that this was always the understanding. However, our proposal for a pilot school had been approved with clearly defined and specialized job descriptions. Only highly qualified individuals were hired for these positions at Fenway and other pilots. How could this process now be overturned in favor of bumping? When we discussed this dilemma with the union president, we were told that the contract was very clear on this matter. Our board took immediate action on this latest incursion into our autonomy and wrote a letter to the superintendent and school committee demanding an immediate assurance that pilot schools would not be subject to union bumping. It is not clear what the results will be.

Until this year, the central Office of Research and Evaluation regarded as its purview the mailing out to Fenway students their annual standardized test (Stanford 9) scores with a letter written "on our behalf," explaining the meaning of the scores. This was done without consulting the pilot-school directors. When we were outraged that such a letter was sent, ostensibly from us but never seen or authorized by us, the central office was perplexed, because every other parent in the district receives such information. After lengthy dialogue, we managed to see that 1998's letter was sent to us for approval first, which gave us the opportunity to send out an accompanying letter explaining how Fenway uses and interprets standardized tests results. It is a hopeful sign that one district department has, in fact, adopted a "customer service" approach and is willing to be flexible with regard to individual school needs and demands.

Significant areas of instructional autonomy remain as yet largely untested at Fenway and at other pilot schools. Autonomy over curriculum has been a hallmark of Fenway since its inception. With the current fervor both in the district and at state and national levels over the development of centralized standards, common products (or assessments) by grade level, and the approach of curriculum-referenced tests, it is unclear whether Fenway and other like-minded schools will be able to hold their ground. Autonomy over curriculum may be, in the end, the fundamental bone of contention. Without it, the other areas of autonomy that we seek may prove relatively meaningless.

The issue of which governance body actually has legal control over the school is another area of disagreement still subject to debate. Fenway has a board of trustees who serve as policy advisors, troubleshooters, advocates, fund-raisers, and overall "keepers" of the health and welfare of the school. This board was also designed to oversee the fiscal health of the school. The 1996 Memorandum of Agreement signed between the superintendent and the board co-chairs describes the board's powers to hire and fire the co-directors of the school, but in consultation with the superintendent. And, as discussed earlier, the issue of fiscal accountability remains hazy. The board has little real authority, because the budget is still within the control of the BPS. Board oversight is largely unnecessary, since money never changes hands into a school bank account. This governance issue will need to be fully clarified in order for Fenway to have a fully empowered board of trustees.

Although the events described above may seem minor to many who work in other industries, each of these incidents saps our strength and causes us to expend energy in areas that do not directly affect student achievement. We are not focusing as well as we could and should on issues of teaching and learning, because we are continually fending off the latest incursion into our autonomy. In addition, we are still advocating for more autonomy in those four key areas.

LESSONS LEARNED

1. There is no substitute for an experienced, caring, and diverse faculty. Simply put, in order to thrive, a school community requires a critical mass of devoted veteran teachers. They provide not only wisdom and experience but also a special personal presence with young people. These are the gifted, "natural" educators, dedicated to their craft and capable of building and sustaining critical relationships with students, counterparts, parents, and collaborators. We have heard that a number of charter schools have, for budgetary reasons, been unable to meet the market demands of seasoned teachers and are top-heavy with transient, less skilled, and less confident teachers. Thus some of these schools have floundered in the crucial early period.

Disappointment is rife in many circles, including university teacher-training departments, that so many schools remain unresponsive, maintaining traditional patterns of organization and perpetuating their culture of isolation and resistance to new ideas. Early retirees from the baby-boomer generation are looking for rewarding new careers in teaching, only to be turned off by the current stasis. Energetic and idealistic young teachers are often almost immediately marginalized by a moribund professional community. As yet, not enough of us veteran educators recognize that without dramatic changes in the ways schools are engineered and operated, not only will schools not improve as they must, but would-be teachers and disillusioned young teachers will continue to deny the profession or leave it in high numbers. In our view, a mix of staff, including veterans, new teachers, and mid-career transition people, will be best able to seize the tremendous opportunity to create a new, fresh, and vibrantly healthy culture of collaboration and high standards. Such a culturally and demographically diverse teaching population will be more capable of looking at itself critically, examining its practices, generating new ideas, diagnosing and solving its own problems, and designing and implementing teacher evaluation and performance systems that really work.

Again, there is no substitute for a good teacher. Not everyone can be a good teacher, not everyone has the desire and determination to do this kind of work. Many charter schools, we hear, for budgetary reasons, must rely on part-time and beginning teachers who cannot contribute in the ways required for a solid beginning under difficult and challenging circumstances. The school is cast as the proving ground for these teachers yet is largely unable to provide the conditions for their support and growth. The long hours and intense pace in a start-up atmosphere undermine teacher practice, and relationships built around teaching and learning fail to materialize.

2. Forming a network is a powerful tool for schools, because meaningful feedback is critical to a healthy school, and networks can provide greater and better accountability than bureaucracies. Friendly, fine-tuned feedback from a variety of sources is indispensable to a good school. Unfortunately, the majority of schools do not seek it out, are often impermeable to it, and are routinely clumsy at receiving and using it when it does get through. This observation is not meant to blame good people but simply to point out that current school culture and traditions, again, have been inherited from another era and do not serve us well in this day and age. District and school-site bureaucracies contribute to the problem by robbing schools of the opportunity to grow and develop. A monitoring-and-compliance orientation, designed to minimize liability, deviations, and conflict, subverts any school's ability to focus energy on problem solving and mission building.

Networks among schools and educators provide the opportunity to grow and learn with and from others who share a clear, common purpose and whose work we know, trust, and respect. Looseness and flexibility are both welcome characteristics of our pilot-network participation, yet we are careful to see that when we criticize each other, we do so constructively, at a negotiated pace and in a friendly style. Feedback from peer schools can have a tough edge to it, taken more to heart perhaps because it comes from those who know young people and the profession firsthand. We often grow much more intimate with these counterparts, even though they may be farther away physically on a day-to-day basis, than with our district-level colleagues. When a network of educators can go to the next and vital step of looking at student work and teaching practice, the stage is set for successful teaching and learning by students and adults alike.

The Rand Corporation study of innovative school practices identified years ago that personal relationships among professionals have the greatest direct influence on successful and lasting changes in education. Paradoxically, just as increasing evidence indicates that day-to-day school business is far beyond the control of bureaucracies, attempts to standardize, monitor, measure, and sanction at all levels of public schooling, and across demographics and geography, have intensified.

Besides providing an invaluable template of principles of school reorganization, membership in a national network such as the CES affords Fenway an important voice in education affairs, the voice of the practitioner, with a democratic and multicultural tone. An articulate and respected reformer such as Theodore Sizer, who enjoys great support from frontline educators, can work persistently and effectively to help counter quick-fix approaches to complex educational problems and create healthy controversy by pushing for realistic time lines and the resources needed for the difficult work to be done. He and others like him, can also bring the weight of the latest research to bear on the problems we face, saving us from the endless and fruitless cycles of state and district-level competency testing, imposed private-sector management techniques, and monitoring and compliance systems. We also learn from the experience of people doing comparable work in contexts similar to and radically different from our own. This is a clear benefit of a national and regional network. An actively networking school can count on the research and development experiences of thousands of member schools and educators.

Regionally, Fenway hopes to join with other members of CES in piloting statewide initiatives that can provide alternatives to present practices in college admissions, in assessment, and in instructional practice. One example is our Massachusetts Education Reform Act, passed a few years ago, whose well-intentioned recommendations for change are only now beginning to get into the bloodstream of the state's schools. Already, however, controversial ex-gubernatorial candidate John Silber, former head of the state board of education, and a group of his handpicked committee members have stated their impatience with the pace, disregarding abundant research on the nature of change in institutions and bureaucracies. The act contains several notable recommendations. One is that more time be spent on learning, requiring a longer school day and year with a focus on the disciplines. Another part of the law directs schools to create more inclusive, clearly defined school-governance mechanisms. Schools are advised to use broader assessment formats that would, in theory, be loosely tied to lean and purely suggestive curriculum frameworks in order to pare down the suffocating amounts of information coursing through the popular and academic cultures. However, schools still find themselves largely hemmed in by standardized testing policies that, although cheap and uniform, are unable to reflect the kind of lasting and powerful skills and knowledge one wants for one's own children. The momentum for progressive changes provided by the Education Reform Act is blocked by the counterforce of reductive assessment practices. As long as parental anxieties and shortsighted university admissions policies continue to drive thinking about learning, we will make schools increasingly unable to teach for understanding. District emphasis on test scores limits the range of instructional strategies and places severe restraints on schools' abilities to design engaging and effective instruction, practices supported by cognitive research and field studies from NCREST, CORS/UWisconsin–Madison, and others.

Working as a bloc of schools, state or regional, our network could join with colleges to look at the work of students differently. We could track our graduates and compare their progress in the postsecondary arenas that really matter. Such collectives could invite a multitude of private-sector collaborators and the Department of Education itself to participate in monitoring their work. The growth and development of such a network would increase our running room, boost credibility, and offer protection unavailable to lone-wolf, reform-minded schools and leaders. Locally, CCE–Metro Boston not only provides a forum for the pilot-school leaders and staff to share efforts and conversation but often plays the important role of intermediary, peacemaker, and translator as central office and the schools struggle to redefine their relationship and create new norms and systems. Our hope is that at some point CCE will succeed in hosting local and regional charter–pilot conversations, allowing us to learn from the collective of progressive educators.

3. Pilotship should be seen as an opportunity for the school to articulate and pursue promising practice or reorganization in management and administration to support teaching and learning and for the district to learn from both. The research-and-design function of the pilots should and must be exploited at all levels. We have wasted the generation since *A Nation at Risk* in trying to monitor educators into compliance, testing students into competency, working endlessly on meaningless standards conversations,

tightening up and "teacher-proofing" almost every aspect of schooling—all to no avail. The game must become one of challenging every basic assumption about school and learning on which the present system rests, followed by the strategic abandonment of almost every vestige of the old system.

We must also take care not to mix apples and oranges when looking at the research and design pilots and charters can perform. Small size and scale, for example, will allow many curricular and programmatic experiments to succeed in a small, focused pilot school but not in a large district high school. It is not that these adaptations are not worthwhile because they don't translate well. The problem is that the size and structure of the large schools generally preclude a deeper kind of pedagogy built on intellectual intimacy. However, there are natural limitations to the research-and-design work, particularly when it comes to transposing simple solutions from other cultures and institutions, as the Edison Project and others are learning. Heavy doses of technology and hardware do not a successful school make. Private-sector wisdom can be a blessing in some areas, but it can also be a curse. The simple adaptation of "corporate" ideas and management techniques is insufficient. If people think that reading an "Eight Step" management book or "work-shopping" a staff in Total Quality Management will change the culture of a school, there will be great frustration and much lost energy and good will. Research and experience over the last 15 years shows clearly that private-sector management techniques do not translate well to public education. These ideas cannot be grafted on, not because they are not good ideas but because the schools are affected by too many complex variables and cultural barriers that are not a part of the private sector. We should, though, welcome and support new approaches to deploying of resources, fund-raising, public relations, budgeting, purchasing, personnel relations, and resolving disputes. These areas can clearly benefit from multiple perspectives.

We must replace the concept of students and teachers as "widgets." To do so, we need to focus on building mission, collaboration, and small learning communities in schools and neighborhoods and providing a range of instructional and organizational approaches for students, parents, and families. In Boston, as elsewhere, a biology teacher is a biology teacher, a student is a student, and a course is a course—all interchangeable parts, a legacy of the factory design on which schools still operate. Teachers are assigned to where an "opening" exists, students to vacant seats. It is time to abandon the idea that we can expect any random constellation of people, and their opinions and working styles, to form a caring and demanding urban school community. We must demand a process through which all our schools can, one by one, mobilize a learning community of parents, students, teachers, administrators, and collaborators with attention to and guidance from those unique circumstances and opportunities that distinguish each school. Without a school-by-school approach to this fundamental issue, we have little reason to expect greater ownership, let alone improved performance and achievement.

In addition, several hundred million dollars will have been spent in Boston to refurbish schools to meet regional accreditation requirements. The irony is that virtually nothing will change within these buildings to reflect new knowledge about curriculum, instruction, assessment, or the like. Time marches on, but the patterns and structures of schooling remain the same. Indeed, much of the refurbishing will help only to cement the older practices into place.

4. There are no consistent forces helping to push schools toward more enlightened policies and structures. Over the past two decades we have accumulated vast new knowledge about the nature of learning, intelligence, and brain function. We also have the fruits of years of research regarding both promising and unproductive practices in curriculum and assessment, school organization, size and scale, institutional change, and professional development. Yet we are unable to break through the cultural insulation that surrounds the American high school; quite to the contrary, there is a tremendous braking effect on progressive schools induced by the practices and trappings of traditional schooling and by the political demands placed on those charged with improving the schools.

Simply put, no forces—pedagogical, economic, or political—support our work in progressive school restructuring. In fact, most of the forces to which we are subject conspire to work against us and undo the changes we have made. Beyond our own sense of dissonance, our own idealism, our own striving for something better for our students and families, we have no outside help—no public, no superintendent, no commissioner or czar, no politician clamoring for smaller, more personalized schools. Instead, Conant's vision of "bigger is better" lives on. We build, rebuild, and refurbish the giant high schools, despite what two generations of research data show about the success of small learning communities. There is no outcry for broader, more inclusive, more informed assessment practices. Cheap and uniform standardized tests rule the day, and norm-referenced testing is just fine, thanks. Real estate values rise and fall with test scores, as do superintendents. No one is lobbying state university systems for headier college admissions policies. Just send in the SAT scores and the GPA. No one is pushing for the sensible integration of curriculum to cope with the suffocating flow of information or for a departure from the information-dispensation kind of pedagogy. It's American history in the morning, American literature in the afternoon, just as it's always been.

This drag on progressive schools occurs across the nation. Dynamic school communities are barraged by traditional expectations and policies. Radical ideas, regardless of their success, are chipped away at by those who want the familiar, recognizable, and comfortable. Leaders pay a high price for bucking the system. Despite what educators know is wrong with today's schools, the public disillusionment reflected in the increasing demand for charter schools and voucher systems, and the corporate community's loss of faith, we insist only on "first-order" change—tinkering, monitoring, doing our best to tighten up a system based on failed principles and assumptions. "Second-order change," a sustained commitment to the strategic abandonment of the things that don't work, may seem all right for small, outside-the-margin schools but in fact requires too much will, too much sacrifice, for the parties involved. Superintendents just don't have the time or the political running room to confess what many of us know and feel deeply: The work will take a generation and will involve throwing out most of what we know about our high schools.

FUTURE CHALLENGES

Many questions remain for us. We are constantly engaged in a balancing act between school-based autonomy and state- and district-driven demand for more central conformity. Has the district been able to work out a method to help and not interfere? Has the reform potential of the pilot schools been recognized, even vaguely, by the school district? Is there any advocacy of this reform initiative from either the union or the BPS? If, as stated in the request for proposals, pilot schools were all meant to have a research-and-design component and cultivate some aspect of their school that could be replicated or modified in other schools, has that been seriously contemplated by the district or union? Fenway has received both national and local accolades and recognition. It is one of ten New American High Schools, designated by the U.S. Department of Education, and it is a "lead" school in the BPS, designated by the Boston Plan for Excellence. It is a school that has been noted for its successes.

Many organizations have analyzed the reasons for the school's success. The school's small size, its clarity about the importance of critically examining student work, and its reliance on strong student–teacher relationships as well as a strong school-to-career program are all key features that have been documented and described in numerous evaluations, news stories, books, and doctoral dissertations. But has its success been used to motivate any other district schools? Have the implications of its pilot status helped to inform any district or school committee or union policies, negotiations, or decisions? Sadly, the answer to these questions is no. There appears to be no new contract language that will promote more pilot schools. There is no movement to dismantle the district high schools. There is no roaring chorus that screams loudly and clearly, "Large High Schools Don't Work!" Rather there is a continuing attempt, albeit very well intentioned, to improve what we have in front of us—to write new curriculum standards, to provide reasonable professional development, to redesign how schools communicate with one another. Yet, in all of this fervor, do we ever ask the very hard, bleak questions about why student success is not improving? What would it mean if we really afforded schools true autonomy? We might actually have some wonderfully successful schools as well as some dismal failures that would have to be closed. Finally, do we ever venture far out on the precipice to ask if we still need the district as we once knew it? It is possible that one of the greatest achievements of the pilot schools will be to show that the kind of bureaucracy we created at the beginning of the 20th century is no longer viable at the century's end.

The current organization of Boston's school district divides up schools into geographic clusters. Discussions include such topics as system-wide initiatives for purchasing and then receiving training for technology; difficulties with meeting deadlines for the next iteration of Comprehensive School Plans; relocation of a bilingual 5th grade; and new trauma procedures for suicide attempts. Sometimes, 15 minutes of each monthly 2-hour-long meeting are allocated for individual schools to report on initiatives. (Fenway has been asked to report on assessment.)

The cluster- and pilot-school networks are both about 4 years old. Their differences are remarkable. Brought together because of shared purposes and visions, the pilot-schools can focus on "real" work that has significant implications for each school and its students and families. The cluster network, purported to be more than an operational network, has no reason ever to gel. The schools do not share common purposes. Their reasons for meaningful communication are as contrived as those of two strangers meeting at a bus station and falling in love.

Could the pilot schools, or for that matter all schools, exist without that district? Could this loosely formed federation of schools, convened by an outside agency, in fact *be* the district? Would that improve the schools' level of autonomy? What about equity? This is usually the first objection raised in discussions of radical reform. Does the district help ensure that each school provides all students with an equitable education? Certainly in the current system, equity is not a right for all students. Most of Boston's high school students are receiving substandard education in the district's public schools. However, the district and the state have played an important monitoring role to ensure that special-education and bilingual-education students receive proper services. If there were no district, as we now know it, would the state assume that responsibility? And what about facilities? The district would need to have some authority to receive bonds for school construction or renovation. Or would this become a function of the city's department of public facilities?

In many respects, the district's most notable contribution lies in monitoring. Is the student assignment process fair? Is testing carried out over certain specified weeks? Do schools understand how to interpret test results? (The district is helpful in analyzing test results and doing various data runs at the school's request.) Do discipline procedures follow due process guidelines established by the school committee? Are all schools complying with public health requirements, such as student immunizations or HIV/AIDS education? Are all budget requisitions submitted by April 15 so that the city can monitor its expenditures and communicate effectively with the public about expenses?

However, in many other respects, the district only confounds a school's ability to run smoothly and determine its own good health and academic strength. For example, Fenway's ability to develop its own curriculum has been a hallmark of the school since its inception. If Fenway were now forced to adhere to district and state curriculum and specific performance tasks, the school's heart and soul would be diminished. Fenway has attempted to incorporate some of the goals of both state and national curriculum frameworks as its teachers develop specific curriculum units and assessments to "test" if students have mastered that material. However, the notion that all 10th graders should be tested on Elie Weisel's *Night* (as defined in the 1996 BPS curriculum guides) defies the logic and pace of Fenway's educational mission. Every 3 years students study *Night* in the context of World War II and the Holocaust. A student might be in 9th, 10th, 11th, or 12th grade. Certainly during that specific unit, students would be well-prepared to grapple with the themes of *Night*. It is not, however, good educational practice to require all students to read a specific book each year even when that book does not relate to a course of study. That renders learning trivial. Rather, students should be required to read books all the time and answer questions and debate themes continually (but, of course, this is a cumbersome approach that creates more work for the district.)

Another example of how centralized policies confound Fenway's mission is the district's recent purchase of math curriculum. The school committee voted to provide each school with math curriculum at no cost to the individual school. It was decided that two math curricula would be available to choose from. Limiting the choice to only two was done because (a) the district could receive a financial break if it bought in bulk, and (b) those students who switch schools during their educational tenure could be better served by having familiar and consistent texts from building to building. Unfortunately, Fenway's math curriculum, The Interactive Math Project (IMP), was not one of the two approved choices and thus the school had to raise private dollars to support the use of its math curriculum. (IMP, as suggested earlier, has contributed significantly to student success at Fenway.)

In a survey done by the Boston Plan for Excellence, a conduit for corporate and philanthropic funds, 60 school principals were asked what central-office services they found indispensable. The principals could not name one. When a Philadelphia superintendent gathered her top brass together in a retreat setting to "reinvent central office," each small group, independently of one another, abolished the central office. They spent the next day arguing that their own functions and job were indispensable. Clearly, one cannot assume that folks will blow up a system that is their livelihood.

But can we envision schools without districts? Can we envision groups of parents and teachers creating their own learning communities and monitoring one another? Certainly, independent schools have been doing this for hundreds of years. Somehow, when the discussion involves tax dollars (or what we call public dollars), we get very squeamish about allowing schools (groups of parents, students, teachers, administrators, and community members) to be in charge. Although our economy is mostly run by supply and demand, we are reluctant to let our schools operate under a similar system. Are we fearful that our poorer areas would have no schools? Do we think that we wouldn't entice excellent teachers into these areas? Do we assume that poorer parents would not want to create good schools for their children? Is it worry about bricks and mortar, that is, good school buildings? Is it fear, or just the weight of history, that keeps us marching on a path that refuses to allow or encourage more Fenway-like schools to grow and flourish? Is it "equity" that says we must continue to reform the district's high schools with each subsequent superintendent's new initiative? When do we decide that enough is enough? We have been in the business of reforming these schools for at least 30 years. They are still broken, dysfunctional, and unsuccessful. We would never send our own children to many of these schools.

What would happen if these schools were closed and other schools opened by groups of parents, teachers, and community members? Would we be any worse off than we are now? Perhaps the district could then provide a supportive role with central-office personnel in charge of ordering furniture and dealing with other capital issues, assisting with food services, or doing any number of operational tasks. Monitoring might be more complex, but student achievement might be much higher. Wouldn't that be a BPS we could all be proud of?

REFERENCE

Sizer, T. R. (1984). *Horace's Compromise: The dilemma of the American high school.* Boston: Houghton Mifflin.

CHAPTER 3

Smarter Charters?
Creating Boston's Pilot Schools

Robert Pearlman

When Ray Budde helped launch the charter-school movement with his seminal work *Education by Charter*, published in 1988, neither he nor any other early proponents of charters, including then American Federation of Teachers President Al Shanker, envisioned that charters would primarily arise from state-sponsored legislation instead of from voluntary efforts by local parents, teachers, and their school districts.

Today, some 8 years after Minnesota passed the nation's first charter-school law in 1991, the nation's more than 1,000 charter schools are almost entirely products of state legislation that bypass what Ted Kolderie of the Minnesota-based Center for Policy Studies calls the "exclusive franchise" of local school boards. Though some state-sponsored charters are formed with local board approval, most bypass it. The result is that most charter schools, although interesting, are marginal to local school districts and local reform efforts, are seen as "hostiles," and in nearly all cases receive no material or moral support from the local districts in which they reside.

Could not an alternative scenario have emerged, as Budde and others envisioned, where local districts, determined to promote educational innovation, would charter local groups of parents and educators to start new schools or to transform existing ones outside the framework of local rules and regulations?

The selection 5 years ago of six teams in Boston to open "pilot schools," or "in-district charter schools," in September 1994, shows that charters can be realized through district as well as state sponsorship. There are now 11 operating pilot schools in Boston. Combined with four state-sponsored charters in the city, Boston has the highest concentration of charter schools of any locality in the country.

How do these in-district charters stack up against their state-sponsored brethren? Can authentic charter schools exist only outside the district? This was the question posed by the Panasonic Foundation (1996) in its excellent study titled "In-District Charters: The Space Shuttle or a Spruce Goose."

Boston's pilot schools are enabled not by state legislation but instead through the 1994–97 contract between the Boston School Committee and the Boston Teachers Union. That contract called for the creation of up to six pilot schools free of the union contract and school-committee rules and regulations during the life of the contract. More pilot schools could be added by the agreement of the two parties.

The contract states that the "Boston Public Schools and the Boston Teachers Union are sponsoring the establishment of innovative pilot schools within the Boston Public School system. The purpose of establishing pilot schools is to provide models of educational excellence which will help to foster widespread educational reform throughout all Boston Public Schools."

The contract further states that the "pilot schools will operate with average school based per pupil budget, plus a start-up supplement, and will have greatly increased decision-making authority including exemptions from all Union and school Committee work rules." This is a far-reaching stance for both a school committee and a teachers union. It has yet to be duplicated by any other school district in the country.

The Request for Pilot School Proposals (RFP), first issued in July 1994 and then reissued in two additional rounds in 1996, spells out even more clearly the autonomy of pilot schools, citing the major characteristics of pilot schools to be models of innovation, to be replicable, to meet student and staff diversity requirements, to select staff from inside or outside the Boston Public Schools (BPS) without regard to seniority, to be free from BPS and Boston Teachers Union regulations, and to be fiscally autonomous, receiving a lump-sum budget that will be equal to the actual numbers of pupils times the average per-pupil spending in the BPS dissemination requirement.

The RFP invited three types of proposals, including New School Pilot Schools, School-Within-School Pilot Schools, and Whole School Pilot Schools. The latter two types, which convert existing schools to pilot-school status, require approval by the School Site Council and by two thirds of the teachers union members at the school. Proposals could come from people and organizations both inside and outside the school district. However, because a major goal of the initiative was to inform the reform process in the district, outside proposers were required to include a Boston principal or teacher as part of their planning team.

Seventeen proposals were received in the first round, and six pilots were selected by a joint union and management committee in October 1994 to start up in September 1995. Among the six was the Fenway Middle College High

School, a nationally recognized member of the Coalition of Essential Schools (CES). Fenway was now faced with the decision to choose between pilot status and becoming a state-sponsored charter school, for which it had already been selected. Fenway's board, and its school community, struggled with this decision. They studied the pros and cons of each and ultimately decided to opt for pilot status because the school's mission included playing a role in informing the reform of all Boston schools, something that would have been impossible from the vantage point of a state charter school.

The six pilot schools in round 1 included the Fenway, the Lyndon Elementary School, the Young Achievers Math and Science Academy (elementary), Health Careers Academy, Downtown Evening Academy, and Boston-Arts Academy. The latter, a collaboration of the six Boston Area arts and music colleges, delayed its opening until 1998, until it could find suitable facilities. This has now been accomplished with the City of Boston's acquisition of a state building that formerly housed Boston Latin Academy.

A second round was held in two parts, with the first group selected in May 1996 for start-up in September 1996. Opening in the fall of 1996 were two small high schools, the Multicultural Middle College High School and the Greater Egleston Community High School.

The second part of round 2 was selected in October 1996 to start up in September 1997. These two new schools were the Mission Hill School, an elementary school led by Deborah Meier, and the Harbor School, a middle school led by Expeditionary Learning, one of the seven New American School Design teams.

THE MAKING OF THE PILOT-SCHOOL INITIATIVE

Boston's in-district charters are unique in this country. What prompted a union and a school district to develop enabling conditions, through a contract agreement, that allows schools to be created and existing schools to opt for a status where they are free of union and school-committee rules and regulations?

Boston was well on the road to reform in 1993. The 1989–92 contract between the Boston School Committee and the Boston Teachers Union was a landmark agreement that not only set reform in motion but additionally cemented a political alliance between the mayor, business community, higher education, school committee, superintendent, and teachers union through the second Boston Compact. This contract established voluntary School-based Management/Shared Decision-making (SBM/SDM) for Boston schools, with the ability for schools to waive any item in school-committee rules and regulation and the union contract; it also gave SBM/

SDM schools the ability to select incoming teachers through the transfer process without regard for seniority.

This alliance faltered during the recession of the early 1990s, when then Mayor Raymond Flynn sponsored, and won, legislation to replace the elected school committee with an appointed one. Frustrated by the power of the schools to win budget share during difficult fiscal times and by what he perceived as the slow pace of reform, Flynn appointed a school committee dedicated to take on, and engage in public quarrel with, the superintendent and the union. This stalled the reform developments but accomplished little else. When Flynn abruptly abandoned the mayor's post in the spring of 1993 to become Ambassador to the Vatican, the committee switched gears. Working with then Acting Mayor Thomas Menino, the school committee attempted to develop a reform agenda in collaboration with the superintendent and union.

Like many large urban districts in 1993, Boston was the capital city of a state where charter-school legislation was being promulgated and was likely of passage. To many Boston leaders—not just school and union but also business leaders and the mayor—state-sponsored charters represented a threat to the reform of the whole Boston district, particularly if state funds for local school support were diverted from the BPS to pay significant per-pupil costs for students in state-sponsored charters located in Boston. Boston wanted to have the ability to sponsor, and finance, innovation in its midst and didn't want to lose that capacity.

It took 250 hours in the summer of 1993 to negotiate a new reform agenda between the union and the school committee. Usually a school committee sends a lawyer to negotiate, but in an unusual move that was necessary because of the high stakes involved—support for public education was on the line—the superintendent and three of seven school-committee members came to the table, along with a mayor's representative. With Conflict Management Inc. (CMI) facilitating the negotiations using the techniques of principled negotiations, better known as "collaborative," "interest-based," or "win-win" bargaining, the parties delivered an extraordinary agreement that included the creation of pilot schools. (For a description of the CMI process, see Wilson & Doherty, 1990.)

Unfortunately the agreement was expensive and fell victim, in the fall of 1993, to the heat of an eight-candidate race for a new mayor. When Acting Mayor Menino was elected as full mayor in November, a 1-year agreement was signed and negotiations resumed for a long-term agreement. The pilot schools had to be put off, because they required a multiyear agreement by the parties. However, in a significant step, the parties extended SBM/SDM to all schools, which meant in practice that all schools could establish personnel subcommittees of their school-site councils with the power to now select incoming staff through the transfer process without regard to seniority and select new hires by school decision and not by assignment from the central district office.

The successor negotiations bore fruit by June of 1994 in a strikingly new climate. The local economy was moving out of its early 1990 doldrums, and the parties of the Boston Compact—the mayor, business community, higher education, school committee, superintendent, and teachers union—set new goals (Boston Compact 3) and a strategic-action plan that incorporated all the key points in the reform agenda emerging in the contract process. According to Neil Sullivan, the executive director of the Boston Private Industry Council, which acts as the convener of the compact, Boston's march toward systemic reform has been built on the synergy of the Compact and the contract between the school committee and the teachers union.

Among the new reforms were the pilot schools; increased parent power on school-site councils; waivers of the union contract and school-committee rules and regulations adopted by the vote of the school only and not requiring school-committee or union approval; and creation of the Center for Leadership Development, a career ladder for teachers. By establishing the status of lead teacher through peer review and the funding for 300 lead-teacher part-time jobs annually (at 10% additional pay for 10% additional work) the center provided incentives for teachers to work on district and school-based reform efforts and professional development.

Thus the pilot-school initiative was realized in a context of a broad reform agenda shared by, and sponsored by, all the parties of the Boston Compact. The union was able to support granting such unusual powers to individual schools owing to 5 years' experience with as powerful a form of SBM/SDM as has taken place anywhere in the United States. This experience showed that, in practice, schools rarely waived union contract provisions. This was not because it was difficult to do but because the real barriers to change, in practice, as perceived by the school-site councils, were school-committee and central-office rules, regulations, and procedures. Giving the power to the schools was, from the union's view, a safe bet: Only reasonable changes would occur through a reasonable, and democratic, process.

Giving the pilot schools the additional freedom to hire teachers from outside the district, and not have to accept current teachers through the transfer process first, was additionally seen by the union as a safe bet, as the district was now hiring 300 new teachers per year. Teachers at existing schools who might be excessed could safely find positions in the regular schools.

State charter-school initiatives start from the premise that the district bureaucracy and its bureaucratic twin, the teachers union, are barriers to reform and that their jointly held "exclusive franchise" needs to be broken in order to enable change. But in Boston, through a high-level partnership and negotiated reform agenda, both sides agreed to give up their powers over the pilot schools. The partnership gave significant wins to both sides and the confidence to sponsor the pilots. Additionally, the union had years of experience with reform and felt confident that the reforms would lead to reasonable innovations and have no negative impact on the jobs and working conditions of the city's teachers.

PILOT-SCHOOL IMPLEMENTATION CHALLENGES

Like any other major reform, pilot schools require not just enabling legislation but also ongoing district support on a range of issues. In Boston both the district and the union appointed coordinators who worked as partners to support the fledgling start-ups. The union coordinator (the author of this article) acted as an ombudsman, pressuring all sides—but especially the central administration—to live up to their commitments. The district coordinator played a major role in finding facilities for the new pilots and coordinated efforts by school-district and city departments to renovate these spaces for fall 1995 opening.

Boston Superintendent Thomas W. Payzant, who was selected as superintendent in the fall of 1995 just as the first pilots opened, has called the facilities piece the major challenge of the pilot-school initiative. Payzant inherited a multimillion-dollar deficit, a significant portion of which was due to an outlay of nearly $4 million for pilot-school renovations. But despite the challenge, Boston has now been able, through leasing, renovations, and new construction, to finance and develop facilities for all but one of its chartered pilot schools. That track record dwarfs that of the state charter-school experiments in Massachusetts and other states, where little or no support is given for financing facilities. Every state has numerous examples of projects that died from failure to acquire facilities and many others that are struggling in inadequate spaces. Several charter schools closed in Arizona this year because of budget problems linked to facilities issues.

From the point of view of the new pilots in the 1995–96 school year, one of the major problems was governance. For all other Boston schools, now SBM/SDM schools, governance was clear: The school-site council, composed of the principal, four to six teachers, and a number of parents equal to the number of teachers plus the principal, was the governing body. The pilots, however, were free to create any governing body they desired, including a board of directors with any composition they desired. They were required, however, to follow the state model under the 1993 Education Reform Law of establishing school-site councils that were advisory (not governing, as in Boston's SBM/SDM schools).

At one pilot school the original planning committee, a group of parent leaders, came into conflict with the people who staffed the new school— the principal and the teachers—and the parents who sent their children there. Ongoing mediation was needed to resolve this lack of common vision between the school's founders and its real-life start-up community.

At another pilot, designed as a teacher-run school with no principal, the teacher management team, composed of three of the school's founders, came into conflict around curricular and management issues with some of the exemplary teachers they had hired into the school.

State-sponsored charters face the same problems. Start-up planning committees usually encounter their real-life parent and teacher communities only after start-up. Despite the exciting mission articulated in these new school start-ups, and the seemingly up-front concurrence about that mission and the school's design among the new staff and the school's parent community, many questions associated with school organization, curriculum, and governance are likely to emerge during the first few years. Additionally, these start-ups often embrace democratic and participatory governing structures that can prolong these early disputes. Process is the way to build, and rebuild, the new school community, but it can be debilitating on the parties involved.

A problem encountered by all the pilot schools was negotiating an annual budget with the school department. Despite clear agreement in the contract that the pilot schools were to be "fiscally autonomous," the school department, despite good intentions, found it difficult to translate that pledge into reality and set up the budget and purchasing systems that ensured "autonomy." Particularly difficult for the department was defining the per-pupil budget for the pilot schools. In regular schools, per-pupil budget is typically 60%–70% of the district per-pupil budget. The rest is expended centrally, some for central administration, some for non-school-based district expenditures (special-education residential placements, insurance, etc.), and some for centrally expended school-based costs (employee benefits, utilities, transportation, etc.).

Little progress was made in Boston's first three pilot-school years in defining what the pilot schools could receive as per-pupil budgets. Representatives from the pilot schools, the school district, and the union met for over a year as the Fiscal Autonomy Working Group and made recommendations. But although the administration remained flexible and did much to increase the per-pupil pilot-school budgets, little progress was made, until just recently, on setting up the systems for increased autonomy for the pilot schools and for increased school-site budgeting autonomy in all the district's regular schools, as called for under SBM/SDM.

LESSONS FOR SCHOOL DISTRICTS

Boston's pilot-school initiative is now 5 years old. Five pilots are entering their 5th year of operation, two are entering their 3rd year, two opened in the fall of 1997, and two more have opened in the fall of 1998. One of those opening in the fall of 1998 is the Boston Arts Academy, a collaboration of six arts and music colleges in Boston that was originally selected in the first round but delayed opening until a proper facility could be secured (Linda Nathan, formerly of Fenway, is now the director of this school).

The Arts Academy illustrates one of the successes of the pilot-school innovation—the attraction of talented and highly capable design teams to develop and manage the new schools. This talent includes one of America's foremost educational innovators (Deborah Meier), a New American School Design Team (Expeditionary Learning), a consortium of colleges, and a school cited by the U.S. Department of Education as one of ten New American High Schools (Fenway). Charters in Massachusetts and elsewhere have, of course, attracted quality leaders, but not at the percentage level achieved in Boston. This is perhaps due to several factors: (a) the district and union's joint support for the initiative; (b) the district's involvement in solving the facilities problem by taking responsibility for securing and renovating appropriate sites; and (c) the opportunity for the innovators to influence reform developments in the district.

If imitation is flattery, then another success is the fact that the pilot schools were the model for the state's second-round charter legislation to increase the number of charter schools in the state. As in many other states, initial charter-school legislation in Massachusetts capped the number of charter schools at 25. The new legislation, passed in June 1997, increased the number of charters from 25 to 50 but went beyond its original "district bypass" strategy when it reserved up to 13 of the expansion slots for "Horace Mann" schools, modeled after the Boston pilots, in that they require the agreement of the local school district and the local teachers-union affiliate to support the proposal by an existing school to take on the charter status while remaining within the district.

Another critical benefit of the pilot-school initiative, recognized by all the pilots, is the freedom to select staff from inside or outside the district, and to "de-select" staff and return them to the regular system.

LESSONS FOR STATES

States may want to follow the Massachusetts example and institute some form of Horace Mann approach. This would allow for both state-sponsored charters and in-district charters. In Massachusetts the new round of charter-school proposals in the fall of 1997, to be selected at the end of February 1998, drew 48 state-sponsored (Commonwealth schools) and 13 in-district (Horace Mann schools) proposals. The Horace Mann proposals included several quality district partnerships involving business, government, higher education, and unions.

Whereas many state charter laws, like that of California, require charter proposers to get local school board approval, the new Massachusetts approach differs markedly in that it retains state sponsorship (bypass) and constructively engages local partnerships for in-district charters. States, however, may want to go beyond just creating enabling legislation and drive the development of in-district charters by offering incentives through grants for start up, including design, planning, and funds for equipment.

Boston's example shows how far it is possible for a district and a union to go in sponsoring innovative new schools. Such a development, when it occurs, surpasses significantly the impact of state-sponsored charter schools, in that the in-district charters inform, and help drive, the local school-reform process. By contrast, state-sponsored charters often are marginalized by the limits of state support and the hostility of local school districts. Lack of state funds for capital financing to build facilities and lack of support and promotion by local educational districts often result in charter schools that fill exotic niches (home schooling, school dropouts, small alternative schools, etc.) but have little impact on reform developments in large urban districts or in the state.

LIMITATIONS OF THE PILOT-SCHOOL MODEL

But the pilot model definitely has limitations. First, it is difficult to get a union and a district to collaborate on such an innovation, in that it requires both to give up their rules and regulations with the concurrence of their constituencies. This is demonstrated by the fact that to date no other district in the United States has copied it, though it was seriously discussed in Minneapolis, San Diego, and New York City.

New York City has been the national success story in promoting the creation of more than 100 new small and innovative schools during the past 4 years. Despite some interesting exceptions regarding personnel selection, however, these schools otherwise operate mostly within the union contract and school board regulations.

Second, school districts are hard pressed to set up the budgetary and personnel systems that ensure autonomy to in-district charters or to the SBM/SDM schools that also desire it. Such a development comes up against the flexibility that districts and unions often need, legitimately, to deal centrally with certain difficult budget and personnel issues. A balance is possible, in a systems sense, but not easily developed.

In the new state charter round last November, four of the original five Boston pilot schools opted to apply for the state Horace Mann status. These schools cited as a rationale their need for "greater budget autonomy" and "additional administrative flexibility" regarding staffing, contracting, hiring, purchasing, and paperwork. Although the state initiative represents an endorsement of the Boston model of district-sponsored charters, this move to state Horace Mann status by some of the Boston pilots can be viewed as a tacit criticism of the pilot-school model, that is, the failure of the district to set up the fiscal systems needed for the schools to have full autonomy. In Boston's case, however, the challenge of Horace Mann status has led recently to a significant agreement on increased budget autonomy for all the pilot schools in the next school year.

Third, in-district charters have lots of start-up problems, like all new schools, particularly in change management and governance. These schools need help to plan, implement, and reflect upon their innovations. A district (and a superintendent) needs to do more than enable the development of pilot schools—it needs to give leadership and support to the process and articulate clearly its role in the reform strategy of the district.

Fourth, the in-district charter model works well for enlisting new schools but has been ineffective in recruiting existing schools to apply for Whole School Pilot Status. As with SBM/SDM waivers of district and union contract rules and regulations, a supermajority vote by two thirds of the teachers, a majority of the parents, and the concurrence of the principal is required for Whole School Pilot School Status. Only 1 of 11 Boston pilot schools, the Fenway, was able to get the two-thirds vote. Fenway at the time of the vote had only 12 teachers, making it about one fifth the size of even the smallest Boston district high schools.

Of course, this is not surprising. Even a vote by a smaller supermajority, or even a majority, might be difficult to get. The total restructuring of the school required for Whole School Pilot Status may be unappealing to teachers who were assigned to the school not because of a common vision but randomly. And giving up a union contract is clearly perceived by many teachers as giving up an insurance policy. Teachers may not be union loyalists, but ask them to give up their insurance policy of contractual rights and they balk.

This is true not just in the Boston experience but also in the many schools across the country involved in the CES and in the many urban jurisdictions where existing schools are being supported by their districts to work with the New American School Design teams.

In Boston this is now a significant issue. The district and the union committed to high school restructuring in the latest contract agreement (1997–2000) and have launched a joint task force to develop and implement this initiative. Although a majority of a school faculty may opt for the redesign of a school, achieving a supermajority vote is difficult, and it is unreasonable to require a two-thirds majority in order to go forward. Boston should experiment with a lower supermajority vote (58% or 60%), or some other enabling option (including reconstitution and start-up), in order to spur some high school redesign. Otherwise, such innovations will be limited to small start-ups.

Finally, what's crucial for both state-sponsored and in-district charter-school initiatives is not just the existence of a capped number of innovative schools but also an ongoing process for creating them. Teachers, and other parties, need an open door to get their act together and create new entities. To Boston's credit, the new contract leaves open the door for the district and the union to get together at any time during the life of the contract, as they did in the spring and fall of 1996, and open up a new round of pilot proposals.

Are pilot schools smarter charters than state-sponsored charters? Boston's pilot-school initiative has its limitations, as does every state's charter-school initiative. But in Boston the now threefold set of charter-school enabling processes—pilots, state-sponsored charters, and state-enabled Horace Mann schools—has led to perhaps the largest and most interesting concentration of charter schools in the nation.

REFERENCES

Budde, R. (1988). *Education by charter*. Andover, MA: Regional Laboratory for Educational Improvement.

Panasonic Foundation. (1996, October). In-district charters: The space shuttle or a spruce goose. *Strategies*.

Wilson, L. & Doherty, E. (1990). The making of a contract for education reform. *Phi Delta Kappan, 71,* 91–96.

CHAPTER 4

The State's Role in Shaping a Progressive Vision of Public Education

Dan French

Recently, a respected teacher wrote me, "As a teacher in a project-based public school which holds high standards for the work and character of its students, I was pleased to see the Massachusetts Education Reform Act generate interest in our efforts. The state asked my colleagues and me to share ideas for building a culture of quality with schools state-wide. Examples of impressive projects, teacher-crafted curriculum, striking portfolios of student work were met with excitement. Then, abruptly, it ended, and a new message appeared. Standards have been replaced by standardization, excellence in work replaced by obsession with test scores."

Even after having recently spent 13 years in the Massachusetts Department of Education, I couldn't disagree with him. Rethinking and reshaping the role of state education agencies and school districts is fraught with perils. We have seen many examples of states and districts that, under the banner of reform and the pressure to increase academic performance, have created policies and requirements that increase their control over schools and compound the bureaucracy under which schools have to survive. This state movement toward increased authority, uniformity, and bureaucracy is a natural tendency for large organizations that are seeking to influence and leverage change. The result has been a proliferation of practices that cause concern among those many educators who are truly committed to building a vision of public schooling that benefits all students.

Is it possible for a state education agency to play a progressive role in shaping public education? And if so, what is that role? Can there be a constructive integration of state influence and democratic diversity of schools? In this chapter, I explore these questions and outline a future agenda for state education agencies to play in transforming public education. In particular, using Massachusetts as a case study, I examine the recent state movement toward adoption of curriculum frameworks and state assessment tests as vehicles in the search for accountability and increased achievement scores.

MASSACHUSETTS: A CASE STUDY OF AN EDUCATION AGENCY

Until 1994, Massachusetts essentially had no statewide curriculum mandates. The premise was that local control ensured that a school district would make more appropriate decisions than the state about providing a quality curriculum to its unique population of students.

Unfortunately, the lesson learned in Massachusetts is that, in a society that is stratified along racial and economic lines, the absence of standards guarantees stratified educational opportunities for students based on where they live and their background. Inevitably, students living in an urban district or a poor rural district received curriculum and educational opportunities greatly inferior to those offered to students in more affluent districts.

Some of this educational disparity had to do with inequitable state funding of the public schools, so that some suburban districts spent more than three times as much per pupil as did less affluent rural and urban districts, resulting in large differences in class size, quality of the teaching force, support services, extracurricular activities, and scope of curriculum offerings. Moreover, academic inequities were equally insidious and doomed low-income students and students of color to an inferior education. For example, a 1986 Massachusetts Department of Education report analyzed course-taking patterns of 3,000 high school graduates from the class of 1984 (Massachusetts Department of Education, 1985, 1986).

Even when students from poor rural and urban districts took courses with the same titles as those offered in suburban districts, students' experiences differed profoundly. In examining college preparatory algebra I and U.S. history high school courses, the study found that suburban students taking these courses were given more homework, had longer class periods, gained greater access to educational materials, and received a more rigorous curriculum than did urban and rural students enrolled in courses with the same titles.

These disparities in access to educational opportunities are fueled by our society's perceptions of students' capabilities based on their racial and socioeconomic background. Simply put, if a student is poor and of color—or both—the majority of teachers and administrators are likely to expect less of that student than they will of affluent, White students. This has been documented time and time again. For example, recent Massachusetts data from the state assessment test indicate that students in low-income school districts were three to four times more likely to state that the curriculum was mostly memorization, a set of unrelated facts, and not very interesting (Massachusetts Department of Education, 1994).

Essentially, in a state that had no standards within a society that has wide and increasing gaps in standards of living based on race and class, the curriculum that students received was shaped in large part by residence, socioeconomic status, and racial-ethnic background. Birth and economic status, regardless of funding inequities among suburban districts and poor rural and urban districts, virtually dictated whether a student would receive educational opportunities that enabled success in the larger society or relegated the person to a lifetime of marginal employment with few chances of promotion and mobility.

A PROMISING START: THE BEGINNINGS OF STATE CURRICULUM FRAMEWORKS

In June 1993, the Massachusetts State Legislature enacted the Education Reform Act, which called for the creation of first-time curriculum frameworks in the major academic disciplines, school improvement plans and school councils, and a new high-stakes assessment test tied to high school graduation (Education Reform Act of 1993). State allocations were realigned to address funding inequities. The act required broad public participation in the creation of the frameworks. There was ample reason for high hopes, despite the uneasiness created by a high-stakes graduation test.

Leadership within the Massachusetts Department of Education interpreted the call for public participation as the cornerstone to developing academic standards and curriculum frameworks. Department staff reasoned that the very act of creating forums in every district, as well as statewide, for teachers to talk about what students should know and be able to do, how teachers should teach, and how to best assess what students know and are able to do, would improve learning, teaching, and assessment in classrooms. Most teachers in most schools have precious little time to discuss their craft, to look at and review student work collaboratively, to develop curriculum, to learn new ways of engaging students. Department staff also reasoned that if teachers were involved in developing the academic standards, their feeling of ownership and understanding of those standards would increase, resulting in a higher level of implementation in the classroom.

Thousands of teachers, administrators, parents, legislators, and business representatives created the Common Core of Learning, a broad statement of what students should know and be able to do, that would form the foundation upon which to develop the curriculum frameworks (Massachusetts Board of Education, 1994). Committees of 25 practitioners were formed to develop a framework for each of seven disciplines: English language arts, mathematics, science, social studies and history, arts, world languages, and health (the mathematics and science & technology committees had a head start, thanks to receiving a National Science Foundation grant prior to the Education Reform Act). Practitioners represented K–12 teachers, principals, superintendents, district staff, parents, special-education and bilingual-education teachers, and community, business, and higher education representatives. Massachusetts also became the first state in the country to recognize that high school students themselves could provide valuable insight into answering the question of what students should know, be able to do, and—equally important—what methods of teaching are most effective.

Public engagement has to be like the ever-widening circles caused by a stone's impact in a pond. An additional 300 to 400 educators, students, and parents were placed in focus groups, which met three or four times over the course of the frameworks' development to provide feedback on emerging drafts and guide the work of the framers. Regional curriculum framework open houses in every region of the state were conducted twice annually to raise the public's awareness of the frameworks and seek broader input, reaching an additional few thousand educators and parents.

At first, there was natural suspicion. "Do you have these [frameworks] already written in your back pocket?" "Is this process designed just to provide the appearance of input?" "Is the state really going to let teachers, parents, and high school students determine what students should know?" After all, it was the state they were being asked to trust and count on. As time went on, these concerns were allayed as the committees freely and flexibly continued to grapple with the meaning of statewide curriculum frameworks. Every month for a year, committee members met in 2- to 5-day retreats, sharing experiences of how students learn best, debating what essential knowledge is, balancing depth and breadth, painstakingly carving out ideas of learning, teaching, and assessment in their respective disciplines. These discussions, sometimes heart wrenching, other times jovial, still others culminating in a group "aha" realization, made enduring impressions on most of the participants. They were actually experiencing the kind of culture that breeds dynamic teaching and challenging and engaging curriculum in schools.

CHARTING THE COURSE: THE COMMON CHAPTERS

Shortly upon embarking on the committee process of framework development, the state education staff and committee members began to cock their ears whenever the committees reported to the larger group. They noted a familiar ring as each committee described the role of the teacher and of the student in the classroom, effective learning experiences for students, ways in which students should be assessed as to what they knew. "Learning by doing is best"; "students need to do the learning, teachers need to become more like facilitators"; "we need multiple ways of teaching and assessing a diverse body of students"; "we're asking questions that have no easy answer"; "tracking prevents all students from having access to knowledge," were comments that echoed and resonated among the groups.

What became clear to participants was that some elements of learning, teaching, and assessment were powerful in reaching students across all disciplines, regardless of particular content. They also noted certain ways of organizing schools that created fertile ground for these effective teaching practices to occur more regularly. Then it dawned on us: Could we create a document that served as the foundation upon which to build all of the discipline frameworks, that provoked dialogue and discussion among educators and parents about what schools and schooling should look like, feel like, and be like? Out of this, *Charting the Course: The Common Chapters of the Massachusetts Curriculum Frameworks,* was born (Massachusetts Department of Education, 1996).

These common introductory chapters to the frameworks were not intended to be a doctrine of how teachers should teach and how schools should be organized for learning. Rather, this set of chapters was designed to communicate a strong message that how we teach, how we assess student learning, and how schools are organized have as significant an impact on what students learn as does the curriculum that states what students should know and be able to do.

Although the common chapters were voluntary for districts, teachers and educators reading them had to grapple with basic beliefs about schools and schooling: How do children learn best? Does ability grouping enable all students to learn a rigorous curriculum? How does one teach in ways that challenge and teach students to use their minds well? What are the best ways of using special-education and Title I staff so that students' diverse learning needs are met? Many a teacher, principal, and superintendent commented at framework forums that the best thing the department of education did was to force educators to talk about learning, teaching, and organizing schools, instead of focusing solely on content.

INTRODUCING STUDY GROUPS:
REFLECTIVE DISCOURSE AND PRACTICE

The original draft frameworks were meant as broad guidelines to what students should know and be able to do, while providing wide latitude to districts in the creation of curriculum that matched the standards. They avoided long lists of specific knowledge students must acquire. The standards were crafted to focus on the concepts and skills that students must know, which they can then apply to learning the facts of whatever discipline.

In December 1994, when the first drafts of each framework were nearly ready for public release and comment, department staff and committee members came to a key realization. It was the fervent discussions of learning and teaching in which the framework committees had engaged that had had the most impact on participants. Merely sending out the framework drafts, without creating the culture for having meaningful discussions about what students should know and be able to do, would have minimal impact. Was there a way to replicate the culture that allowed a diverse group of educators to have fruitful and meaningful conversations about their craft and discipline?

The solution we arrived at was simple yet powerful. In January 1995, the Massachusetts Department of Education distributed $3 million across the state by formula, providing each of the approximately 350 districts with funds to create teacher study groups to discuss the drafts of the frameworks, try them out in the classroom, and provide feedback to improve them. More than 1,000 study groups were formed, with about 10,000 educators participating. Nearly 1,000 study-group facilitators, selected by their peers, were trained by the department to conduct these groups. It was recommended that study groups meet a minimum of 15 times, each meeting lasting 90 minutes, to discuss the frameworks. Study groups were encouraged to send in products of their work. Videotapes of classrooms, curriculum units based on the draft academic standards, and plans for school restructuring flooded the department, providing evidence that sustained dialogue about learning and teaching can be the most potent tool for improving schools.

Many teachers expressed both orally and in writing that they had never before had this kind of forum to talk about the practice of teaching. One 30-year veteran social studies teacher related his reluctant revelations through his study group. He had joined the district's social studies study group just to ensure that his curriculum would not be altered by others. He listened as the group discussed the core concept of the discipline—uncovering social studies through asking questions. One morning, as he was starting a new unit on immigration in his U.S. history class, instead of writing up the unit questions on the blackboard, he left it blank and asked students what questions they would like to explore. Quickly, the blackboard was filled with questions: Why did immigrants come over to the United States? What were living conditions like for them? Was it always like the American Dream for them? Are immigrants today better off than in the past? When the teacher stepped back, he realized these questions were almost the same ones he would have written on the board, but now they were the students' own questions, in their own words.

This is a small but pivotal step for a teacher to take, one that can deeply affect how he approaches learning and teaching in the future. Similar stories were abundant from other disciplines: helping students to construct their own meaning in English language arts, assisting students to learn and feel the power of mathematics in interacting with the world, for example.

CREATING REFORM NETWORKS
COMMITTED TO DEMOCRATIC SCHOOLS

Schools have a greater chance of being successful when they have opportunities to collaborate with other like-minded schools. Just as we need to break down the egg-crate isolation of teachers within their closed-door classrooms, we need to reduce the provincialism that many schools experience from trying to improve in a vacuum.

Realizing this, in 1990 the Massachusetts Department of Education had launched a group of reform networks, many affiliated with national reform movements, that included the Coalition of Essential Schools, Accelerated Schools, Project Zero, Carnegie Turning Points, and High Schools That Work, focused primarily on urban and rural schools. The goal of this initiative was to engage network schools in school-wide dialogue and change that resulted in models of learning, teaching, assessment, and organizing schools that improved student learning. Selected schools had to demonstrate school-wide faculty commitment to undertake a multiyear process of transformation. Schools within each network received multiyear small-scale planning and professional-development grants, funded using a combination of Title I, special-education, and state funds, as well as on-site coaching, networking opportunities to collaborate with other member schools, and professional development for faculty and principals.

For those schools not wanting to affiliate closely with a particular school-reform model yet seeking a collaborative relationship with other schools, the Massachusetts Department of Education formed professional development alliances, or clusters of grade-level schools and universities that were committed to collaborating on a joint professional-development agenda. Each alliance was required to organize a steering/governance committee on which each member school/institution had representation. This committee was responsible for creating a democratically built agenda of sustained professional development for all faculty. Out of this process grew study groups, minigrants to teacher teams to develop curriculum, "chalk talk" sessions, college courses, and action research projects.

Upon the initiation of the state's Education Reform Act, it was decided that these network schools could play a key role in implementing the curriculum frameworks. Schools that are engaged in school-wide conversations about learning, teaching, and assessment are more primed than other schools to talk formally about what students should know and be able to do. While continuing to retain their separate identities, these networks were thus integrated under a larger umbrella, the Education Reform Restructuring Network (ERRN), to reflect their key role in implementing the state's new Education Reform Act. All told, at its peak in 1996, the umbrella ERRN network contained more than 150 schools, primarily urban and rural, in the school-reform initiatives, comprising almost 10% of the state's schools, and about 300 schools in the professional-development alliances.

THE TIDE TURNS: WHEN STANDARDS CAN CONSTRICT INNOVATION

Although broad state academic standards can serve to spark dialogue in schools about curriculum, teaching, and organizing schools for learning, there is also a downside to the state and national standards movement. As we have experienced in Massachusetts, promoting academic standards without a larger vision of democratic schools is a dangerous proposition. A rigid framework canon can reinforce educational inequities because it doesn't provide a vision of learning, teaching, and assessment that embraces diverse learners, or it doesn't address rigid tracking that relegates some students to a second-class education. Standards that are mandated without input from the field do little to establish a culture of teachers who discuss improving student learning and the craft of teaching. Ultimately, rigid standards create winners and losers among students by narrowing the focus of curriculum and by creating pressure to cover material rather than using diverse instructional approaches to reach more students. In a stratified society, these winners and losers are invariably identified by their income status and race.

In 1996, former Boston University President John Silber was appointed chair of the state board of education. State legislation overhauled the board membership, allowing Chairman Silber and Governor William Weld to stack the deck by bringing in more conservatives. The new board majority had multiple associations with organizations such as the Pioneer Institute, a conservative think tank.

Along with these new board members came a new conservative philosophy regarding curriculum frameworks, academic standards, and statewide assessment tests. The common chapters, which had spearheaded much discussion in districts about how to teach all students, were essentially put in mothballs. The pedagogy of high expectations, inquiry and project-based learning, interdisciplinary curriculum, and authentic assessment was in conflict with many of the conservative board members' views on education. "The best active learning I know of is sitting at your desk taking notes on a good lecture," retorted one board member in reaction to a guiding principle in the draft social studies framework calling for active learning. Board members were opposed to discussions about tracking and ability grouping, breaking large schools into smaller learning communities, and inclusion being discussed within a frameworks document. A larger vision of democratic schools was being snuffed out.

Under the reconstituted board's leadership, the curriculum frameworks for social studies and English language arts underwent significant transformation. Teacher committees were dismissed, and new drafts were created by conservative board members and handpicked practitioners who shared their political viewpoints. In the new social studies drafts, lists of facts about people, places, dates, times, and events predominated and a strong Eurocentric point of view was emphasized, virtually omitting key areas of the world. In the English language arts section, English and U.S. authors were stressed, with only a token mention of authors from Asia, Africa, and Latin America. The emergent framework with its rigidity, prescriptiveness, and much expanded focus on coverage forces innovative schools and teachers to make difficult choices in order to change and adapt successful curriculum to align with the new standards.

The focus on the emerging new state assessment system was equally distressing. The original Education Reform Act language called unequivocally for a state assessment system that included multiple assessments designed to improve teaching and learning:

> The [state assessment] system shall be designed both to measure outcomes and results regarding student performance, and to improve the effectiveness of curriculum and instruction. . . . The system shall employ a variety of assessment instruments on either a comprehensive or statistically valid sampling basis. . . . As much as is practicable, especially in the case of students whose performance is difficult to assess using conventional methods, such instruments shall include consideration of work samples, projects and portfolios, and shall facilitate authentic and direct gauges of student performance. . . . The

assessment instruments shall be designed to avoid gender, cultural, ethnic or racial stereotypes and shall recognize sensitivity to different learning styles and impediments to learning . . . (Education Reform Act of 1993)

While the proposed 10th-grade test was tied to high school graduation, the language engendered much hope that the eventual state assessment system could be a blend of varied local and state assessment measures that were designed both to stimulate improved teaching and to measure performance.

Unfortunately, with the new state board of education, this did not happen. A number of the state assessment committees were dismissed with equal disdain, as were the curriculum framework committees, to be replaced by others who disproportionately held positions on assessment that mirrored those held by conservative members of the board. The vision of the state assessment system was quickly reduced to a single, high-stakes, annual, on-demand test for grades 4, 8, and 10. Testing mania obscured the original intent of the Education Reform Act and reinforced the board's belief in the narrow, prescriptive frameworks they had developed.

Simultaneously, the department of education was told that it needed to have a sole focus on implementing the new curriculum frameworks and state assessment test, and that all other initiatives needed to take a back seat. In this context, it was decided that the ERRN was siphoning time and resources away from this goal, and the entire network was disbanded after the 1997–98 school year. This decision came despite evidence from an evaluation report that showed cautious optimism that schools in the reform networks, especially at the middle and high school levels, had a greater chance of improving student learning as measured by the state assessment test (DePascale, 1997). Fundamentally, the concept of creating a diverse array of school-reform networks that promoted democracy and equity clashed with the bureaucracy's vision of standards and testing. (Fortunately, federal Porter-Obey funds will continue to fund 50 schools adopting a reform model.)

LESSONS TO LEARN

What can we learn from this case study? Harold Howe II, former commissioner of the U.S. Department of Education, once said, "If you have to have state and national standards, they should be as broad as possible" (1997). Howe was acknowledging that standards can be valuable in ensuring equitable opportunities for all students. At the same time, he was pointing out the fine balance between creating broad standards that can help provide a level playing field for students, and ensuring wide latitude for schools to be innovative in how and what they teach students.

In Massachusetts, what started out as an initiative to walk this balance beam of reform has turned into an effort that is fraught with the problems that frequently characterize too many bureaucratic, authoritarian, state-sponsored initiatives:

1. *Excluding practitioners from the development of education policies that affect them.* Removing teachers from the frameworks' development process eliminated valuable professional growth and eroded trust. The new process reinforced the factory model of schooling, in which teachers cannot be trusted to take a leadership role in deciding what students should know and be able to do and are regarded as merely the conveyors of already prescribed information.

Unfortunately, this policy weakens not only teachers' understanding of the curriculum frameworks and how to use them in the classroom but also their commitment to implement them. It is a fallacy to believe that we can improve schools and raise academic achievement when we do not involve in the decision-making process those who are responsible for teaching students each and every day.

2. *Academic standards that are overly prescriptive and narrow.* In the content disciplines, it is too often the case that students must learn an endless lists of facts, facts that often educated adults don't even know. Certainly U.S. students need to learn facts, but there must be a good balance between coverage and depth. Overbearing coverage of facts precludes the ability to focus in depth on essential concepts, leading students to superficial knowledge about the world that is easily forgotten over time. Coverage forces teachers to reduce or even exclude teaching methods that are more successful with diverse students, such as project-based learning, small-group work, and student exhibitions, because these activities take more time. Too often, especially in English language arts and social studies/history, coverage lists reflect the political viewpoint of those with decision-making power. This is particularly true when the standards are constructed in a vacuum devoid of democratic input and inquiry.

3. *High-stakes tests that promote teaching a narrow range of facts rather than knowledge and understanding.* State assessment tests, especially high-stakes tests that are used to determine who graduates and who doesn't, are all the rage in this nation. It is as if the act of testing students, divorced from the actual classroom practices of learning and teaching, is going to somehow make students smarter. Yet little evidence indicates that a single, high-stakes test improves and sustains student learning and the effectiveness of curriculum and instruction. At the same time, ample evidence indicates

that the use of a single, high-stakes test helps widen the achievement gap between White, Black, and Hispanic students, as well as between affluent and low-income students.

Inevitably, high-stakes testing encourages uniformity rather than diversity in building successful schools. It focuses on punitive measures for schools that are under the designated cutoff score for acceptable performance, rather than analyzing and creating the conditions under which more schools and more students can be successful.

More important, most high-stakes state assessment tests are being developed using a process that far too often excludes, rather than includes, those who have to do the real work with students. Large testing companies use predeveloped data banks of questions to mix and match ready-made state assessment tests. Or, as in the case of Massachusetts, assessment committees are stacked with people representing a narrow political perspective. When the very people who are responsible for educating our students are not involved in the assessment development process, there is every reason to believe that the assessment test will be an intrusion in the classroom rather than a benefit to the learning and teaching process.

4. *Ignoring the conditions that need to be in place for democratic schools to flourish.* Many of the new state assessment tests, like those in Massachusetts, are characterized by an incorrect belief that academic standards and high-stakes assessment alone will raise achievement levels of students. Unfortunately, this is not true, especially for low-income students and students of color. For example, academic standards and high-stakes testing are going to be ineffective with many students if the content is biased, if the teacher's expectations of students is low, if student grouping practices condemn some students to never catching up, or if there isn't a nurturing learning environment that accepts and embraces diverse approaches to learning.

In the end, although this narrow, authoritarian approach to standards and assessment may result in minimal overall increases in student achievement and pockets of significant improvement in some districts, the gap between low-income students and students of color will likely continue to remain large and possibly even increase.

LOOKING TO THE FUTURE: CAN STATE EDUCATION AGENCIES PLAY A PROGRESSIVE ROLE IN PROMOTING INNOVATION, RIGOR, AND EQUITY IN ALL SCHOOLS?

The public schools of the United States house a global diversity of students representing many races, ethnicities, cultures, and languages. Similarly, our schools represent a broad diversity of educational philosophies and practices. This is our strength.

Our schools also reflect the deep-seated and pernicious effects of social-class and race stratification in our larger society. This can be seen in rigid ability-grouping and tracking practices that bunch disproportionate numbers of low-income students and students of color in low-level classes, in the curricula of urban schools and districts that reflect lowered expectations and dumbed-down standards, in the creation of warehouse schools that are large and impersonal, and in the disproportionate emphasis on narrow instructional practices that reach only a small percentage of students. This is our challenge.

Public education has been all too successful in fulfilling the time-honored purpose of molding our young citizenry to take their rightful places in U.S. society, as pre-determined by their race, culture, and socio-economic status. We need to break the mold. Yet small, innovative schools are doomed to be educational islands unless we forge a new progressive role for state education agencies to create the conditions that these schools need to proliferate. To not do so condemns the vast majority of our public schools to mirror the race and class inequities that exist in our larger society, while a few isolated schools, almost in spite of their state and district, thrive, much like the wispy trees that cling to rocks and soil particles in alpine conditions, somehow finding just enough nurturance to grow.

CRAFTING A PROGRESSIVE AGENDA
FOR STATE EDUCATION AGENCIES IN
PROMOTING SUCCESSFUL EDUCATION REFORM

We need to create a movement for successful schools, one that reaches beyond individual examples of excellent schools. One piece of the puzzle is to radically reshape the institutions of educational democracy so that they serve and support our schools, teachers, parents, and students, rather than control them. State education agencies need to devote their leverage and resources to marrying rigor and diversity, equity and democracy, high expectations and multiple intelligences, rather than promoting a shotgun wedding featuring uniformity, rigid standards, and narrow high-stakes tests. Our educational institutions need to act and behave democratically, in the truest sense of the word.

What does this look like? I offer the following five guidelines around which state education agencies can organize themselves to promote successful schools:

1. *A philosophy and practices that are fundamentally based on the principles of democracy and equity.* State education agencies should be driven by the belief that those closest to students and the students themselves should be the critical players in making decisions and creating policy that shape public education. For society to invest in creating good schools, those on the front line must be involved in the discussion that shapes what those schools will look like—teachers, parents, students, and administrators, as well as representatives of higher education, community institutions, and business. Through study groups, focus groups, working committees, drafting and redrafting, each and every district and school must be significantly represented. This messy process is necessarily neither linear nor final, but it is the only way to invite and sustain a lasting culture of commitment to creating successful schools.

Just as the *process* of democracy is a critical step in creating a movement for successful schools, so too is the *practice* of educational democracy and equity. Schools need to look and act democratically and equitably. As Carl Glickman (1993) notes, successful schools are marked by high levels of collaboration and collegiality rather than individual autonomy. The language one hears in these schools is "we" and "our" rather than "I" and "my." Teachers are not treated as subordinates but rather granted the authority to make decisions and act on these decisions. In these schools, there is also a constant, sustained focus on raising the learning ceiling and closing the academic gap between low-income and affluent students and between White students and students of color. All practices promote rigor and equity for all students. All members openly invite dialogue and debate, express diverse viewpoints, and offer rich ideas as they work together.

State education agencies and school districts have tremendous leverage and power, and the public and schools listen to what they advocate. Imagine if these institutions actually used their power to promote a vision of democratic schools that are shaped by a commitment to equity!

2. *Broad standards, not standardization.* Standards have a role in a just, equitable society. They offer one important means of creating a more level playing field by stating that we want all students to be held to similar standards. In fact, the best schools already do this for their students.

Broad standards are helpful in shaping effective schools if they

- Are created by and for teachers, students, and parents;
- Are one piece of a broader effort to realize a new vision of learning, teaching, and assessment as well as how schools should be structured for learning;

- Articulate a vision of democratic schools and democratic schooling;
- Are used to promote sustained forums for teachers to discuss what students should know and be able to do, and how best to teach them and assess what they know;
- Allow local schools and districts to interpret and shape them to their students' needs.

Broad standards can spark dialogue and discussion among teachers about what makes good schools and classrooms, and what students should know and be able to do. Rather than promote exhaustive, narrow lists of bite-sized information for students to swallow, these standards should allow schools and districts flexibility to develop their own more specific standards if they so choose. A key piece of the standards puzzle is placing equal emphasis on the structures and practices of schools that promote engaged learning.

3. *A multileveled assessment system that is focused on improving student learning.* We do need some way of assessing what students know and are able to do and a means of reporting that information coherently to the public. However, ultimately the foremost goal of any state assessment system must be to provide teachers with a concrete tool to assist them in improving student learning.

Such an assessment system should be based on broad rather than narrow academic standards. It should allow students to express their knowledge and understanding in multiple ways and in more than one test.

Most important, high-stakes tests at the state level do little to improve teaching (Muncey & McQuillen, 1993). Dangerously, such tests become sorting mechanisms of the haves and have-nots, and all too often the have-nots are students from those groups that have historically been shut out from access to power. Rather, state education agencies should be assisting districts and schools to develop their own performance measures, including awarding diplomas on the basis of mastery of a range of competencies and promoting a movement away from the tradition of graduation by course counting and seat time.

4. *Commitment to the professionalism of teachers.* Public schools will improve only if teachers are at the center of the reform movement. Yet all too often teachers are only marginally involved in shaping the reform efforts that they are then asked to implement. In many respects, the current standards-reform movement epitomizes the old-school notion of teachers as factory workers rather than professionals. As in the Massachusetts case study, standards development in many states and nationally has all too

often been taken out of the hands of teachers and placed in the hands of so-called experts. Ultimately, however, it is always teachers who must put into practice the educational policies that are developed and who are responsible and held accountable for student learning in school.

We need to start trusting teachers and stop telling them what to do and how and when to do it. We need to redefine teachers as the professionals who take the leading role in deciding how learning, teaching, and assessment in schools should be done. The essence of developing them as professionals lies in giving them the responsibility to develop a body of knowledge about their profession and a means to ensure that knowledge is up to date, much as doctors are required to do. For states and districts, this means always including teachers as critical voices and decision makers in reform discussions through study groups, committees, and other forums.

5. *Diverse networks of like-minded schools that are committed to working together on whole-school reform to achieve excellence and that are provided the support needed for them to be successful.* Democracy implies an embracing of diversity. Just as students have multiple intelligences that require diverse instructional approaches, our schools should reflect variable responses to meet these needs. Each school is a unique learning community, with its own culture and shared beliefs. There is no one uniform educational philosophy or school-reform process that works for all schools.

At the same time, we know that most schools that are successful in significantly improving and sustaining student learning have embraced certain principles of education: collaborative and democratic decision making, personalized learning communities, high expectations, diverse curriculum and instruction, an instructional focus on inquiry and discovery, multivaried assessments, and active family and community involvement. These schools embrace a unified vision for their school community and link with other like-minded schools to collaborate in their journeys.

State education agencies can play an important role in creating democratic schools by establishing an array of reform networks through which schools can work collaboratively to grow and improve. Essentially, we need to create a plethora of schools that are committed to radical reform and that work toward creating a statewide and, ultimately, national democratic schools movement.

6. *Creating conditions that provide districts with opportunities and incentives to grant increased autonomy and flexibility to schools.* Just as a farmer needs to till and fertilize the soil to produce a bumper crop, we need to create conditions under which schools can thrive, that is, an atmosphere that encourages risk taking, setting lofty visions, and experimenting. Too many

barriers now stand in the way of schools, preventing them from becoming laboratories of innovation—lack of budget flexibility, lack of hiring and firing power, lack of control over district-wide specialists, purchasing and contracting requirements, bureaucratic paperwork and reports, and over-reliance on standardized testing, to name just a few.

Rather than supporting thinly veiled efforts to privatize our public schools through vouchers and the charter movement, we need to create the same conditions of flexibility and autonomy for all of our schools *within* school districts. State education agencies and state legislatures need to enact legislation, policies, and regulations that provide districts the opportunity and incentive to grant maximum flexibility and autonomy to their schools with a minimum of state bureaucratic hindrance. Some of the flexibility provisions should include:

- Total lump-sum budgets based on average per-pupil district expenditures, and freedom to purchase and contract services other than through the school district;
- Freedom to hire and release all staff with due process, while providing union wages and benefits;
- Flexibility from district policies, rules, and requirements.

In this scenario, the school would remain a vital member of the school district, sharing and working with other district schools. And the relationship of the district office to its schools would naturally change from regulating to assisting and coaching them to become high-performing learning communities.

In addition to creating the means for schools to become small, democratic learning communities, other provisions that a state education agency can enact to promote these schools are:

- Incentives in the form of grants to districts and schools to adopt increased flexibility and autonomy;
- Facilitated dialogue among teachers unions, superintendents, and school-committee associations to arrive at a common vision of supporting maximum flexibility to create high-quality schools while protecting teachers' wages and rights;
- The promotion of exemplars—successful autonomous schools that embody the principles of democracy and equity.

In return for increased flexibility and autonomy, these schools should be held accountable for improving and sustaining improved learning for all of their students, accountability systems that are determined by and for reforming schools.

THE BOSTON PILOT SCHOOLS NETWORK

One exciting example of district and state policies and legislation that promote small, democratic schools is the Boston Pilot Schools Network. Pilot schools were established as part of the Boston Public Schools in 1994 under a new contract agreement with the Boston Teachers Union. As part of the contract, Boston agreed to allow groups of parents and educators to submit proposals to become pilot schools. These schools, while ensuring union wages and benefits for faculty, would be freed from most union and district requirements, allowing them to become laboratories of innovation. For example, they would have hiring and firing flexibility, lump-sum budgeting, flexibility in setting the school day and year, and freedom from curriculum requirements. The pilot schools were conceived of and created with the hope that successful practices used in pilot schools could be replicated in other Boston schools.

In September 1995, as a result of an extensive review process, five new pilot schools opened their doors—three high schools and two elementary schools. All five schools served 300 students or under, had active faculty and parent participation, and engaged in collaborative decision making. Over the next 4 years, six more pilot schools joined the founders. All told, the current 11 schools serve about 2,200 students. These schools are among those most often selected by families in Boston. When the first pilot middle school, the Harbor School, opened its doors, more than 500 families chose the school as their first or second choice, despite the availability of only 60 openings for the first year. This outpouring of interest indicates how strongly families desire small, personalized, and democratic schools. There is ample evidence that the pilot schools are educating many Boston students who would otherwise not be in the system today.

Initially, the pilot schools were provided little infrastructure of support and no means to link them with other Boston schools. Until 1997, in many ways the pilot schools represented islands of educational innovation, separate from one another and from the Boston Public Schools (BPS). However, during the 1995–96 school year, the Center for Collaborative Education (CCE), a nonprofit education organization dedicated to working with networks of reform-minded urban schools, began working with the pilot schools and in the spring of 1997 both the pilot schools and the BPS agreed to have the CCE become the parent organization for the new Boston Pilot Schools Network.

In a short period of time, the CCE and the BPS have taken significant strides toward becoming a high-performing network of visionary schools. First, the network agreed on a set of shared beliefs and vision about education:

- Pilot schools should have high expectations for each and every student, and the education that students experience should reflect these expectations;
- The people closest to students should be the policymakers and decision makers, including teachers, administrators, parents, and students themselves. This requires democratic forms of school governance and facilitative leadership;
- Schools should be small and personalized, so that teachers and students know each other well;
- The school culture should promote innovation and risk-taking, and professional development should be an integral part of daily school life;
- Learning should be purposeful, authentic, challenging, creative, and build students' capacity to take responsibility for their own learning;
- Authentic forms of assessment, such as portfolios and exhibitions, are key to improving learning and teaching.
- Families are critical partners in creating high-performing pilot schools;
- The people who are responsible for the learning and decision making should be held responsible for the impact of the school in the lives of learners and of the community.

CCE staff have also worked with the pilot schools to plan and convene monthly pilot-school directors' meetings, conduct the annual leadership retreats for pilot-school leaders, and establish a minigrant program for pilot schools to work collaboratively with each other to improve learning and teaching. Recently, in collaboration with the Annenberg Institute for School Reform, CCE staff and the pilot-school directors have developed an accountability system for the pilot schools, based on a school portfolio and school quality review model (Annenberg Institute for School Reform, 1997).

This system replaced the evaluation process previously used by the BPS and shifted ownership of accountability to the pilot schools, where it belongs.

HORACE MANN SCHOOLS

One result of the pilot schools' success is legislation recently enacted by the Massachusetts State Legislature creating Horace Mann schools. These schools, modeled after the Boston pilot schools, provide the opportunity for schools across the state to gain expanded flexibility and autonomy similar to that afforded to Boston pilot schools while retaining membership within the school district in which they currently reside. Similar to pilot schools, a Horace Mann school, while ensuring union wages and benefits for faculty, would negotiate with its respective school district and teachers union to be free from specific union and district requirements, affecting hiring and firing, lump-sum budgeting, setting the school day and year, and planning curriculum.

Massachusetts has set aside 13 slots for new Horace Mann schools to be created over the next 3 years. In many respects, this is ground-breaking legislation that enables public schools within public school districts to receive the same privileges granted to charter schools. Public schools can thrive in significant numbers only when the shackles of bureaucracy, mandates, constrained budgets, and rigidity in staffing patterns and school-day/school-year determinations are removed, leaving the schools the freedom and flexibility to be innovative while remaining contributing members of their respective school districts. With this in mind, we find it interesting that many conservative members of the current state board of education have opposed the Horace Mann schools, stating that these schools were created by the state legislature solely to undermine the proliferation of charter schools. Subsequently, in February 1998, the board of education granted only four charters for Horace Mann schools, a move that included denying Horace Mann status to two Boston pilot schools that had already demonstrated their value to the students they serve. At this same meeting, the board approved eight new charter schools, four of them contracted to for-profit corporations.

One problematic aspect of Massachusetts's new Horace Mann legislation is that it does not provide the opportunity for groups of schools within one district to apply jointly for Horace Mann status. Therefore, for example, schools in the Boston Pilot Schools Network must apply individually for Horace Mann status rather than as a network. As well, the paltry 13 slots afforded to Horace Mann schools preclude the possibility of having large numbers of schools from one district receive Horace Mann charters. The legislation does require the department of education to conduct a study regarding the feasibility of granting district charters to enable a district to grant Horace Mann charters to groups of schools like the Boston pilot schools, but this potential legislation would face opposition from the current board of education and possibly from state teachers unions.

Although just beginning, the Boston Pilot Schools Network and Horace Mann legislation provide a vision of how districts and states can create the conditions to build a movement for small, democratic schools.

CONCLUSION

Can state education agencies play a pivotal role in building a movement for small, democratic schools, or are they too aligned with society's power structures, too prone to the changing tides of politics, too enmeshed in their own bureaucracy, too geared to control and authority to be collaborative players in progressive reform? The answer is that it depends on the leadership and its commitment to a progressive vision of reform. As we have seen in Massachusetts, some signs offer hope that indeed a state education agency can play a constructive role. The department of education continues to promote positive professional-development opportunities for teachers and administrators on standards-based curriculum and improving learning, teaching, and assessment. Yet, in the same case study, we see that a circumstance like the takeover of the state board of education can create conditions that as often as not stifle innovation and attempts to create small, democratic schools. At the same time, the requirement for high-stakes testing virtually guarantees that more students will drop out of school and experience academic failure than have done so in the recent past.

We also have seen that, without districts and states that create the flexibility, autonomy, and vision for schools to thrive, there will be only a smattering of successful individual schools isolated from one another. Under these conditions, we can expect to continue to see the strong push toward increased privatization of public schools through charter schools, vouchers, public funding for private and parochial schools, and for-profit education organizations vying to take over our public schools.

We need a national movement for broad academic standards, small, democratic public schools, and increased accountability through multiple measures.

Yet this national movement is not going to take shape until and unless states and the federal government reverse course from the current rage for high-stakes testing, standardization through rigid curriculum frameworks, punitive measures rather than support to raise school performance, and continued bureaucratic and regulatory controls. President Clinton's recent push for voluntary national tests reflects this blind allegiance to high-stakes testing, tests that just confirm that our current public education system is designed to sort the haves from have-nots. Yet evidence indicates that such a strategy of high-stakes testing does little to change how teachers teach and what students learn (Kellaghan, Madaus, & Raczek, 1996; Koretz, 1997; Muncey & Quillen, 1993; Smith and Rotenberg, 1991).

We need to change our federal, state, and local educational institutions to become supporters of this new vision. We need institutions that (a) create conversations in the field among teachers, administrators, parents, and students in order to develop educational policy that will ultimately benefit and shape the ability of schools to be successful; (b) set broad standards, crafted by practitioners, of what students should know and be able to do, while promoting local innovation and flexibility in order to achieve them;

(c) design multiple assessments to aid students in demonstrating what they know, rather than tests that serve solely as a sorting mechanism; and (d) create and support networks of like-minded schools committed to fundamental change and provide schools with the flexibility and autonomy to accomplish wonderful things. Then, and only then, will we truly have a national movement for excellence and equity for all of our students.

REFERENCES

Annenberg Institute for School Reform. (1997). *Boston Pilot Schools Network, Center for Collaborative Education, Annenberg Institute for School Reform, Boston Public Schools, Boston pilot schools accountability Process: Self study guide.* Providence, RI: Author.

DePascale, C. (1997). *Education Reform Restructuring Network: Impact documentation report.* Portland, ME: Data Analysis and Testing Associates, Inc.

Education Reform Act. (1993). *Chapter 71 of the Acts of 1993: An act establishing the Education Reform Act of 1993.*

Glickman, C. (1993). *Renewing America's schools: A guide for school-based action.* San Francisco: Jossey-Bass.

Howe, H. II. (1997, April). Speech delivered at Haward Graduate School of Education Forum.

Kellaghan, T., Madaus, G. F., & Raczek, A. (1996). *The use of external examinations to improve student motivation.* Washington, D.C.: American Educational Research Association.

Koretz, D. (1997, Summer). Arriving in Lake Wobegon: Are standardized tests exaggerating achievement and distorting instruction? *American Educator, 12*(2), 8–15, 46–52.

Massachusetts Board of Education. (1994). *Massachusetts common core of learning.* Malden, MA: Author.

Massachusetts Department of Education. (1985, June). *Course taking among Massachusetts high school students.* Quincy, MA: Author.

Massachusetts Department of Education. (1986, April). *The high school experience in Massachusetts.* Quincy, MA: Author.

Massachusetts Department of Education. (1994). *Summary of 1994 MEAP results.* Malden, MA: Author.

Massachusetts Department of Education. (1996). *Charting the Course: The common chapters of the Massachusetts curriculum frameworks.* Malden, MA: Author.

Muncey, D., & McQuillen, P. (1993). Preliminary findings from a five year study of the Coalition of Essential Schools. *Phi Delta Kappan, 74,* 486–489.

Smith, M. L. & Rotenberg, C. (1991, Winter). Unintended consequences of external testing in elementary schools. *Education Measurement: Issues and Practice.*

PART II

Voices from the Front Lines:
New York City

CHAPTER 5

A Day in the Life of a Teacher in a Small School

Meredith Gavrin

In September of 1993, the Institute for Collaborative Education (ICE), a combined middle school–high school in New York City, opened with 7th and 9th graders. (The school opened in 1993 as the Institute for Secondary Education. The name was officially changed in January 1996). The school was one of four pilot programs formed in a collaboration between the Manhattan High School Superintendency and District Two. The two districts hoped to create greater continuity between the middle and high school years, maintain small school size, and explore alternative ideas in education. In September 1995, I joined the faculty as a humanities teacher. By the fall of 1996, the school ranged from 6th to 12th grade. The school, accepted as a member of the Coalition of Essential Schools (CES) in 1995, is part of the New York City Public School System, and it is now fully under the auspices of the Manhattan High School Superintendency. The students are academically, economically, and ethnically diverse, and they come to the school from all five boroughs of New York. ICE differs significantly from other middle and high schools in the Manhattan High School Superintendency. With a faculty of approximately 16 teachers and an administration of 2, ICE lacks the middle-level administration many schools have. As a result, policy decisions, scheduling, curriculum design, and advising all involve the entire teaching faculty. The curriculum itself also differs from the New York City public school norm. All course curricula are designed by the faculty with an emphasis on critical-thinking skills, hands-on activity, and project-based assessment. Recently, ICE received a waiver releasing its high school students from the state-required Regents Competency Examinations required in New York State; ICE graduation requirements will instead use portfolio assessment to measure students' mastery of skills and content areas. Finally, ICE is determined to maintain a student body of approximately 300 students and class sections of 25 at a time, whereas the New York City class average falls at about 37. Teaching at ICE has a culture of its own. Each member of the faculty works hours well beyond the teachers union guidelines, with additional administrative responsibilities but few "planning" periods. We hold high academic standards for our students, and they in turn demand that we provide attention, energy, and creative approaches to teaching. Once a friend told me that he would never become a teacher because "you do the same thing day in and day out, and I just don't think I'd be challenged enough." Teaching at ICE is, above all, a challenge.

   7:00 A.M.: Coffee in hand, I walk the five flights of stairs through the building we currently share with two other schools to reach my classroom. My desks have been, once again, rearranged—there must have been an adult school class in the building last night. Drop my bags, finish my coffee, erase yesterday's notes from the blackboard; fill the board with today's class agendas, a "do now" for students to complete when they enter the classroom, and an announcement to remind my advisees about their permission slips for next week's trip to the Metropolitan Museum.

   7:30 A.M.: Rearrange the desks. My 7th graders come in first, so they'll need to be set in a circle to focus the first activity I have planned. I want the desks in clusters for advisory, but I'll have to rearrange again during the 5-minute break between classes. "I found something in the *Times* last night that I think I'm going to use with the 9th grade. What do you think?" Constance walks in as I'm pushing desks and hauling chairs. She hands over a clipped article about parent–child relationships, her lesson plan notes attached to the back with a paper clip. "This is great," I tell her as I skim through the first few paragraphs. "Why don't I pick up the topic with them again in advisory? We've been skirting around issues about their struggles with their parents for weeks." We discuss the connections we can draw between her humanities class readings and my advisory group, and she leaves to organize her own classroom for the day.

   7:55 A.M.: Mark and Julius, two of my 7th graders, arrive and make themselves comfortable, complete with basketball trading cards, breakfast, and a pen to make last-minute additions to last night's homework. I hurry to the office to photocopy 45 copies of a short story for my 7th graders. The office has run out of white paper and our supplies budget is low, so the blue sheets will have to suffice.

   8:00 A.M.: The building bell rings loudly. It signals nothing for our school, but the bell schedule is dictated by the school that occupies the first three floors of the building.

   8:15 A.M.: Classes begin. My 7th-grade class is missing several students, and I know that at least two of them will wander in within 10 or 15 minutes with excuses about a malfunctioning subway. I fill out the attendance form according to who's there at 8:15, and I begin class with the "do now" from the blackboard, a quick writing exercise to generate thoughts for today's short story: "Write about a time when you thought someone misjudged you." With a double class period of 1 hour and 40 minutes, I'll be able to have students read aloud together, discuss part of the reading in groups, and also begin tonight's writing assignment in a "writing workshop." When everyone has finished the "do now," I lead a quick discussion of the ideas students have just written. Some students have written pages, others have struggled to put a few sentences on paper. For each, however, the exercise has, I hope, begun to shift the focus from thinking about home and sleep toward today's class work. For the next 20 minutes or so, we will read the short story "The Kind of Light That Shines on Texas" out loud together. I begin the reading, then take volunteers to continue. After about 5 minutes, I notice that James is doodling in a notebook and has not turned a page. He has difficulty reading, and so he resists it. As Amy continues to read aloud, I move to stand behind James, point to the paragraph Amy is reading, and whisper, "You do the next one—I'll help." With a few sentences left in Amy's paragraph, James can look ahead and prepare. When Amy finishes, he reads smoothly with some assistance from his friend Doug, who sits to his right. At 9:15, we have finished the story. I give the students a 5-minute break, and I remind them to be quiet in the hallways. Nevertheless, I need to stand in the hallway with them to stop a few from making faces in the doorways of their friends' classes, still in session. The last part of class will be writing workshop, where they will begin a several-day-long writing assignment. I explain the assignment, spend several minutes trying to encourage a few distracted students to start working, and then set out to help the students who have questions. I kneel by Shendo, offering advice about how to start his story. I feel a tug on my sleeve; it's David, who needs paper. From across the room, Carlos calls, "Meredith! I need help! Can you come here?" Within 10 minutes, Amy has finished a page and a half, and she wants to know if she "has to" write more. I read her story quickly, then write down four questions for her to consider, to take her story to another level. Too soon, I have to ask students to pack their belongings and leave for their next class.

9:50 A.M.: My 9th-grade class arrives. One student walks in just as I'm about to close the door, and he slams the door with his fist as he passes. "Wait," I say, resting a hand on his shoulder. "What's going on?" "I think I should be in the other section. So I'm not with my friends who distract me. I'll do better." "What happened?" "I'm just getting in trouble all the time and it's not all me." He asks me if he can go talk to the principal. While sending a student to the principal's office is a feared punishment in many schools, our students seek out our principal when they are unhappy, feeling ill, wish to share an accomplishment, or believe they have been treated unfairly. Because I don't want this student to miss class, however, he and I agree that he should wait until the mid-class break before taking his side of the story to the office.

10:50 A.M.: I'm about to switch from a group discussion of an excerpt from Machiavelli's *The Prince* to a writing workshop when Tania, one of the 10th graders, appears at my door. "Can I make an announcement, Meredith?"

"Sure, quickly." "There's going to be a meeting of the student government today at lunch in Andrew's room. Anyone can come. We're going to try to write down all of the students' suggestions about how to change the lunch policy, so it's very important. Andrew's room, lunchtime." We begin the writing workshop, to start a "Passage Paper" essay that requires the students to connect their close reading of a brief passage from the novel we've been reading to the themes of the novel as a whole. When the Humanities Department worked in July to restructure our entire curriculum, grades 6–12, we agreed that making connections is one of the important skills (or "Habits of Mind," in the language of the CES) for the 9th grade to master. This "Passage Paper" will allow me to assess their progress.

11:30 A.M.: I have taken 5 minutes after the end of class to arrange an after-school help session with one of the 9th graders who has been chronically absent; now I'm running late. Today is the day I share cafeteria duty with another teacher. Although the building places two security guards at the door of the cafeteria, they don't know our students well. We prefer to be on duty ourselves, even though that means we lose precious planning time. Mostly, we're there to make sure that our students stay in the cafeteria we use, while students from the other schools in the building file past into the cafeteria at the opposite end of the hallway. Luis, a 9th grader, and Pete, an 11th grader, ask permission to go to art class, held once a week during lunch and taught by a visiting artist. Although they are supposed to have permission slips granting them the right to leave the lunchroom, I know both students well and I accept on good faith their explanation that the artist only arrives at 11:30 and is not present in the morning to write permission slips. As other students sign out for meetings or activities, I realize I've finally learned the names of all but a few students in the school.

12:35 P.M.: My 10th-grade advisees arrive, demanding the cookies they know I've made for Nadia's birthday. When I have taken attendance (on my own form, on the board of education form, and in the notebooks one teacher uses to coordinate attendance and call the homes of absent students), I ask if anyone has any issues to discuss. I'm prepared to use

Constance's article for discussion today, but I'm also willing to postpone that topic. "What happens if you don't complete a class?" Lin asks. We are approaching the end of the "cycle," and the students know that their teachers are writing narrative progress reports for each of their classes. The progress report, in addition to extensive comments about the student's understanding, project work, class work, work habits, and progress, will include a system of "grading": Each student will receive an indication of one of five levels of achievement, ranging from "Completed With Honors" to "Failed to Meet Standards for the Course." The students aren't yet accustomed to the grading system, which is new to us this year. In part, the system is a result of a series of frustrating conversations with college admissions officers who refuse to accept our seniors' narrative reports. "Put it all into numbers," they have told us; we have agreed not to abandon the narratives, but the added "grade" should help. Although I repeat for my advisees the policies regarding course completion and grading that they heard in last week's "town meeting," I emphasize the fact that there is plenty of time to complete the work for all of their courses. "Your teachers *all* stay after school to provide you the help you might need. They will *all* sit with you to finish work that has given you difficulty or to explain assignments you still owe. You can come in any time before school starts or after classes end—everyone's here until at least 5:30 or 6:00. And if a particular teacher can't help you, I can try to help you too." When I confer with Greg and Caitlin later, they tell me that their 11th- and 12th-grade advisees raised the same concerns and they each took the same approach.

1:10 P.M.: My last class for the day: a double period "senior circle" elective. When I took this teaching job last summer, I was given the opportunity to create my own elective, to design a course I "would love to teach." The elective, "Laws and Limits," covers the Bill of Rights, Supreme Court cases, and the issues the cases raise. The only difficulty I've had with the class is scheduling: The class meets three times a week, in the afternoon. One of our graduation requirements is that students take a college course sometime during their 11th or 12th grade ("senior circle") years. Several of my students are taking courses at New York University and Borough of Manhattan Community College, and their courses often conflict with my class. They've made concerted efforts to keep up with work they've missed, and I can usually find time to meet with those students briefly after school. When they have missed a class, however, the next class discussion or case reading is often more difficult for them to follow.

2:50 P.M.: Class has ended, I have Kishara and Jonathan in my room for extra help on an assignment, I have to make four phone calls home to students who owe me a major project that was due last week, I haven't eaten lunch, and the faculty meeting begins in 20 minutes.

2:55 P.M.: Manuel, a 7th grader, stops by to announce that he's running errands for several teachers. "Would you like anything to eat or drink?" Caitlin also stops by to schedule a graduation committee meeting. Despite a waiver from the Board of Regents, we have determined that the 12th graders will have to pass the state-required exams in math, science, reading, and writing. We are concerned that the waiver may be rescinded or that our students might receive criticism from institutions unaware of the waiver system. However, we need the committee meeting to discuss the history exams. If the students are required to pass them, we may have to alter our current humanities curricula. At this point, we have designed our curricula to achieve in-depth coverage of selected topics in literature and history. The state exams demand a survey approach in order to cover, briefly, the scope of American and global history. The dilemma involves not only our students' graduation requirements but the state's view of our curriculum and academic success as a school as well.

3:10 P.M.: I run into the office to call the homes of the four students who owe work. The student intern at the front desk hands me two more messages: one from the mother of one of my advisees, who would like me to call right away to discuss her daughter's work habits, the other from the speaker I have arranged for next week's town meeting.

3:15 P.M.: Andrew has written the agenda for today's meeting on the blackboard: "Attendance reminders, 5 min. Eighth Grade Graduation, 10 min. Portfolios and Presentations, 45 min." The attendance reminder comes from Andrew. In many schools, attendance coordinator is a full-time job; here, Andrew serves as attendance coordinator and coordinator of student activities in addition to teaching and advising. Other teachers serve as admissions coordinator, organize athletics, create after-school programs, or design and coordinate class scheduling. The attendance reminder is an important one: If we do not complete our attendance forms promptly and correctly, our per-pupil funding may be in jeopardy. The 8th-grade graduation committee plans a meeting for next week. Although our school spans middle school and high school years, we signal the passage of our students from lower school to upper school and recognize the fact that some students will choose other schools for their high school years. Our discussion of portfolios and presentations is difficult. Ideally, we believe, students' midyear and end-of-year assessment should consist of projects that incorporate the material and skills they have learned; they then present and defend those projects before panels of teachers, students, parents, and outside guests. "Every time kids demonstrate the work they've done it should happen in front of a panel." "How can we do that? We can't let the middle schoolers go during Regents week, they have to have their full schedule of classes. With them here, how am I supposed to schedule panels for my 11th grade class? And I want to have the 7th graders present their projects as well." "Presenting to a whole class just isn't the same experience." "That's right. We just can't . . ." "But we can't necessarily do right now what we ultimately want to do." "What if we had panels for just the high school?" "Or just at the end of 10th grade, to move to senior circle?" "If we compromise what we want to do now, though, when do the kids grow accustomed to presenting to panels? I thought the whole idea was that that experience just couldn't be replaced by a typical report in front of a class." "It wouldn't be a typical report. . . ." Our immediate concerns and time constraints make realizing our ideal vision more difficult, and the situation may call for interim solutions like scaled-down class presentations. Compromising raises fears, however, and the meeting is a heated one. Although decisions by administrative dictum or by small committee might be easier, we feel that this is an important issue and want everyone to express ideas. After 2½ hours of discussion, we agree to meet in smaller groups to answer some of the questions raised today. We set ourselves a deadline of next Monday's meeting for agreeing on the details of our policy.

6:00 P.M.: Before I leave the building, I stop to say goodnight to the group of students, teachers, and parents who have just gathered for a College Information Night. I realize that I have forgotten the folder of papers I need to evaluate and the book I will need to use when I create tomorrow's group activity at my computer tonight. I return to my classroom, find the folder and book, and write myself a note on the blackboard about tomorrow's special schedule. I look around the room. The desks are all wrong for tomorrow's activity, but I suppose I can rearrange them first thing in the morning.

CHAPTER 6

Why Wasn't I Taught This Way?

Ellalinda Rustique-Forrester

From my perspective as a beginning teacher, the problem of "new schools and old systems" is about two conflicts that I experienced as a student, a learner, and a teacher: first, learning to teach in ways that I myself had not experienced as a high school student; and second, attempting to teach differently in school environments still mired in traditional, conventional thinking.

The profound contradictions between interpreting my past experience as a student, on one hand, and understanding the classroom and school environment as a beginning teacher, on the other, were revealed to me at three significant points: first, during my experience as a college student when I decided that I wanted to teach high school history; second, during my experience as a student teacher in a large, traditional school in suburban St. Louis; and third, as a classroom teacher in two small restructured schools in New York City. At each point, I realized that the teacher I wanted to be—someone who could teach for understanding and intellectually empower diverse students—required teaching skills and a school culture that I had not really experienced as a high school student. Thus I needed to learn how to become the teacher I envisioned.

Though I had been a "good" high school student—an Asian minority female who earned straight A's, was named class valedictorian, and hoped to someday become a doctor—I realized during my freshman year of college that the way I learned in my small Kansas high school had not prepared me to think critically in college: I could not recall, in a deep and meaningful way, the big ideas about what I had learned in my high school classes. I could not provide any real-life application of the different mathematical rules of algebra. I could not explain, at least in simple terms, basic scientific laws or principles. Though I could remember how to change scientific coefficients, I could not explain why the concept of a "balanced equation" was important in chemistry. I could recall only the floating bits and pieces of skills I needed to demonstrate competence in chapter tests, but I had not retained my knowledge in a way that allowed me to explain these ideas to another person. I did not know how to do the kind of higher level thinking that I was now being asked to do in my college classes. Only a year after graduating from high school, I had only a superficial understanding of what I had learned.

I tried to criticize my high school teachers for how I had been taught but found this rather hard to do. I could not see anything "wrong" with how or what I had learned. Yet, as I attempted to recall the details of daily life in high school—my seven-period schedule and the 4-year sequence of my college preparatory track of classes—I realized that what exactly happened during my 45-minute classes was vague and hardly meaningful. I remember reading short, boring textbook passages and answering questions at the end of the chapter. I recall studying and memorizing vocabulary lists of random words and copying notes and formulas from the chalkboard. I remember doing my homework for the next class while periodically listening to the teacher, or reading a novel in my lap while pretending to do my assigned work in class.

In high school I just did the work, never questioned it, and got A's. I could not think of anything that my teachers specifically did "wrong," nor did I believe that they were incompetent, uncaring teachers. But somehow the subjects I took in high school had not translated into a deeper, acquired knowledge or enabled me to make connections to the real world. What could my teachers have done differently? Mrs. Richman's writing assignments, Mr. Hall's problem sets, Mr. Smith's multiple-choice tests had all seemed fine to me (all teacher names are pseudonyms): Mrs. Richman was a good teacher; she always gave great writing topics that fit neatly into five-paragraph themes. Mr. Hall was known as a tough, hard-working math teacher; he always gave us long algebra assignments, which we would check against the solutions that he had neatly written out on transparencies. He would display these on the overhead, we would exchange and grade our homework with another classmate. Mr. Smith wasn't boring; we conducted chemistry experiments in class and often watched science documentaries. But now in college, I was barely passing the subjects that I did well in high school. I was struggling in chemistry, withdrawing from biology, and lost in calculus. I was even having a hard time with English composition. A sudden insight about how I had been taught in high school occurred when I received a note from one of my English professors that read, "Please see me." I had received a C on the latest paper assignment and dreaded this moment. Trembling, ashamed, and in tears, I sat down in my professor's office. He began by asking me what I thought about the books that I had chosen to write about. I looked at him blankly, confused. "What do you mean?" I asked. He said, emphasizing certain words as he spoke, "Let me ask you in a different way. Did you like the books? Did you agree with the author's analysis?" He continued, "Look, when you read, you should question. The problem here is that you are simply reporting what you read. When you write a paper, you need to cast the author's interpretation in a new light. What I want you to do is write about your opinions and use the text to support your conclusions. I want to understand, after reading your paper, what you thought was important and, most of all, why." And as we began to talk about the themes and ideas raised by the author, my professor pushed me to articulate my thinking. "And how do you know this?" he kept asking. And as I defended my opinions, he said, "Now you've got it. Now tell me in the paper. Explain it in writing." He handed me another student's paper, and said, "Here, read this. This should help you to structure and organize your ideas. It's a good example of how to do it." As I raced back to my dorm room to rewrite my paper, I realized that I had rarely been asked by my high school teachers to do what my college professors were now asking of me: to question or criticize assumptions; to construct and articulate my own ideas; to defend my interpretations with evidence; and to talk about my thinking with other students.

As I read over the model paper, I began to see the difference between writing as a simple reporting assignment and writing as a process of thinking and reflection—the former what I had been "trained" to do; the latter what my English professor now required of me. I began to make new connections between the books I was reading and our class discussions. Determined to revise and improve my paper, I realized that the difference in my learning was not so much that my college professors were any smarter than my high school teachers, but that they demanded that I think in an entirely different way and reflect about what I was learning. My math and science professors, in particular, expected me to interact with what I was learning in a more complex, conceptual way, to consider hypothetical applications, and to draw connections to the real world. After struggling through my freshman year, I decided that being a doctor and scientist was simply not the path for me, and I transferred from the premedical/engineering program into the college of arts and sciences. I discovered in government and history, two subjects that I always thought I hated, a new source of intellectual passions. Enrolled in two social science seminars, African Americans and the Civil War and Constitutional Issues, I found myself being inspired by the teaching of two brilliant professors, both female and both of color: an African American and an Asian American. These professors had two things in common: Both were knowledgeable and passionate about their subjects, and both were teachers with whom I could identify as a Filipino American.

I experienced for the first time a kind of teaching that pushed me beyond the cursory learning that I had done in high school. Each class was a weekly seminar filled with 2 hours of stimulating discussion, enlightening lecture, and fierce debates about questions of equity, race, and social justice. Organized around a few essential questions rather than random, unrelated topics, my weekly reading assignments were rigorous intellectual exercises in comparing and contrasting multiple perspectives. Writing involved weighing evidence presented by different viewpoints. I discovered that there was not one answer (always available in the back of the book) but rather different ways of interpreting and seeing the world. Unlike my high school experience, learning history was now not about recalling names and memorizing dates but about grasping concepts, understanding the chronology of ideas, and knowing how to locate dates and confirm facts.

I had discovered in the social sciences a discipline filled with controversy and debate, and I saw in teaching tremendous possibilities for intellectual challenge, social rewards, and personal satisfaction. Galvanized by my new realizations about learning, I decided that I would teach high school social studies. I wanted to be the kind of history teacher who would inspire students to interpret the world in ways that I had not been taught in high school and had to wait until college to learn. Most of all, I wanted to teach in the urban setting—in schools where I thought that the kind of teacher I aspired to be was who was needed most—and where I might be able to make a difference. I was thrilled when I found out that it was not too late to apply for the college's teacher preparation program and enthusiastically began my 4th year of college in a one-year preservice program (the university's M.A.T. program) to become certified to teach high school social studies.

LEARNING TO TEACH "OTHER PEOPLE'S CHILDREN"

As do many university-based M.A.T. programs, mine required that I begin my teacher preparation by taking courses in the theory, rather than the actual practice, of teaching: methods in pedagogy, methods in reading, methods in social studies, educational psychology, the history of schools, and current issues in education. I found these ideas helpful in understanding some of the theoretical and contemporary issues about schooling, and trusted that this kind of background knowledge would be applicable in my teaching practice. Overlapping my course work were two practice-based experiences in the classroom: first, in a small, urban elementary school where I observed a 3rd-grade classroom; and second, in a large, suburban high school where I did my student teaching.

But confronting my social and academic expectations of "other people's children" was my first real lesson in becoming a teacher, when I realized how pedagogy becomes translated from a teacher's expectations into student expectations in the classroom. After my first visit to a 3rd-grade classroom in North St. Louis where 30 African American children sat in rows quietly reading, I found myself remarkably surprised that the children were so well-behaved and intellectually engaged. I found their questions intelligent and was equally impressed by their teacher, also African American, whose classroom was very structured and whose expectations of her students appeared very demanding.

My delight and surprise at what I was observing turned quickly to self-horror when I realized the implications of my honest but racist conclusions: I would not have been so surprised by what I observed had the children and their teacher been White. That I, a potential teacher and minority female, could hold such prejudiced assumptions about the intelligence and behavior of students because of the color of their skin was a stark and sobering self-discovery. I realized that teaching was not simply about content or teaching methods but about how these were applied in the context of the classroom. I began to comprehend the complexity of my own social expectations, and the impact that my opinions would have on students who would be diverse in race, social class, and background. I began to see how powerful a teacher's individual beliefs about students can be in the process of a student's learning. What role had my elementary and high school experience as a student played in the shaping of my social attitudes and expectations as a teacher? I wondered. I then realized that although the schools I attended may have been racially diverse, the composition of the reading and math groups in which I was placed was not. Like many of the student teachers in my preservice program, I learned in ability-tracked schools—sorted by intelligence tests and divided by race. Missing from my theoretical preparation was a way to confront my past and deal with current issues of diversity—a way for potential teachers like me to understand the complex interrelationship of race, culture, and pedagogy. Although the theory I was learning as part of my preservice preparation was helping me to describe in pedagogical terms what occurred in classrooms, I was not adequately equipped with the language and tools to teach diverse students. Even as a member of a minority, I began to see that teaching for diversity required a continuous process of self-examination—a kind of teacher preparation that I could learn only by being inside a real classroom with real students, and perhaps by finding a school that did not track students by ability. But I would not find this in the school where I would soon do my student teaching. Instead, I would quickly realize how deeply the problem of teaching for diversity was embedded in the culture and structure of schools.

STUDENT TEACHING: EXPERIENCING THE CONFLICT
BETWEEN THEORY AND SCHOOL REALITY

Later that spring, when I began my 12 weeks of student teaching in a large, "shopping-mall" high school in suburban St. Louis, I began to see contradictions between the goals of my preservice preparation program and the reality of the school where I was being prepared to teach. At odds with the pedagogical goals that I hoped to try to accomplish as a student teacher—building on students' prior knowledge, translating content knowledge into interdisciplinary lessons, getting to know my students well, and encouraging them to be self-reflective, metacognitive learners—was the harsh reality of the big high school: its overwhelming size, the way classes and teachers were divided and organized, and the anonymity that the school's vastness and daily regimens reinforced.

Every day I saw thousands of students moving between four separate buildings, several floors, and various wings. I saw divisions and compartmentalization by department, by race, by grade, by ability—and student learning fragmented the same way. Six times a day I saw students shuttling from one 45-minute class to the next. As students rushed and piled into my cooperating teacher's classroom, I wondered what kinds of connections they were making between classes and how much they could remember of what they had learned there. When I asked my cooperating teacher why schools couldn't be organized differently—classes longer, tracks eliminated, and students and teachers teamed together so we could all know each other—he replied, "Is that what you're learning about at the university?" He laughed, agreeing that these were good ideas, but not offering a feasible explanation of why it could not be done. I suddenly realized how strikingly similar in feeling and appearance were the structures and routines of my own high school to those of this school in which I was now learning to teach. Both appeared to function efficiently, and there was nothing "wrong" with teachers teaching as if each class was unrelated to the next. In high school, however, I was oblivious to how my college-preparatory track resulted in different levels of expectations for students set on tracks different from mine. As a college-bound high school student, I wanted to take challenging courses. I naively assumed that other students had the same access I had. Now as a student teacher, I saw what happened "behind the scenes"—how certain students were assigned to certain teachers and why. Reflecting on my own high school schedule, I recalled that classes always seemed long, though the most interesting ones often flew by, and I remembered feeling rushed on the days that we had chemistry lab experiments. Now, as a student teacher, I struggled to create lessons that could be taught in 45-minute periods and wondered how I would find time to prepare when I actually had a full load of classes. My high school teachers had always seemed prepared for class, and I figured that having different students moving from class to class simply kept things interesting for them. I thought that, like my teachers, I too would have plenty of opportunities to consult with other teachers from other disciplines, to talk about other students, to seek advice about dealing with a parent, or to grapple with issues about learning. I soon realized that this was far from the school's reality. As I watched teachers rush about with myriad administrative tasks, I realized that teachers had very little time to prepare and even fewer opportunities to discuss curriculum ideas or lesson plans with other teachers. Teachers taught and planned their classes without knowing what other teachers in other classes were requiring students to do. I realized that any connections students might have made between their classes were lost in the daily shuffle. Occasionally a teacher would comment about a successful lesson plan, talk about what he or she was doing in a class, or remark about a specific student's difficulty grasping a concept. On these rare occasions, a conversation would spark among those who happened to be sitting in or passing through the teachers' lounge. For me, these collegial exchanges were always valuable but often occurred haphazardly, without notice, and almost always without closure. When our staff discussed content standards and subject matter during weekly department meetings, I wondered what other teachers in other departments were talking about. The monthly staff meetings were filled with teachers whose faces I did not recognize, assembled to vote on issues that to me seemed unrelated to teaching. By the end of my 12 weeks of student teaching, I was plagued with questions about how curriculum was organized and the way schools were structured. Unlike the three or four essential questions my college professors expected students to grapple with over the course of a semester and answer in a paper or an essay exam, the hurdles confronting these high school teachers I saw as tremendously daunting: galloping through curriculum, racing to cover many subjects and topics that were often out of context and in a sequence that didn't always make sense. Though I had assimilated all of this wonderful theory of teaching, I now had doubts about the reality of schools and wondered if I had been prepared to teach in a school that simply did not exist. How was I to address students' developmental needs and build their prior knowledge when I received a different group of students each year? How could I attend to each of my students' individual needs if I saw an average of 150 students a day? How could I get help with my interdisciplinary lesson when the English department was two buildings away? How could I create in my 45-minute class enough time for reflection, discussion, reading, and multiple pathways for learning? I had thought that an important difference between my high school teachers and college professors was simply the different levels of content and pedagogical expertise; but now I saw other factors, beyond subject matter, that made it difficult to teach in new and powerful ways. I knew that it had to be possible, but under what circumstances? After confessing my dilemma to one of my professors, I learned of a "restructured" school that was attempting to tackle these very same issues. The school was entering a partnership with a local university's school of education to set up an internship program for beginning teachers. Would I be interested? Would I be willing to move to an urban setting—New York City? Excited, I called the principal, talked about the dilemmas I was experiencing with student teaching, explained what I was looking for in a school, and found myself several months later at Central Park East Secondary School.

CPESS: A SCHOOL RESTRUCTURED FOR STUDENT LEARNING AND TEACHERS' PRACTICE

Central Park East Secondary School (CPESS) was unlike any school I had experienced, observed, or thought possible. Unlike my own high school and the school where I did my student teaching, CPESS was not organized into a traditional high school with four grades but into three multi-age divisions: Division I, which included middle school grades 7 and 8; Division II, which included 9th and 10th grades; and the Senior Institute, which included 11th and 12th (and sometimes 13th) grades. Teachers in Divisions I and II were divided into several houses, which were further broken down into small, interdisciplinary teams of four teachers who taught the same group of students for 2 years. Every student had a 2-year advisor, who also served as a teacher on the teaching team assigned to the student. In the Senior Institute, students were similarly placed in a 2-year advisory, but students took courses in different subjects to complete work in 14 graduation portfolio areas, which included subjects such as math, science, and history as well as social issues, fine arts, and autobiography. Seven of these portfolio areas were to be defended by the student before a graduation committee composed of the student's advisor, one or two teachers, a parent or adult, and a student. In all divisions, classes were small and longer.

The entire school fit on two floors in a single building. There were no bells and no teachers' lounge. Rather than the predictable offering of classes by department and the grouping of students into ability tracks, CPESS had mixed-grade classes with a heterogeneous grouping of students. Built on the belief that "less is more," a mantra that reflected one of the key principles of the Coalition of Essential Schools, or CES (of which CPESS was a member), the schools functioned under a set of assumptions about school size and the depth and breadth of the school's curriculum, which would focus on key concepts and "essential questions." Toward this end, teachers in Divisions I and II developed a 2-year core curriculum organized around a set of interdisciplinary themes, such as "The Peopling of America," and essential questions such as, "How does our body work?" and "How do we measure time?" In the Senior Institute, teachers developed curriculum to encourage habits of intellectual inquiry that reflected the kinds of cognitive skills that enabled students to use their minds well. Known as the Five Habits of Mind (Viewpoint, Relevance, Evidence, Connections, and Alternatives), this framework defined the process of learning and teaching. The habits of mind helped teachers organize curriculum and lessons around a set of expectations and standards upon which students would be assessed and served as the framework for the school's system of performance-based assessment. Toward this end, student achievement was not measured by test scores or determined by school psychologists but was based on a student's performance and what the student demonstrated through "class exhibitions" and "portfolios." The teachers and staff of CPESS believed that teaching students to use their minds well was best achieved through a core curriculum that was organized around a few core ideas rather than discreet subjects and state-defined competencies. At CPESS, I found what I was looking for as a beginning teacher: a school that was able to provide multiple ways for diverse students to engage in meaningful learning; teachers with an increased understanding of the complexity of teaching for understanding; principals with an appreciation for supporting teachers in their workplace; and a working environment that considered teaching the most important activity and organized the school around teachers' professional needs.

EXPERIENCING THE SENIOR INSTITUTE

I reached a pivotal point in my continuing preparation as a teacher and my induction into CPESS when I was assigned an experienced, mentor teacher in the Senior Institute, who helped me understand how the school functioned as an organization and also helped me translate and connect my earlier ideas and notions about teaching into the unique philosophy and culture of the school.

Having a mentor allowed me to safely ask questions about lesson planning, organizing a cooperative learning activity, preparing lectures, and assessing students' work. Because I shared a classroom and advisory with my mentor teacher, we were able to talk nearly every day about the classes we co-taught as well as the needs of our students and advisees. We often had lunch with other Senior Institute teachers, allowing me the benefit of hearing veteran teachers talk about some of the classroom challenges they too were experiencing.

My mentor and I attended whole-school staff meetings together in which these same issues of student standards and assessment were discussed, and in biweekly, discipline-based team meetings teachers looked at examples of real student work. I heard teachers talking about the same issues that I had learned and read about through my university-based preparation but had rarely heard discussed during my student teaching experience.

At CPESS, questions about school accountability, pedagogical conflicts, and raising levels of students' intellectual engagement were openly debated and discussed by the entire staff in both formal and informal ways. By October, I was co-advising with my mentor, counseling graduating seniors on how to revise and synthesize their work for their final portfolios, and trying out different lessons under my mentor's supervision.

By second semester, I was teaching on my own and developing curriculum for a history class that I called "The Vietnam Conflict." I was writing narrative reports that assessed students' habits of mind, and I was serving on graduation committees with other teachers from other grades and subjects. Most of all, I was learning to teach and enjoying it. At CPESS it was possible for me to know, by name, virtually all the students in the Senior Institute. I could ask other teachers about the content and courses they were taking and was beginning to know more about students' individual needs by hearing their advisors talk to each other. I saw Senior Institute teachers consulting with students' previous advisors in Division II. I heard teachers talking across subject-matter disciplines about planning interdisciplinary projects and assignments that would meet the particular needs of specific students. I heard teachers across grade divisions discussing whether the curriculum at one level was providing students with the skills and knowledge to succeed at the next. In discovering the Five Habits of Mind, I finally understood my cognitive limitations as a high school student and found the source of my intellectual liberation as a college student.

As tools of historical inquiry, the Five Habits of Mind were, in fact, what had enlightened and empowered me to become a high school teacher. Now these habits were my most useful pedagogical device and tool for organizing curriculum—enabling me to teach history in ways that made people and events interesting, controversial, and relevant to students. I developed lessons to provide multiple opportunities to identify and compare viewpoints. I organized student debates and trials for students to defend their opinions with evidence. I required students to keep a journal so they could explain the relevance of what they were learning. I assigned essays based on essential questions to encourage connections to other historical themes. We had class discussions to consider different historical alternatives.

Through the Five Habits of Mind, I was able to assess each of my student's cognitive development and figure out how I could help each of them reach school-wide expectations for intellectual expression. Because CPESS focused on teaching students to use their minds well, I could encourage students to express their understanding in diverse ways and work with individual students on their different needs. After one year, I had been prepared in ways that made me feel ready and excited to teach. Moreover, I had experienced how much more challenging, as well as socially and intellectually rewarding, the process of teaching and learning at CPESS was from the way I had been taught as a high school student and as a fledgling student teacher.

I saw the difference between following the simple "scope and sequence" of a standard textbook and developing curriculum that built on students' prior knowledge. Unlike teaching out of a textbook, this kind of teaching required a deeper, more conceptual understanding about history, the subject I would be teaching. Moreover, my pedagogical effectiveness depended on how well I knew my students. I also learned that this kind of teaching involved more labor-intensive planning and time-consuming narrative forms of student assessment. Although I still had plenty to learn about teaching, and plenty of room for improvement, I could see opportunities for professional development structured into my daily schedule. I could get ample help from, consult with, and observe other teachers as I learned about the diversity of students' abilities and how to help them meet the school's graduation standards.

More remarkably, I saw other teachers, more experienced than I, working to improve their teaching as a result of the work their students produced. I found that when teachers were provided with time and professional support, they were able to reflect and improve upon their own practice, revisit school-wide goals, and continue to focus on the needs of their students.

At CPESS, I felt immersed in a culture and set of structures designed to facilitate and sustain a process of continuous learning for a beginning teacher. After teaching 2 years at CPESS as an intern, I finally felt I had a working understanding of the theory I had acquired during my 1-year university program; and I had a set of real classroom experiences that allowed me to articulate, describe, and make sense of the kinds of practices that I would continue to test, work, and experiment with.

Cooperative learning, interdisciplinary teaching, authentic assessment had seemed elusive, even impossible, goals in the traditional schools where I had learned and student taught; but CPESS changed all that. Though it had taken 2 years in two different schools, I now understood what it meant to successfully integrate theory into practice. I was convinced by my experience in developing a curriculum that "less is more" helped my students successfully engage in and appreciate history. I discovered that teaching students to use their habits of mind was effective in encouraging them to become critical, self-reflective learners. In short, I had been professionally empowered by CPESS's school-wide pedagogy and educational philosophy and felt confident that I would take these tools wherever I taught. By June, I had interviewed and received offers for a full-time teaching position from two newly created schools. Both schools knew about CPESS's success as a restructured school and were inspired by the opportunity to create their own versions. Having just completed the first year, each school was run by an enthusiastic principal whose commitment to students and teachers was very apparent. Though both were honest about the difficulties of starting a new school, I learned from talking with each school's individual teachers that both schools wanted to create a rigorous intellectual, learning environment, based on the habits of mind, small classes, team teaching, and portfolios.

I was pleased that I had two good choices but saw two important differences. One school was part of the CES, the network of which CPESS was a member, and thus would continue to organize the school on the basis of CES organizational principles. The second school was considering membership in the CES, but had not yet decided. But a second, more critical difference—the composition and experience of each school's teaching staff—became the deciding factor in my choice. Whereas the entire staff was returning for a second year with the non-CES school, only one teacher was returning for a second year with the CES school. Worried about lack of collegial support, which I had relied on so heavily at CPESS, I accepted the offer from the second school, assuming that membership in CES would come later. I was comforted by the fact that the principal and staff were experienced teachers who seemed to believe in and appreciate a similar goal: to create a school with high expectations for students and teachers.

BLOCKS AWAY, WORLDS APART:
LEARNING TO TEACH IN A "REAL" SCHOOL

Fourteen blocks away from CPESS, I would experience, once again, the challenge of teaching in a school environment in which my goals as a teacher would be translated into concrete classroom practices. Now in a new school with new colleagues, I began to realize the ingeniousness of the structure and organization of CPESS, and the complexity of creating a school culture where teaching students to be critical thinkers and encouraging them to use their minds well were what drove student–teacher interaction. I had interpreted the school's acknowledgment of CPESS's success as agreement about the way the school would be structured. I quickly realized that my assumption was naïve: The structures that supported the pedagogy and philosophy of CPESS had not yet been established and, more significantly, still needed to be debated and agreed upon by teachers.

Among the fiery topics of debate during the months prior to the first day of school were how to organize the school year, structure an advisory system, and decide what classes would be taught. But instead of focusing on the kinds of learning experiences we wanted to create for students and the standards that students would be expected to meet, the discussion centered around the traditional, conventional system: what the state required for graduation and what was required to earn a Regents diploma. Instead of discussing what we wanted students to be able to demonstrate through their work at the end of each year, we debated over the sequence and scope of the curriculum—who would teach what and in what order. Consensus was reached by agreeing that students would follow a rigorous sequence of course work, rigor defined as 4 years of math, 4 years of science, 4 years of English, 4 years of foreign language. The "skills" students should develop were largely to do with computer literacy, interview techniques, and included learning to balance a checkbook. These were all important, I thought, but I felt that something was missing.

I was accustomed to thinking holistically about the curriculum and structure of the school, and I felt lost in this conversation. I tried to pose a question that made sense to me: "What if we tried to plan our curriculum by working backwards. We should try to figure out what we want students to know and be able to do when they graduate—after 4 years." I tried to explain my approach to teaching: "It's not enough for me to know that I will be teaching social studies for two periods; I want to know what I am preparing these students for, and what I should be aiming for as a teacher. How will we assess our students' learning? How will we communicate to ourselves how students are developing in different areas of their intellectual development?"

My questions were met with blank stares. I wondered if I made any sense. A teacher confirmed that I did not. Putting his arm on my shoulder, he said, "Elle, you're no longer a CPESS cadet, you're now in a real school." I realized that whether or not this was a "real" school, this environment was now my new reality. As the staff decided to put off until the next staff meeting the task of assigning teachers to classes, I realized that I was indeed alone in my abstract reconceptualizations about schools and teaching. Though I saw the traditional structures we were creating to be at odds with the goals we wanted to accomplish as a new school, I found it difficult to explain this to anyone. To my new colleagues, I was indeed a "CPESS cadet"—with too much theory and idealism about teaching and too little experience. I also learned that although my new colleagues were inspired and motivated by what CPESS had been able to accomplish as a small school in East Harlem, many teachers felt that CPESS's success resulted from special treatment from the district, specially selected students, and a unique, visionary principal. That CPESS was an exception, for reasons other than structure, was easier for my new colleagues to conclude than to look at how CPESS created new ways of organizing teachers and students, conceptualized curriculum into essential questions and habits of mind, and developed a teaching schedule around teachers' needs. Looking back through my notes from that day, I can appreciate how difficult it is for teachers to think about schools, students, teaching, and curriculum in ways that they have not seen or experienced. Even though I could explain in a literal way how CPESS had redesigned its curriculum and its requirements for graduation, I was only a beginning teacher without much practice. And the more I talked about CPESS, the more difficult and awkward it was to explain to more experienced teachers about the pitfalls of thinking about teaching and learning in traditional ways. How could I, who had never really taught in a traditional school, ask my new colleagues to consider the impact that traditional structures might have on practice? I had neither the confidence nor the years of practical experience. Away from CPESS, I realized how difficult it would be to translate and transfer my pedagogical practices into a school where the routines, habits, and practices that would shape how teachers and students would interact were being conceptualized differently. I recalled the remarks of visitors who came into my classroom and commented about how different CPESS was from the rest of the world. Perhaps it was true. Perhaps this was what teaching in the "real" world was about. But I found this difficult to accept in light of my previous experience at CPESS. The unique structures that allowed me to be an effective teacher there—2-hour classes, classes that met every other day, and dividing students among teams of teachers—were simply unfamiliar to teachers in my new school, who found these reconceptualizations difficult to translate into their own practice. Without time during the school year for the staff to visit other schools, to see how schools organized their curriculum, and to examine what different models of teacher schedules and student work loads translated to in practice, the staff's ability to develop new ways of thinking was severely limited. As a result, our meetings that summer ended with the re-creation of a traditional schedule and conventional way of assigning students to teachers: Every student would be required to take a certain number of courses in specific subjects. Each student was required to take math and would be placed according to ability displayed on a Regents competency test. Each teacher, beginning or experienced, would teach five classes and have one planning period. Despite purporting goals similar to those of CPESS—creating a safe, personalized environment for learning and setting high student expectations for rigorous, intellectual activity—our summer discussions did not lead to the creation of structures that facilitated the accomplishment of the CPESS components: small classes, a flexible schedule, a reduced teaching load, ample time for planning and talking with teachers, a school-wide curriculum. The traditional ways of organizing teaching and learning—dividing the day into seven periods, assigning teachers four "preps" and one planning period, separating students by grade and math ability—became the most efficient way to deal with each school day. In short, it would be the responsibility of individual teachers, rather than that of the entire school, to address the diversity of students' abilities.

Though CPESS was only 14 blocks away, it seemed a world away. By the end of my first month at the new school, I realized that the kind of teaching that I had hoped to continue to build and improve on would be greatly influenced by my new environment. I was now teaching five 50-minute periods daily. The CES limited a teacher's daily student load to 80, but I was seeing more than 100 students a day. I had one planning period and lunch duty once a week. I no longer had a mentor to consult with or access to other teachers during the school day. I realized that "success" did not necessarily transfer across school settings. In one year, I would experience the deconstruction of the pedagogical framework I had built at CPESS and find the tools of my effective practice—the concept of less is more, essential questions, planning backwards, and the habits of mind—rendered ineffectual as I felt a deep sense of helplessness and lack of collegial support.

LOSING MY HABITS OF MIND

In my new school, less was not more; *less* meant demanding less of students. I found this ironic, because the greater my work load, the less effective I felt and the less I expected of my students. By November, I began to see the practical impossibility of doing narrative reports for 150 students and implementing a portfolio system without a school-wide system of assessment. I found it difficult to balance and focus: I had an advisory with 20 students; a writing workshop; an elective called History Makers (which I struggled to find time to plan); and two periods of the American Social

History Project. Although there was much potential in the kinds of learning experiences I wanted to plan for my students, I did not have enough time or flexibility in my schedule. Classes met every day. I had one planning period. Because each teacher planned and implemented lessons differently, no advantage was gained among teachers teaching the same classes (as with the American Social History Project), nor did this practice translate to a common set of school-wide expectations. When students began skipping advisory, the issue of tardiness was raised at a morning staff meeting. What was revealed, however, was that different teachers saw the purpose of advisory differently. Some felt that advisory was simply a place to take attendance. I, and a few other teachers, on the other hand, considered advisory as a time for counseling, helping students with work, and discussing social issues. We suggested that advisory be longer and also be graded. Maybe students would come then. Other teachers strongly disagreed, pointing out that advisory would cut into "academic" classes. We decided that the purpose of advisory was an individual decision. Soon I began hearing students say, "Mr. Schmidt doesn't make his advisees keep a journal," and "You can't give me a grade for advisory." By second semester, my advisory became a morning study hall.

In my other classes, a similar lack of school-wide consensus made teaching and assessment difficult. In my history classes, I wanted to encourage students to revise papers and decided that I would assign grade based on their habits of mind—clarity of viewpoint, strength of evidence presented, and their ability to make connections. I developed a rubric that reflected the Five Habits of Mind, but I found this set of intellectual standards and expectations lacked meaning to my students, who wanted a simple letter grade, who wanted to know how the rubric translated into the school's 100-point grading scale. By December I had given up on many of the teaching practices I had used successfully at CPESS and began to see the failures and struggles of my students as overwhelming barriers to their learning and my teaching. My confidence level and enthusiasm for teaching were in serious jeopardy. I felt like a plant, previously thriving in a nutrient-rich environment, now repotted in regular soil and struggling to stay alive. Overwhelmed and discouraged by the challenges of my new school environment, I began to rely increasingly on rules and routines to find order and consistency. I was relieved when students were absent because my classes were smaller. I showed lots of videos and frequently assigned reading during class. I felt terrible, and my students knew that I was having a difficult time. I was further conflicted because I could not provide multiple opportunities for students to really deepen these cognitive skills. I felt inadequate and incapable—how could I justify giving grades, assessing habits of mind that I could not help all of my students to develop?

By May I realized that my posters of the Five Habits of Mind, which I had posted proudly above my desk at the beginning of the year, were in sorry condition. "Viewpoint" and "Alternatives" had fallen off the wall. I found them crumpled and face-down on a bookshelf; "Connections" was missing; "Evidence" was covered in chalk dust. Discouraged, I took down the last habit of mind, "Relevance"—it sat in a stack at the corner of my desk for the last few weeks of the year. Another new teacher asked me if she could have a copy of my habits of mind. "Sure," I replied, only to realize a few days later that both of us had forgotten about her request.

My aspiration to teach students for understanding, which I had been so galvanized by in college and through which I had found extraordinary professional satisfaction at CPESS, now seemed lost as I struggled to stay positive about my classes. My communications with other teachers about students' needs were infrequent and disjointed. Though some days were better than others, and I could find some evidence that certain students responded favorably to my teaching, my overall ability to assess and address the individual needs of classes was confined to only a few selected students, at unpredictable moments, and was difficult to sustain. By the end of the year, I had failed several students: literally, by assigning them F's, but—worse—philosophically, because I could not help them find ways to achieve individual success. Whether students had met the goals that I, and other teachers, had hoped to achieve in creating a new school was at best undetermined—at worst, missed entirely and misunderstood. What had appeared to me in the beginning to be subtle differences in school structure and the organization of teachers and students resulted in the end in profoundly different teaching practices and beliefs about how students learned. Though my new school was small, its structure and culture relied upon the traditional ways of organizing students and classrooms. Even though teachers were at the center of decision making and given primary responsibilities for managing the school, we did not have time to focus on our most important activity: figuring out how to meet the cognitive and social needs of our adolescent students. The process of creating a new school, certain aspects of the curriculum, and the school's small size and relatively small classes may have made it appear that the school's approach to education was new and different; thus I had difficulty realizing that underlying the newly created structures were traditional practices and assumptions.

THE OLD AND NEW THINKING OF RESTRUCTURED SCHOOLS

Though both schools were considered restructured, among the acute differences between CPESS and the newly created school were the ways in which each school functioned and the structures that were created to keep daily routines for teachers and students in place. Unlike at CPESS, bureaucratic notions about teaching at my new school were seen as the most efficient way of organizing teachers and students: Teaching load was determined by the division of labor; students were assigned to classes by subjects; and student behavior was set by building rules. Although these ways of organizing teaching and learning appeared to work, they worked in opposition to the school's goals and resulted in a school culture that felt and looked profoundly different from that of CPESS. A newly created school can resemble a smaller version of a traditional school, which raises another critical difference: the quality of relationship between teachers and students between the two schools. At CPESS, students were assigned to groups of teachers so that teachers could know students well and have other colleagues to consult with about common students. Though smaller and more personalized, the newly created school felt more like the traditional school where I had done my student teaching: My role as a teacher was formal; my work load was equal to that of other teachers; my identity was defined by my subject matter; my students were divided among all the teachers in the school; and my practice was regimented into daily, regulated routines. Defined along behavioral lines of formal authority, the relationships and interactions between my students and me were not unlike my own in high school—where I floated in and out of classes, learning different things for different reasons, none of which made sense in the real world.

In short, CPESS created a school ethos opposite to the traditional, bureaucratic model: a communitarian school in which the individuality of teachers took on more importance than the role they filled. Teachers conceived their work based on the exchange of new information and ideas about conceptual understanding and shifted their practice according to the developing needs of students. The results of the school's reconceptualization of teachers' practice were stable, trusting relationships between teachers and students, and a school guided by a common ethos of intellectual well-being rather than by the restrictive pressures of externally imposed, economic objectives for student achievement. CPESS's emphasis on student development and the relationships between students and teachers regarding learning thus became the way that teachers organized their practice. A demanding but nurturing environment emerged, motivated by the diverse learning of individual teachers and students united in their aim for common intellectual and social goals, not by the scope and sequence of curriculum. Sometimes I wonder if, as a beginning teacher, I expected too much too soon, particularly from the newly created school which, after all, was beginning too. Here I am not so unlike my students, for whom there is much to learn about learning itself. Indeed, the process of creating a new school in an old system is inevitably the kind of task that requires time for change, adaptation, and reflection among students and teachers who are teaching and learning in ways that represent new practices and conceptualizations about previous experience. I wonder, here, if perhaps the critical difference between the two schools was simply that the school culture achieved by CPESS resulted from many years of hard examination of trial and error and different stages of creating stable, trusting relationships between teachers and students. Only time will tell whether both schools can stay focused upon meeting both teachers' and students' needs; their ability to do so will be critical in creating the kind of schools and genuine learning communities that will begin changing the old system.

CONCLUDING THOUGHTS AND FUTURE CHALLENGES

I had set out to become a teacher because I wanted to teach in ways that I had not been taught. I was able to realize that this was indeed possible. I experienced it—intellectually and practically—through a mentor and induction program in a successfully restructured school where teaching and learning were the most important activities. I found out how difficult achieving that ideal of teaching for understanding and diversity could be through my own experience of the bureaucratic organization of teachers' and students' daily routines. I saw how resilient schools can be in changing and sustaining new ideas about learning, and how fragile a school's organizational structure can become when faced with transforming old ways of teaching.

To understand the problem of new schools and old systems is to understand the ways that the schools in which I learned and taught each sought to accomplish goals for students and teachers but produced profoundly different learning environments. Although each of these schools was dedicated to creating an encouraging learning environment for students, the way in which each school translated this good intention into students' and teachers' activities inevitably characterized the school's functions and ultimate culture. In the newly created school, at best, the result was the kind of teaching and learning that resembled the superficial learning I did in high school. At worst, the process of teaching and learning did not occur at all. For me, the difference between CPESS and the new school was not simply about a change in school building, staff, and students but about the contrasting learning environments created by each school, the extent to which each school organized itself around the cognitive and social development of students, and the integration of collegial support into teachers' practice. Although bureaucratic constraints certainly operated at both schools, and often at external levels, the most difficult constraints to identify and confront were those that characterized our own thinking. Creating schools that are better structured to meet students' social and cognitive needs requires support beyond the district level and, more profoundly, within the staff itself in our approach to teaching. The elements of class size, time, and planning for teachers are important functions in how schools operate. But the process of questioning, challenging, and reconsidering how these elements relate to the goals of teaching and learning was largely bypassed by the teachers at the new school; at CPESS, the subject was continually challenged and revisited during teachers' discussions.

Understanding the impact that each school had upon my development as a teacher goes well beyond the simple explanation that every school is different. I had to recognize the habits of a long-standing bureaucratic school culture and the extent to which these habits translated into the old system of teaching and learning and prevented a genuine, sustained transformation of schools into optimal learning environments for both teachers and students. Indeed, a successfully restructured school is a place where the cognitive, social, and intellectual development of children and adolescents provides the central basis for how a school establishes its schedule, structures, policies, and procedures—all of the things we commonly think of as bureaucratic. A truly restructured school is one that has completely rethought itself down to the structures of its existence in the school system—including the use of school time, how students learn and grow from their understanding, and how and why teachers teach they way they do. Schools like CPESS exist and are successful because of the staff's ability to stay focused on how to help students use their minds well and how to create working conditions under which teachers can facilitate this process. My experience the year after I taught at CPESS shows how easy it is to have the "right" ideas and goals, but how difficult it can be to translate these abstractions into practice.

For what may appear to be subtle differences and negotiable factors in class size, teaching load, and curriculum choices are factors that impact enormously on the predictable success of teachers and their students. The process of creating a new school, without time for ongoing professional development for veterans, structured supports for beginning teachers, and systematic reflection back to the school's goals for students can result in a school that looks a little different in some places, but is really a brand-new, traditional school. To take CPESS's apparent successes without a deep understanding of its underlying goals and assumptions about students, and the impact of its structure on teachers' practice is like trying to cut random pieces out of one tapestry and sew them onto another create the same picture.

Creating new schools and restructuring, I think, depends on whether teachers in a school can unlock old structures, examine their assumptions about how children learn best, and structure the day around teachers' needs. Genuine school restructuring must be considered as a whole package of new ideas and new practices: It is about reconsidering the whole process of how children and teachers learn. To take one idea is like pulling on a single thread of a tightly woven tapestry, only to realize that the whole picture is unraveling. Herein lies a final lesson that I have drawn from my experience. For teachers to teach students in new and powerful ways, we must visualize schools differently, as places that we may have not experienced ourselves as students. We must reconsider the ways that most schools are organized and carefully examine how teachers are supported. And we must be aware of the profound influence of bureaucratic school routines that most of us, both as students and as teachers, still carry with us.

Efforts to restructure that place to provide ideal working conditions for teachers, to meet adolescent needs, and to put nurturing, trusting relationships at the center of a school's activities will not happen simply with time but only when we teachers are freed from the old system of thinking. How to empower new schools and enable teachers to realize this will be the future challenge for creating schools that are genuine learning organizations; how we meet this challenge will also ultimately determine whether beginning teachers like me stay in teaching and have the chance to be successful with all students.

CHAPTER 7

The Transformation of One Large Urban High School: The Julia Richman Education Complex

Ann Cook

It's almost a cliché: the large inner-city high school, symbol of the crisis in public education—out-of-control kids, harassed, incompetent teachers, bullhorn-toting principals. So powerful is the symbolism, we hardly need the dropout statistics or incident reports to prove what politicians, newspaper editors, and taxpayers have been saying for some time: Large urban high schools are failing.

Once such schools held great promise. Often stretching an entire city block, these five- or six-story buildings were regarded as an almost perfect metaphor for our thriving cities. Advocates, like James Conant, regarded them as "collections of inner communities"—the very essence of democracy. Built to hold 3,000 or more adolescents, they seemed to reflect stability and certainty, employing an efficiency of resources and serving as a gateway to an American society abundant in employment and higher education opportunities.

Today, these same facilities are compared to factories, still worse, to prisons. They have become emblematic of the most impersonal and unwieldy of environments, routinely reporting a high incidence of violence, absenteeism, and poor achievement. What begins in some large schools as a freshman class of 800 often dwindles to a graduating class of 120. Morale is low, dissatisfaction high.

According to one report (Darling-Hammond, Ancess, McGregor, & Zuckerman, 1998), New York City has at least 20 such high schools, accounting for some 60,000 students. Factoring in the dropout rates in such schools, one study calculated that these schools cost the system more than $150,000 per student to produce a graduate. (See Chapter 11.)

THE SMALL-SCHOOL ALTERNATIVE

By contrast, small schools offer possibilities once thought inconceivable. As Deborah Meier argues in *The Power of Their Ideas* (1995), small makes it possible for entrenched faculty to change habits; it allows for access and provides a way to "create a culture in which staff and students [can] interact in an atmosphere of mutual respect" (p. 107).

Over the past 15 years, the emergence and success of dozens of small high schools in New York City underscored the wisdom of exploring a new strategy that might transform the large high schools. If small, free-standing schools could work, why not find a way to bring small to scale, restructure the big schools in such a way as to incorporate the benefits of small, autonomous learning communities? If this could be done, dozens of failing schools might be salvaged and students provided with new opportunities to succeed.[1]

In the past, attempts had been made to reconfigure or downsize the factorylike high schools, but success had often proved elusive. Large schools have been redesigned into houses, schools within schools, mini-schools, clusters, sub-schools, and academies—yet each has met with only limited success. Moreover, those efforts that seemed to work often raised other issues. As one study put it:

> Too often, the redesign has been directed at the students rather than the school, and some failing old schools have become successful new ones by dint of who their new students are, giving credence to the wisdom that good kids make good schools. . . . [and as] these redesigned schools have frequently found themselves once again sabotaged by those very conditions that initially qualified them for closing down . . . we are reminded that recycling is not reform. (New Visions for Public Schools, 1996)

THE COALITION CAMPUS SCHOOL PROJECT: AN OVERVIEW

In contrast, some school reformers argued that it was the very design of large high schools that was inherently flawed. Deborah Meier, president of the Center for Collaborative Education (CCE), New York City's affiliate of the Coalition of Essential Schools (CES), articulated the position of the organization, noting: "[Large schools] had plenty of opportunity to succeed and didn't. That may not have been [the administrators and teachers'] fault. We think these schools are based on a failing design." Proposing a new strategy that could restructure large failing schools, Meier and the CCE challenged conventional practice by offering to "take approximately the same population served by one of these schools, and recreate [it] as a group of smaller schools" (Jacobson, 1995, p. 11).[2]

The proposal quickly became known as the Coalition Campus School Plan (CCSP). It called for a three-pronged approach: the closure of a large high school; the creation of small, autonomous schools to serve that school's student body; and the transformation of the former one-school structure into a multi-age, multiservice complex. Conceptually, the plan drew on a growing body of national research that has documented the academic successes achieved by small schools.

The plan seemed simple enough: Students attending the designated high school when the plan went into effect would continue there until the last senior class graduated; staff of the school was to be offered the choice of transferring to another school or applying to one of the six new schools; the new schools were to begin with 9th graders and add a class of students each year; and the designated school would close, undergo renovation, and reopen as an education complex housing several small schools as well as a number of services.

In some respects the CCE proposal resembled familiar central-board of Education restructuring efforts, but with some essential differences: Given CCE's sponsorship, it was understood that the new small schools would adhere to a quite different set of assumptions than those existing in typical high schools. Following principles established by the CES, there were specific expectations affecting school culture: school size, student–teacher relationships, curriculum, and assessment. (Adherence to CES principles is required for membership in CCE.) Moreover, unlike most board redesigns, there was an overall conceptualization of the restructured building as an educational complex.

Meier proposed that established CCE schools mentor the new schools, providing support in a variety of ways, from the hiring of staff to the preparation of purchase orders for equipment.[3] This strategy had the effect of focusing the mission of the new schools on a set of assumptions, and, although each of the mentoring schools differed in structure and curricular design, all shared a commitment to these basic principles: student-based assessment, school-to-work experiences, and innovative scheduling.

As implemented, the proposal demonstrated a clear understanding about how to create new schools and close and redesign old ones; it also revealed a considerable level of political sophistication, for, as had been anticipated, once Julia Richman High School had been selected as the school to be closed, there were some staff members and parents who did not believe the school warranted closure and were prepared to derail plans for the redesign proposal altogether. Thus support from the teachers union

(UFT), the central board, and the superintendent of alternative schools was essential if the project was to proceed. Support from the UFT was critical with respect to the transfer and reassignment of staff from the designated school, and from the board with respect to endorsement and then implementation of the plan's multiple phases. The infusion of $3 million of foundation support also helped establish the project's credibility and, on a practical level, made it possible to bring directors of the new schools into the planning process months before the schools actually opened.[4]

In time, two of the six new schools (Manhattan International High School and Vanguard High School) moved into the complex; however, they were not located there initially. Instead, all six new schools were "hothoused" in temporary space.[5] Although the long-range effect of this strategy may not have been fully appreciated at the time, in retrospect, it is clear, it allowed the new schools to develop their own culture, unaffected by the negative tone and climate of the downsizing school. And, as it turned out, hothousing also served as an effective way to provide "swing" space for the extensive building renovations required; thus, for the first year at least, construction work could proceed more efficiently.

The redesign of the single school involved more than simply "condominiumizing" the former one-building, one-school structure. The recognition that a new form of building-wide governance would need to evolve was seen as critically important. Similarly the redesign plan called for the creation of a multi-age environment that would include elementary and junior high school children, young adults, and infants and toddlers. Finally, the inclusion of a professional-development facility was also regarded as a central feature of the redesign. As the idea moved from the proposal to the implementation stage, each of these ideas became more focused.

PORTRAIT OF A FAILING SCHOOL

By most accounts, Julia Richman High School was a prime candidate for closure. As the local paper noted in an article written shortly before the school's selection:

> In addition to its shoddy academic programs, the school has long been known in the neighborhood more for its shoplifting than for its scholars. . . . It was a school whose academic and attendance record clearly show[ed] a row of unbroken F's. (*Eastsider*, 1993, p. 3)

Like many other New York City high schools, it had quite a glorious past. Named for an early pioneer in public education ("the socializing power of the school is limitless"), Julia Richman opened in 1913 and moved to its present location a decade later. Built on the site of a former plant nursery, the new structure was typical of many high school buildings of its day. Occupying almost one square city block, it stood five stories high alongside a six-story annex that housed two gyms and a swimming pool.[6]

Like many schools for girls, Julia Richman initially focused on commercial skills, but within a short time the curriculum had expanded beyond typing and stenography to include a full range of academic courses including Latin, Greek, and the classics. By 1928, Julia Richman High School was regarded as one of the city's premier academic schools for the young ladies of New York City.

Notwithstanding current board policy, which defines a school's "admissions zone" by its geography, Julia Richman was never regarded as a neighborhood school. Instead, as a check of student addresses will show, Julia Richman, even in those early days, was regarded as a magnet school, drawing its students from across the borough, indeed the city. Some girls came to attend the Country School, which existed as a gifted-and-talented program within the larger high school. Eventually court challenges put an end to single-gender public education in New York, and in 1968 Julia Richman, like many other New York City schools, became coeducational.

Although there were some early warning signs that all was not well, the school began what now appears to be an inevitable decline during the mid 1970s. As an *Education Week* article noted:

> Only 37 percent of Julia Richman's students graduated in four years, graduating classes came to represent less than a third of those who entered as freshmen and fewer than three-quarters showed up each day. And many students failed to earn enough credits to advance to the next grade. (Bradley, 1995, p. 37)

As failure rates skyrocketed, discipline, even violence, became endemic. At one end of the large room that housed the vice principal's office, a wire-mesh cage was used to separate adversaries or hold unruly students until police arrived. By 1993, in what can now be seen as a last-ditch effort to control safety within the building, metal detectors were installed. Still, security remained a troubling issue. Neighborhood merchants continued to complain about an increase in the number of incidents, and local residents reportedly moved from the area, citing street danger and falling property values.

Inside, the building's once glamorous appearance deteriorated dramatically. Beyond the lack of attention paid to basic repairs required by any building more than 50 years old, vandalism had become chronic. Given the general condition of the building and the shrinking budget available for maintenance, the repair schedule for the school became impossible to maintain. John Broderick, who came to Julia Richman as its custodian, describes what he found when he arrived in 1993:

> When I took the job at Julia Richman, my custodian friends asked me whether I had seen the condition of the school. It had a bad reputation among the custodians and people told me I would have to get a whole new crew. It was that bad.
>
> And when I walked through after I arrived, the condition of the building was deplorable: the roof had leaked and had caused considerable damage on almost every floor. Some rooms were completely unusable. The bathrooms were covered, ceilings and all, with graffiti. Bathroom partitions were torn down; urinals were broken. Ceilings and walls hadn't seen a coat of paint for years and had turned cocoa brown; they blended in with brown trim on the doors.
>
> The lunchroom was a disaster. There was spot painting all over from where graffiti had been covered up. It looked like a jigsaw puzzle.
>
> The building's condition was hard to believe.

What accounted for the decline? Observers offer a variety of explanations ranging from the massive budget cuts that peaked in 1975, then continued for several years after, to the frequent turnover in principals (4 in 12 years), to charges by union members of administrative incompetence, to an increase in "over-the-counter" admissions (students who have no say in selecting their school). Others single out the indifferent attitude of a central bureaucracy that allowed large numbers of disaffected students to register without the provision of an adequate support system. Reformers argue it was the school's factory-model design and the overwhelming number of students that made sustainable change impossible to achieve.

FAILED EFFORTS AT RENEWAL

Whatever the actual cause, Julia Richman seemed to occupy a permanent place on the list of failing secondary schools in New York City.[7] By 1993, Julia Richman had appeared on New York State's list of failing schools for 14 years.

The board of education responded to the school's decline with a number of familiar strategies. As Darling-Hammond and colleagues point out,

For many years, the Board of Education responded to the plight of the comprehensive high schools by cycling a variety of expensive Attendance Improvement and Drop-Out Prevention packages through them. These programs were unable to dislodge the organizational structures that kept the system of failure firmly in place. (Darling-Hammond, Ancess, McGregor, & Zuckerman, 1998, p. 4)

One solution called for the creation of programs such as nursing, child care, food service, performing arts, medicine, or law. At one time, Julia Richman High School had special programs in at least three such concentrations. Proponents of this "thematic" approach argue that in addition to attracting and holding on to interested students, the ideas also promote decentralization within the school, foster personalization, and eliminate the alienation often occurring in the large factorylike schools.

There are drawbacks to this approach—some obvious, some more subtle. Partial decentralization within a school creates a structure of haves and have-nots—of insiders and outsiders. Those who are assigned to the mini-school, cluster, or school-within-a-school might indeed feel special, but the rest of the students soon feel threatened and on the defensive. "They (the mini-school or special program) get more" is the common charge leveled by those in the "regular" school. Perhaps this explains why so-called special programs seldom change the overall culture of a school. A special program may survive, but the strategy itself does little to turn around an entire school.

Still another popular strategy was the house plan, which called for an entire school to be subdivided into smaller units. Promoted widely during the late 1980s by the Division of High Schools, this approach mandated that principals divide their schools, usually by year, into self-contained mini-schools (e.g., freshman house, sophomore, etc.).

Though introduced and promoted energetically system-wide, this idea too eventually fell by the wayside. Perhaps this resulted from a lack of clarity: were "houses" meant to promote administrative decentralization, or were they a strategy meant to foster more student-centered educational goals? Or perhaps the idea never clicked because, like so many other reforms, it was introduced and administered from the top down. Principals were told to create houses and they, in turn, told their faculties. As a result, little planning and discussion occurred among those responsible for spreading the house idea.

It wasn't clear whether faculty was to join with like-minded colleagues to form a house, or whether the house assignment was to be arranged by the administration. The selection of house leadership also lacked clarity. Were houses to be led by assistant principals or by teachers? Who was to decide? How much autonomy was to be afforded to the houses? How much could one house differ from another, and what was the process for deciding the focus? Such questions remained unresolved. Even changing principals, an approach endorsed by some of the research literature, failed to reverse the process of decline.

No matter what strategy was employed, Julia Richman's performance continued to decline and it joined the short list of schools considered for closure by the board. Discussions with board personnel suggest that three factors finally proved decisive in its selection as the school to be redesigned: growing alarm at the level of internal disorder (the number of suspensions, etc.), mounting pressure from neighborhood residents and merchants regarding safety issues, and the school's continued poor performance with respect to academic achievement. Some think that the lack of a tenured principal also contributed to the school's selection (Darling-Hammond, Ancess, McGregor, & Zuckerman, 1998).

THE REDESIGN

With the designation of Julia Richman and the selection of the six new school directors in place,[8] the next phase of the project—the actual redesign of Julia Richman—began. Several operating principles detailed in documents submitted to the central board shaped the overall redesign:

- The single structure was to be reconfigured into a complex that would house multiple schools and programs;
- Each school in the complex was regarded as an autonomous unit having control over curriculum,[9] educational philosophy, staffing pattern, schedule, and organization;
- Each school was expected to create a community in which participants could develop a sense of "ownership" and in which they would be able to exercise control over their working environment;
- No single school in the complex was to exceed 300 students in order to promote both quality education within schools and a sense of community among schools;
- Each school was to be allocated a secure and autonomous space— traffic patterns in the building were to support and define each space;
- A governance structure was to be created within the complex that would foster and support democratic decision making, school autonomy, and a building-wide community.

The complex was to become a multi-age facility, serving children from infants and toddlers through young adults and was to provide a variety of services designed to support both students and staff.

Although the board accepted these concepts in principle, it took several months of lobbying for the resolution creating the Ella Baker Elementary School to be approved. The development of an infant–toddler program occurred without delay.[10] A special-education program was also to be housed in the building. The program that had existed in Julia Richman was ultimately replaced by a junior high school for autistic children.

THE TRANSITION TO A COMPLEX

As plans for the school's redesign moved forward, politics—education-style—moved to center stage.[11] From the outset, the CCSP proposal had positioned the six new schools within the Alternative School Superintendency and the redesign plan called for housing some of the new schools in the Julia Richman complex. However, as a large comprehensive school, Julia Richman was part of the Manhattan superintendency; this meant that jurisdiction of the building would become an issue. Because the Manhattan superintendent had not agreed with the selection of Julia Richman as the school designated for closure in the first place, resolving the issues of authority would become quite important.[12]

At this juncture, the issue became even further complicated by the unexpected departure of Schools Chancellor Fernandez, who had been an outspoken supporter of the redesign plan. His leaving caused uncertainty about several issues still in need of resolution.[13] What, for example, was to become of Talent Unlimited—the performing arts program within Julia Richman High School? Although originally slated to move to another site, the program, it was suddenly announced, would remain in the Julia Richman building. In addition, in what some regarded as a show of strength, the Manhattan superintendent, through a board resolution, ensured that Talent Unlimited would become an independent high school.[14] This meant that at least one school in the complex would report to the Manhattan superintendent. Thus, one year into its redesign, the complex had students, parents, faculty, and a principal under the jurisdiction of the Manhattan High School Superintendency. Perhaps, in response, the central board reassigned jurisdiction of the building, placing it under the Alternative School Superintendency.

As the redesign moved forward, the superintendent of alternative schools assumed a key role in the building's future. With multiple schools slated to relocate within the complex, building management became a focus. How was it to proceed? How were internal decisions to be made? The building still had an acting principal responsible for the Julia Richman students who remained in attendance; it still had scanners; and it still had a disturbing number of incidents. To complicate matters further, several Julia Richman teachers who remained on staff were miffed at what they perceived to be the school system's capitulation to woolly-minded reformers.

Although the initial design had called for hiring a building manager, details about this new position were not spelled out. Who was this building manager? How would such a person be selected? With hindsight, we now understand how central this position has been in assuring the overall success of the redesign. Yet this was one of those areas that lacked precise definition and thus was subject to the vagaries of the system's political agenda.

As the building's jurisdiction passed to the Division of Alternative Schools and Programs, the superintendent made a decision that provided some of the answers to the problem of building management. He proposed that the Urban Academy, one of the senior CES schools that had been active in the overall design, move into the complex and that Urban Academy's co-director assume the role of building manager. This proposal extended the mentoring strategy that had been a central theme in the development of the new schools. As a 10-year-old school with a reputation for professional development, Urban Academy seemed well suited to offer the sort of support the new schools might need and to help provide stability during the building's transformation. As it turned out, Urban Academy's style of consensus-building leadership worked well as the need to create a unique approach to building management became essential to the success of the complex's future development.

THE JULIA RICHMAN COMPLEX TODAY

Remarkably, the redesign of the Julia Richman High School into an education complex has been implemented almost precisely as designed. Five years after the project began, the Julia Richman Education Complex (JREC) included the following:

- Manhattan International High School and Vanguard High School, two of the six Manhattan Coalition Campus Schools;
- Urban Academy, a 14-year-old coalition school that became the anchor school;
- Talent Unlimited, formerly a professional arts program in Julia Richman High School that became an autonomous school in 1994;

- The Ella Baker School, a pre-K–8 elementary school;
- First Steps, an infant–toddler center and day-care program serving the children of students who attend one of the schools in the complex;
- Transitional College, an institute for high school seniors;
- P226M, a special-education program for autistic children of junior high school age.

In addition to the schools, the complex also includes the following:

- The Center for Inquiry in Teaching and Learning, a professional-development institute providing a resource library as well as a full program of workshops, courses, and seminars for in-service and preservice work. The center collaborates with university-based teacher-education programs and assists in coordinating the School-based Teacher Education Program (STEP), which grants state-approved teaching certification.
- The Teen Parent Resource Center, a training facility for staff and parents affiliated with NYC's school-based child-care programs. The center provides staff-development opportunities and includes a library of resources related to the growth and development of infants and young children.
- The Student Health Center, an on-site clinic providing a range of medical services for students, including emergency care, social work assistance, referrals, and dental care. The center is administered by Mt. Sinai Medical Center.

FOR CHILDREN OF ALL AGES

Certainly one of the most far-reaching aspects of the original plan was the insistence that the complex become a multi-age facility. Planners believed that the presence of younger children could, first, significantly alter the tone of the building; second, promote continuity of experience; and, finally, strengthen building-wide accountability. The age mix could offer what Headstart's Ed Ziegler has called a "dovetailing of experience."

CREATING SYNERGY: THE BUILDING COUNCIL

In a building housing multiple schools, there is always the need to balance interests of individual schools tenaciously guarding their autonomy with the interests of the building-wide community relying on collaboration and compromise. Both require support: Without question, the schools provide a critical connection for the students. On the other hand, schools must co-exist; they must share common spaces[15] and react together in an emergency. The Building Council, composed of all the principals and program directors in the complex, is responsible for creating and maintaining the balance, and its facilitator must see to it that disagreements are resolved through consensus.

As Lucy Matos, principal of the Ella Baker Elementary School, put it:

> I think what's different here are the assumptions that are made; before I came to the complex, I worked in a building that also had several schools. But we were not equal partners the way we are here. In the Complex, although each school is quite different from the others, philosophically we exist as one body with a unique commitment to an idea—that of creating a collaborative community. Little by little we find opportunities to relate and to create traditions together. Certainly one of the pluses for me is the opportunity to see how other individuals work as leaders in their schools—we can have conversations and all of us bring ideas to that conversation.

As the Building Council (consisting of the directors of the original schools, Urban Academy, Vanguard, Manhattan International, and the principal of Talent Unlimited) invented itself, several issues emerged as central concerns: determining which additional schools or programs should occupy space in the building; selecting individuals to direct new or shared programs in the complex (First Steps, the infant–toddler program, the Ella Baker Elementary School principal, sports director, etc.); scheduling the use of common space; determining the management of internal security; and outlining the nature of and time line for renovation work. Whereas some of the more tangible concerns involved the day-to-day operation of the complex, others relied on a shared trust. Indeed, establishing the very concept of a building-wide governance structure became an evolving reality, not only within the complex but also with respect to the central board of education.

As the central board devolved responsibility and decision-making power to the complex, defining the practical reality of such a shift required patience and determination. Early on, in one memorable meeting in the office of the deputy chancellor, an agreement was struck in which the central board acknowledged the expanding role to be played by the Building Council and agreed to allow its continued development.[16] Surprisingly, to a degree perhaps not imagined at the outset, the experiment has resulted in a growing number of building-based decisions: The Building Council's decision to remove the security scanners was endorsed; its determination to play a key role in approving new programs for the complex was honored; and even the reassignment of a special-education program that the board had placed in the building prior to its redesign and its replacement with a program for autistic youngsters was determined jointly by the Building Council and the central board, not by the board alone as would normally be the case.

Without exception, policy decisions affecting the complex are reached by consensus, perhaps the consequence of having the co-director of the Urban Academy serve as building manager and facilitator of the Building Council. The complex's governance model mirrors the leadership style operating in that school. Building Council members credit the role played by the building manager with helping to create a process for effectively discussing and resolving difficult, even tense, issues. As Lucy Matos, principal of the Ella Baker Elementary School, noted:

> In contrast with that of a principal who supervises the entire building, I strongly prefer the concept of a building manager who convenes and facilitates the building council. The building manager concept supports the idea of equity—all of us being on an equal footing with equal authority.
>
> Also, I think it matters a lot that the building manager is one of us; Herb is a practitioner so he's coming from a place which is like ours—he thinks like a teacher who relates to all the other teachers and he does for the building what I try to do for my single school. But, since all of us are advocating for our schools, he reminds us constantly of the need to consider the larger picture. It's also important that we know that his own school relies on a consensus style of leadership as well.

Louis Delgado, principal of Vanguard High School, agrees:

> We are all equal members of the Building Council and while one person organizes the agendas for the meetings and follows through from one meeting to the next, everyone has an equal voice and role in shaping policies in the complex.

The fact that consensus building could succeed at Julia Richman is, in some respects, remarkable. Incredibly, the schools in the complex report to no fewer than three different superintendencies.[17] Clearly, the potential for dissonance and discord is great.

Louis Delgado continues:

> For me, the biggest surprise was the tone we were able to establish in the building from the beginning. Initially, I was very skeptical

about the three superintendencies and infants and toddlers to 12th graders in the same building. I wasn't clear how it would all unfold. But, in time, I think we have become real partners in this effort. And, I think the younger children really provide a soothing component to the building. Their presence gives a broad vision of what the school was proposed to be from the very beginning.

There is an emerging sense among those in the complex that they share a common perspective and that decisions about the complex are best made by those in it. When three of the principals received letters calling for an increase in enrollment, the schools responded collectively as well as individually. In a convincing demonstration of unanimity, the schools drew attention to the negative impact such a size increase would have on individual school communities as well as the functioning of the overall complex.

Similarly, the Building Council has recently begun to address the budget needs of the complex. At the outset of the project, attention necessarily focused almost exclusively on the development of the new schools. As the restructuring effort moved ahead, issues of governance, building security, renovation, and space allocation took priority. Increasingly, discussions in the Building Council have focused on the critical need to generate and sustain support for educational positions and programs that service the entire complex—positions such as librarian, athletic director, computer technician, and building-wide secretary. Such positions require a new category of support and budgeting from the central board to provide adequately for multisited buildings. Thus it is with a growing sense of independence and shared determination that the Building Council continues to evolve its role. Three concerns may serve to demonstrate how this high-stakes exercise in synergy actually works.

SHARED SPACE

Shared space is an issue revisited with regularity by the Building Council. From the beginning, the Building Council insisted that all common spaces be shared by all schools on a scheduled basis: This includes the gyms, the auditorium, the mini-theater, and other areas not within a school's designated area. Thus a request by one school to have exclusive use of a lecture/chorus room was refused. Because this school had existed as a program within the Julia Richman building before it was ordered closed, "prior custom" was cited as a justification for the room's continued use. Still, although acknowledging that its decision would overturn former practice, the Building Council held firm as it sought to establish a new tradition: All rooms outside a school's own area were common spaces and needed to be shared on a scheduled basis.[18] Increasingly, therefore, there is an understanding that if a school's curriculum requires a specific kind of space almost full-time, it is the school's responsibility to adjust its own space to make the program work.[19]

TEAM SPORTS

Membership in the Public School Athletic League (PSAL) also became a tricky issue to resolve. Should each school join the league and field a team of its own, or should the complex join the PSAL and create teams drawing players from all the schools? Some felt that individual school teams would pit one school within the complex against another. Such a prospect was regarded as a troubling possibility, given the council's concern for building positive interschool relations (there is already a building-wide student government, a building-wide lunch committee, library committee, etc.). Moreover, given the size of each school, there was a real possibility that female players, in particular, might be adversely affected if individual schools fielded their own teams. Thus, in the interests of strengthening the spirit of community and putting the interests of all students above those of individual schools, it was decided that the complex should apply for PSAL membership. Coupled with this decision was a commitment to support the development of a JREC intramural supports program that could serve all students interested in playing team sports.

MAKING THE COMPLEX SAFE

From the outset, security has been regarded as a top priority in the building. If students and staff felt unsafe, any attempt to restructure the building would surely fail. Thus creating small schools in which staff and students knew one another well was regarded as a first step in satisfying everyone's natural desire for security while allaying mistrust and suspicion: Controlling each school's size would make it possible to create an atmosphere in which students and staff could resolve potential conflicts through dialogue and negotiation.

To promote such environments within the complex, great care was taken to allocate self-contained space for the schools so that each could patrol its own space effectively. Schools were positioned so their students could come and go without passing through another school's space. Every individual using a designated area would be known to the school assigned to that space: Thus intruders would be quickly identified. Such a strategy has paid off already: Strangers are quickly spotted and asked for identification.

When the initial traffic plan inadvertently required groups of students from one school to walk through the space of another on their way to the cafeteria, the Building Council devised an alternate plan: The school previously occupying the corridor was relocated and the linking corridor reconfigured to become common space, housing a dance studio, pottery room, culinary arts room, and guidance suite.

The emphasis on creating safe spaces for each school led, quite naturally, to a shift in building-wide security. Each school was to be responsible for security in its own area. Still the scanners that had been in place prior to the school's closure remained, and their presence created an unwelcoming tone.

The scanning process was time-consuming. Students arriving at school on time lined up outside the school to pass through the electronic devices. As a result, they were often late to class. Moreover, there was evidence that, because of the building's many exits (15), the scanners were not a particularly effective way to prevent dangerous items from entering the building. Most important, scanning suggested a siege mentality— that the building was on the edge of losing control, that its student body couldn't be trusted.

However, removing the scanners was no easy decision. It represented a calculated risk and demanded a high level of commitment from students, staff, and parents. Nor did the scanners' removal imply that all problems in the complex had been solved. Assuring safety in a building the size of the complex will always demand close attention, particularly in large spaces like the school cafeteria. But the decision firmly established the relationship between security and trust and underscored the need for each school community to take responsibility for making that connection a reality. Finally, it solidified the role of the Building Council as the critical decision maker in determining policies that affected the entire complex.

THE BUILDING MANAGER

Over time, as the Building Council tackles the problems before it, routines and traditions become established. Some are in place already. It is the building manager, for example, who prepares and brings a building-wide security plan to the table for discussion and approval. Though security is best monitored by individual schools, the deployment of the six guards in a building that takes up almost one entire city block demands coordination.

Similarly, maintenance issues involve both a school and a building-wide response. What has emerged is a working relationship in which individual principals communicate directly with the head custodian regarding immediate problems but rely on the building manager to sort out building-wide concerns. Thus problems with the contractors responsible for a major roof reconstruction were handled by the building manager and the on-site project director. Repairs to the auditorium were coordinated by the custodian and the building manager, who brought the scheduling problems caused by the temporary closing of the auditorium to the Building Council for discussion and planning.

Working with the custodian, the building manager has also had major responsibilities for representing the Building Council in an ongoing capital improvement project in the building, but again the manager is guided by the Building Council. As a result of decisions made by the Building Council, resources have been allocated to create or renew various common spaces: the library, an arts center (housing a gallery and a small theater space), the band room, a dance studio, a culinary arts and pottery studio, and the lunchroom. In several instances, teams of teachers from the schools also contributed ideas to the upgrading or creation of these facilities.[20]

IMPLICATIONS

At a moment when education has moved to prime time, when political campaigns routinely feature schools and student performance as central issues, the transformation of Julia Richman High School into an educational complex is a story worth telling. Turning a school around—one that only 5 years ago saw fewer than 10% of its entering students finish high school—and replacing it with schools that graduate almost 90% of their entering students is certainly major news.[21] So too is the transformation of a building where security scanners once occupied center stage to a complex where safety, without metal detectors, is now taken for granted by students, teachers, and neighborhood residents as well as by parents whose small children attend the early childhood classes in the elementary school. Instead of housing one failing school, the building now houses six small schools defined by a sense of purpose and serving a widely diverse group of children. The Julia Richman Educational Complex is now a place where, as the custodian points out," the kids leave the building before the teachers— the first time I have seen that in all my 35 years of working for the Board."[22]

Upon close examination, four factors appear to have been critical in creating and sustaining this effort at reform:

- School autonomy. From the outset, each school came to the collaboration as an equal partner: Each had its own sense of mission (clearly articulated and revealed in its overall structure), its own faculty, student body, curriculum, time table, and set of priorities. Program autonomy extends to space allocation. The need for each school to have its own space is as important for creating school identity as it is for establishing security.
- Building management by consensus decision making. Participation in the complex must be by choice, and all agree to adopt a management by consensus with no single individual making final decisions for all. School leaders make time to participate in a Building Council that, following a process of discussion and compromise, reaches decisions through consensus building.
- System Support. The importance of unequivocal support from the central educational bureaucracy cannot be overstated. Without support from the chancellor's office and the teachers union, redesign, on even the most elementary level, is problematic; in the case of total school reform, such as Julia Richman, their commitment is essential. Commitment from the central board requires development time, flexible funding, and a willingness to make necessary adjustments to well-established rules and procedures.
- Small schools. Schools that are able to create a sense of community for both students and teachers provide the best environments for teaching and learning. Controlling schools for size makes it possible to concentrate on what matters most—engaging students in intellectually challenging pursuits.

NOTES

1. A recent study, conducted by the Institute for Education and Social Policy at New York University, found that small schools get better results for their money than do large schools because more students graduate in 4 years, thereby reducing costs overall. (Stiefel, Iatarola, Fruchter, & Berne, 1998)

2. The proposal called for six new small schools to replace the one large school; together they would serve the population formerly housed in the single building.

3. At the outset of the plan, six established secondary schools—all members of CCE—agreed to participate in the proposed plan and serve as mentoring schools. Meier and her co-project director Marcia Shelton Brevot provided critical support during the project's initial stages along with the CCE board and staff.

4. The funding supported work to redesign two failing large high schools: Julia Richman in Manhattan and James Monroe in the Bronx; all together, the redesign accounted for 11 new schools. In addition to providing a planning period for new directors, the funding also supported a range of staff-development ac-

tivities and helped two of the schools survive when leasing arrangements fell apart during their first year of operation.

5. Although Coalition School for Social Change, Landmark, Legacy and Manhattan Village Academy were initially placed in temporary space, all are now permanently housed in renovated leased space.

6. Ironically, from its earliest days (1924), concerns were voiced about the enormous size of the building and the impact this size would have on teaching and learning. (See Rousmaniere, 1997.)

7. Local residents had dubbed the school "Julia Rikers," after Riker's Island, one of the city's jails. Sloan Kettering, the large medical complex located one block from the school, routinely warned its new employees to avoid 67th Street, which passed by the school's front entrance.

8. The downsizing of Julia Richman began by redirecting the 8th graders who would have been its freshmen class to one of the six new small schools. The plan had specified that students who entered Julia Richman as freshmen in 1992 would be allowed to remain in the building until their graduation four years later. Consequently, at the outset of the project's official beginning—September 1993—the school still held the sophomores, juniors, and seniors enrolled in Julia Richman High School.

9. There are indications that, in the name of standards, the new state assessments introduced in 1999 by the State Education Commissioner will result in standardization, thus curtailing the degree of school-level autonomy, particularly with respect to curriculum. This is occurring, despite strong evidence that many of the small schools have been particularly successful with formerly disaffected students who demonstrate a high level of academic success. The most senior school in the complex annually sends more than 95% of its student body on to college.

10. The structure for school-based day care has existed within high school buildings for some time and was, therefore, less controversial than the creation of the elementary school.

11. Some observers, including the local paper, wondered aloud whether the redesign would work. In an article appearing in April 1995, the paper asked: "Can the city really transform a failing, violence-plagued school into a model for educational reform?" (Jacobson, 1995.)

12. According to one source, her disapproval was based primarily on not being consulted adequately during the selection process.

13. An article appearing in the *New York Times*, May 15, 1994, documented the chaotic effect the Fernandez ouster had on citywide school reform; the article noted: "Small schools' achievements had come despite adversities." (Dillon, 1994.)

14. Various reports suggest it was New York's Senator Moynihan who intervened on behalf of a personal friend and persuaded the board to leave the program at Julia Richman.

15. These include the gyms, library, auditorium, dance and pottery studios, distance learning lab, presentation room, and culinary arts room.

16. Present at that meeting were the deputy chancellor, the head of high schools, the special assistant to the chancellor, the CCSP directors, the JREC building manager, and the co-director and the on-site CCE project manager, among others.

17. Four of the schools report to the alternative superintendent, one to the Manhattan superintendent, and one to the superintendent for special education.

18. Members of the Building Council, in an acknowledgment of the school's need for a chorus room, proposed, then helped implement, a plan to assist the school's purchase of new risers, which were then installed in a room within the school's own space.

19. When Ella Baker, for example, decided that dance and movement were central pieces of its school's daily curriculum for all its children, reliance on the complex's common-space dance studio was seen to be inappropriate and the school designated a room in its own space to accommodate its needs.

20. From the outset, an on-site project director representing the CCSP has served to coordinate a number of building-wide projects: for example, the school-based day-care center, library renovation, teachers' center, culinary arts room, etc.

21. All of the CCSP schools have successfully graduated their first and second graduating class.

22. From John Broderick's speech at the Dedication of the Leon Raphael Library; December 2, 1997.

REFERENCES

Bradley, A. (1995, March 22). Thinking small. *Education Week, 14* (26) p. 37.

Darling-Hammond, L., Ancess, J., McGregor, K., & Zuckerman, D. (1998). *Inching toward systemic change in New York City: How the Coalition Campus Schools are reinventing high schools.* New York: National Center for Restructuring Education, Schools, and Teachers.

Dillon, S. (1994, May 15). 30 new high schools report first-year success. *New York Times,* Sunday Metro Section, p. 1.

Eastsider. (1993, April 15).

Jacobson, L. (1995, April 5–11). Reform school: Notorious Julia Richman High School changes its course. *Upper East Side Resident,* p. 11.

Meier, D. (1995). *The power of their ideas: Lessons for America from a small school in Harlem.* Boston: Beacon Press.

New Visions for Public Schools. (1996). Unpublished report.

Rousmaniere, K. (1997). *City teachers: Teaching and school reform in historical perspective.* New York: Teachers College Press.

Stiefel, L., Iatarola, P., Fruchter, N., & Berne, R. (1998). *Effects of size in student body on school costs and performance in New York City high schools.* New York: New York University Institute for Education and Social Policy.

CHAPTER 8

Birthing New Visions Schools

Beth Lief

New Visions for Public Schools, founded in 1989 as the Fund for New York City Public Education, has from its start worked with educators, parents, students, city leaders, and community partners to develop initiatives that lead to better instruction, higher student achievement, and greater school accountability for all children in the city's public schools. By the time we began working on small-school creation, at the beginning of 1992, the fund had programs in more than 150 schools as well as efforts aimed at reforming system-wide, state, and national policies, framing our positions from the real-life experiences of the schools in which we worked.

Although the creation of small schools had not been one of our explicit goals, our work to create and foster New Visions Schools represents all that is at the heart of our values. Systemic reform has always been our aim, and well it should be. New York City has its educational gems, but spreading great schooling throughout the system never seems to happen. Working first with individual teachers, then teams of teachers, both within and across school boundaries, we became increasingly convinced that a good school system had to be responsive to and responsible for schools that provided, or are working hard to provide, rigorous and caring education. Sounds obvious, and yet too many policies and practices in the bureaucracy could not answer the simple question, How does it improve teaching and learning?

We also became convinced that a sense of community, of belonging, of being known and respected, on the part of both educators and students was a critical element of successful schools. Although far from guaranteed, attainment of these goals was certainly much easier in small schools. And it would be a Herculean feat to create this environment in the large schools where more than 2,000 students crowd the hallways, unknown by name to teachers acting like traffic cops between periods. Our participation in the wave of small-school creation in the 1990s was thus a natural outgrowth of our work.

Small high schools from the 1960s when they emerged until the early 1990s were housed at the time exclusively in the Alternative High School Superintendency and not in the five other high school superintendencies that were defined geographically. Most of these schools were for students who had not succeeded in other schools. A minority, like Central Park East Secondary School and International High School, were not second-chance schools. They took students in the 9th grade but were and still are radically different in culture, scheduling, pedagogy, and assessment from the city's traditional, large high schools. Regardless of the nature of their student populations, all these small high school communities appreciated the flexibility (some would say protection) that was the hallmark of the Alternative Superintendency. The educators in most of these schools felt—rightly or wrongly—that they would have a much rougher time of running their schools the way they wanted under the traditional high school superintendencies.

The small schools that existed at the elementary and middle school level were clustered in the early 1990s in three of New York City's 32 community school districts: in East Harlem's District Four; District Three on the west side of Manhattan and tip of Harlem; and District Two, which wraps around Central Park to the south and where Superintendent Tony Alvarado nurtures innovation the way he did earlier as a superintendent in East Harlem. A few small schools had started in other places, but the school system didn't consider, let alone discuss or support, the notion of small, distinctive, autonomous schools as an important way to increase achievement for all students.

The conversation about creating a critical mass of new small schools began for us at the end of 1991 in the offices of the Aaron Diamond Foundation. The Aaron Diamond Foundation, which unfortunately has since gone out of existence, was a bold, supportive place for folks and groups seriously interested in improving public education. Irene Diamond, its founder, is a feisty, determined, and smart woman who did not want tinkering at the edges, and she urged those of us she supported to push ourselves and the system as far as possible in pursuit of lasting reform. The senior education program officer was Norm Fruchter, an educational reformer of long-standing. Norm brought me together with Steve Phillips, the head of the Alternative High School Superintendency, Mark Weiss, his deputy and a former principal at an alternative high school that had included the first urban dormitory in the system (and who was to become in the next year the principal of School for the Physical City, one of our initial New Visions schools), and Alan Dichter, the principal of Satellite Academy, an alternative high school. The purpose of the meeting was to discuss how to end the practice of small, innovative schools as well-kept secrets, how to make them part and parcel of the entire system. I don't recall whether we were bold enough to talk in terms of small schools' becoming the norm, but we did begin the process of imagining many more such schools and discussed how we would begin, whom we would work with, and so forth.

At about the same time, then Chancellor Joseph Fernandez had been studying the student-achievement patterns at high schools throughout the city. He and his deputy chancellor, Stanley Litow, became convinced that an effort to create significant numbers of small high schools would do much to improve the system. Our nonprofit status had been set up as a result of an earlier chancellor's request for an organization to help with philanthropic and other private offers of support, and we had an excellent relationship with Chancellor Fernandez and Stanley Litow, who had actually helped set up New Visions when he was himself the head of another nonprofit organization. The chancellor called me in with Norm Fruchter to see whether New Visions would be interested in helping to set up some number of these schools. The Aaron Diamond Foundation had offered to help by giving us a grant to support the development of such schools.

THE FRAMEWORK

We accepted but asked for certain conditions. The first concerned the governance and grade structure of the schools. New York City's public school system, in addition to being the largest in the country, has a unique governance structure. Responsibility for education in kindergarten through 8th grade resides in 32 community school districts with elected school boards who, until April 1997, had full power to select their individual superintendents. Responsibility for high schools resided in the central administration, which had in turn created six superintendencies—the Alternative Superintendency and five geographically based superintendencies. Finally, a separate, central superintendency oversees the education of the most severely disabled student populations, and there is a chancellor's district that is small in size and whose function has varied over time.

The elementary and middle school structure thus operated entirely differently from the structure for high schools—different superintendents, different school boards, different funding systems, and, for some purposes, even different computer systems. Continuity in education from the middle years to the high school years was tenuous, to say the least, at a point in adolescent students' lives when continuity was very important. We therefore asked that the schools we helped create span these years and range from schools with grades 7 through 12 to schools that range the full gamut from kindergarten or pre-kindergarten through grade 12. We knew that given the then statutorily defined governance system, we would have to craft individual governance agreements, often with two superintendents, but we agreed to do so.

The second condition was more a mutually agreed upon understanding concerning the superintendencies under which these schools would reside. Going back to the discussion at the Aaron Diamond Foundation, we wanted small, innovative schools to become familiar to the system. The best way to do that, we thought at the time, was to put these schools in superintendencies throughout the city, not just in the Alternative High School Superintendency or in Anthony Alvarado's District Two.

The third concerned the manner by which we would create these schools and paved the way for the distinct nature of New Visions Schools. We suggested opening up the opportunity to the widest, most diverse groups and peoples imaginable. Let the public help create, and thereby to some degree redefine, public schools. Thanks to the courageous advocacy on our behalf by Joseph Fernandez and Stanley Litow, there was no argument to this or to the two other conditions. We were off.

It was the third condition that probably made New Visions Schools most distinct. New York City has had a rich and long-standing tradition of linking nonprofits, universities, and other "outside" organizations with public schools. Key to the reform efforts of New Visions for Public Schools has been our attempts to maximize the power and potential of such partnerships. We believe that schools cannot serve students well without the help of others who have an impact on their lives; that in a fiscally strapped school system, partnerships bring needed supports and resources; and that, perhaps most important, they bring the public into public schools, with perspectives on students' lives that are invaluable to nurturing their intellectual and emotional growth. We wanted to extend the benefits of connecting schools to community and outside organizations in a new and much deeper way. We wanted to create an inextricable link between community and school.

Thus in the spring of 1992 we sent out a very public call to start new schools. Ads appeared in newspapers and on the radio. We organized meetings and mailings. Sixteen thousand individuals and groups received our first Request for Pilot School Proposal (RFP), an invitation, as it were, to set forth their conception for a small, innovative school. We had certain non-negotiables—small size (which we at the time defined as no more than 500 to 700 students); heterogeneity; connection to and respect for parents and community; and a rigorous college-preparatory curriculum, to name the most important. The chancellor gave us the authority and private donors gave us the finances to award ten planning grants with the expectation of creating five actual schools. The response to the RFP was so over-whelming that the first round ended up with 16 planning grants and, even-tually, 15 schools. A second RFP in 1996 resulted in planning grants to 31 teams. The initiative had grown to include approximately 50 schools by the summer of 1997, 20 of which were in the planning stages and planned to open in September 1997 or in 1998. We continue to receive calls on a regular basis from communities and educators about the possibility of our supporting more schools.

THE SCHOOLS

The small schools that New Visions has helped start have origins, unlike many small schools sponsored by other organizations. Some New Visions Schools adhere to and are part of the Coalition of Essential Schools (CES). Others are quite different. The array of pioneers is extraordinarily diverse. These school communities were launched by, as one close observer wrote,

> unions, churches, community based organizations, groups of teachers, pock-ets of parents, colleges, museums, folks who swear off standardized tests and folks who swear by them, educators committed to Afrocentrism and those committed to Western civilization . . . educators who work from a position of activist democracy and those who work toward high test scores by "what-ever means necessary." But all responded to the invitation to create small schools because they were committed to trying to build and sustain high-quality public schools for *all*. (Fine, 1996, p. 12)

The three conditions we'd agreed upon—a grade structure that at-tempted stable, continuous schooling for the majority of a student's pre-collegiate career; the decision to engage as many superintendents as possible in working with small, innovative schools; and the opening up of school creation and school-based governance councils to outside organizations—were radical departures from the system's usual way of doing business. As a result, the birthing, strengthening, and survival of these schools has cre-ated a state of fairly constant tension within the school system—sometimes healthy, sometimes heated. Major changes in systems built to withstand change, especially changes advocated nosily by folks unaccustomed to being at the table who are pushing for new ways of defining schooling, don't come easily. We sometimes marvel with the "family"—members of our staff and the school communities—how hard so much of the experience has been. But then again, this business of *creating* and sustaining successful public schools is, even under the best of circumstances, exceedingly tough.

NURTURING SCHOOLS THROUGH THE EARLY YEARS

These New Visions Schools are young. The first wave is 7 years old and still maturing. But there is no question that these schools have generated a sense of new possibilities for what education can be. They have ignited the imagination of many who had become too accustomed to the status quo. Today the city's educators, policymakers, and parents know there can be a museum school whose classrooms are the galleries of five of the top museums in the country. In a former church, there is a community school focused on peace, justice, and human rights and built upon notions of collective self-help; its leader says to her students every day, "You do not come to the El Puente Academy to study history. You come to make history."

These pioneers join a more mature set of small schools that grew under the wings of just a few superintendencies. Their results to date, although not uniform, are impressive. These schools as a whole admitted a greater number of students who were below average academically, were poor, and come from minority groups than did schools in the system taken as a whole. Yet in the first eight graduating classes, in 1997, the graduation and college acceptance rates were terrific, averaging more than 80% and even reaching 100% in two of the schools.

WORKING TOGETHER

New Visions has established with these schools a variety of supports to help strengthen their educational communities and develop their leadership. Some supports are quite specific and came about in response to particular requests from schools. In 1996, for example, as the specter of our first graduating classes approached, we began our College Bound program, training teachers to offer SAT courses, organizing college fairs and financial aid workshops for students and families, building relationships with specific colleges, and producing a guide in Spanish and English that details how to prepare students for college.

Ongoing opportunities for professional development are critical to making a reality out of our vision, particularly for so many schools with high percentages of young teachers and new school leaders, and we devote much effort to building such opportunities. We have educators from within and without the schools who serve as a New Visions faculty. They visit schools and help them assess their goals and needs with respect to teaching and learning. These consultants and practitioners work with teachers and administrators to plan and implement activities in such areas as the use of standards-based instruction as a tool for improving student achievement; on-site support for the development of strong leaders; and technical assistance in areas such as curriculum development, scheduling to promote common planning time, budgeting, personnel selection, and parent involvement. One practitioner, for example, assisted educators from a group of schools in researching, evaluating, and assembling appropriate high school and middle school curriculum materials in mathematics. With her assistance, these educators developed a transitional curriculum for 9th-grade students who enter high school without an adequate mathematical foundation. We have supported other sets of schools in different curriculum areas.

We also sponsor a set of forums, usually in collaboration with others, for discussing educational issues to which members of all school communities, educators, parents, community partners, and students, are invited. A series of "Loft Talks" are offered for discussing important issues with nationally recognized educators and authors.

Interschool organizations are emerging as promising mechanisms for school support. There are permanent networks of schools and groups of schools that vary by topic and need. In the more permanent arrangements, schools have joined in groups of three to eight, receiving flexible private funds to engage in joint staff development and other projects. One network, for example, is comprised of six schools that have a particular focus on the needs of Latino students. Some of the schools are set up as dual-language communities, others are not, but all are concerned with the system-wide failure of Latino students to flourish academically.

Another network is the natural outgrowth of the desire of four schools that share the same building to pool their resources and brainstorm toward collaborative and collective improvement. One result is that library resources and the talents of specialized teachers are now shared across school lines. Other networks are more fluid, as exemplified by a group of schools working together on community-service learning. In some cases, however, issues resulting from the distance between schools, different superintendencies, and the ever-present crunch for time frustrate the best of intentions. Technology offers a partial and welcome solution. So too does flexibility—in defining networks, allowing for their reorganization, and shaping their purposes and styles.

Our aim in all these professional-development endeavors is to help school communities develop their own capacity for sustaining constant, continual intellectual inquiry and personal growth on the part of the educators as well as the students. These educators' time is stretched to the limit, even given the 10-hour-plus days and the weekends these committed people put in. They lack the time to construct all curricula from scratch or to research what best suits their students' needs and school goals. That each school is small enough for teachers and students to know each other is undeniably a great advantage in creating a culture of learning. But searching for and sharing of successful strategies among the network of schools and across school lines is also important for the building of each school's pedagogy. We hope it will shed light on successful approaches for all schools in the system.

THE OUTSIDE PARTNER

In reflecting on the role New Visions as an outside organization has played, I keep coming back to a few, perhaps less obvious considerations. We offer a safe space for educators, community, and parents to be honest, even brutally so, about their fears, their frustrations, their failures. The school system is changing in some respects, but overall (again, with important exceptions), reasonable risk-taking is not appreciated or encouraged, despite the fact that doing business as usual is not resulting in the kind of success we want and need. We encourage risk.

New Visions is also a place for celebration, and we try to celebrate regularly to remind ourselves not to become overly obsessive about the challenges the schools continually face. We work to get good news stories about the schools and the people in them into the press, and we've had gratifying results—two *New York Times Magazine* stories, many newspaper articles, television snippets, speaking engagements, and the like. These schools are pushing themselves to the limit on a daily basis; to become media celebrities, even temporarily, offers them a welcome and deserved lift. Seeking and encouraging good publicity also has another benefit. As Michael Rose observed in *Promised Lives* (1995), the news about public education is almost uniformly bad. Without whitewashing the harsh realities of overcrowding, underfunding, poorly prepared teachers, and insufficient supplies, it is important to present some balance in the profile of public education.

We also nurture. Our first director of the school-creation initiative, Naomi Barber, has an extraordinarily nurturing personality, which was as important as any of her insights on school reform. She taught us that giving succor to school leaders—at all hours of the day and night—is necessary psychological and emotional support. The school system is often portrayed as the boogie man, but educators constantly feel battered not by the system but by the devastating circumstances of so many of their students' lives, and by the lack of adequate resources, human and otherwise, to compensate for so much of what the children need and lack. The extraordinary professionals who take on these challenges deserve and need to be told they are special.

But the role that consumes most of my time as head of New Visions is that of broker, negotiator, interpreter, and advocate for the place of small schools in a big system. The form these negotiations take has varied over time. In the beginning, we spent hours with David Sherman from the teachers union, working out variations to the collective bargaining agreement that would modify seniority provisions to allow teachers to choose particular schools. Naomi, other senior staff, and I appeared before groups of teachers, union delegates, and representatives from the supervisors union to explain what we were trying to accomplish, to answer questions, to allay fears. ("Are you suggesting," taunted a veteran teacher from a huge high school, "that everything we do is terrible?") As David Sherman describes in greater detail in Chapter 10, the agreement to modify hiring practices became a formal part of the teachers' contract within 2 years. We also spoke with members of the central school board and their staff on a fairly regular basis, and, as the time for formally recognizing the schools grew closer, we met with top school-system and teachers-union staff to hammer out governance details, including agreements for including community-group representatives at the table when school leadership and staff were being selected.

The granting of official status for the initial round of schools does not end the need to broker. For the vast majority of the system's management unfamiliar with this type of school, hours of explanation are needed to make the case for the potential these educational communities offer. Some have suggested, quite reasonably, that the system shouldn't need an intermediary. In fact, in the 8 years since those initial meetings in 1991 concerning small-school creation, understanding and appreciation of the value of our efforts have increased enormously. In many cases, educators, supervisors, school board members, and legislators today not only know what these small schools can be but see them as one important method of building successful learning communities and of restructuring failing schools. For example, at the board of education's request, we helped adapt our application process and worked with a broad-based community advisory council to select planning teams to restructure a large, failing high school in Brooklyn, Eastern District High School, into four smaller schools. Superintendents from community school districts (other than the usual suspects from Manhattan) have in the past few years asked us and some of our partners in the Annenberg project, New York Networks for School Renewal to break down larger schools into smaller ones.

But even when superintendents and other supervisors want these new schools, there is still a need to foster a tolerance for difference, for the entrepreneurial spirit they engender. The leaders and creators of these schools tend to be a gloriously prickly lot. To those accustomed to passive or silently rebellious school staff, this group comes as a shock—with character-istics that tend to go hand-in-hand with a dogged refusal to be deterred from creating the very best school.

There has been change. These schools are no longer well-kept secrets. But, except in rare instances, are these schools still treated as exceptions? Has the system changed to support, nurture, or at least accommodate them? Or it is only our individual and collective tenacity that enables us to continue?

A few changes have come easily. In at least one area, the system re-sponded with alacrity and grace. Perhaps the hardest issue for the first wave of New Visions Schools was space. Until permanent space was found and renovated, schools moved as many as four times in a year, with consequent upheaval that made concentrating on teaching and learning very tough. These conditions were a function of our terribly overcrowded school sys-tem overall. Happily, when we did begin to work on construction and reno-vation with system officials, they did not balk at working with architects hired by school teams and accepted the notion that space, as much as any-thing else, should reflect individual school themes. In 1997, under Chan-cellor Rudy Crew's stewardship, we achieved another first. El Puente, the nonprofit organization that started the El Puente Academy for Peace and Justice, was able to purchase its own building with the system's agreeing to pay for the lease of the facility.

But in many other areas change has not progressed as far or as smoothly. Yes, there are explicit regulatory impediments that need to be or are in the process of being removed. But the most important changes needed do not, for the most part, involve the elimination of specific written rules.

Some change in that regard is, of course, necessary. Special education is a good example. The present New York State funding stream and defi-nition of special education actively discourage the kind of inclusionary practices that characterize these schools' approach to teaching all children. Regulatory provisions regarding both special and bilingual education gen-erate resources and supports based on numbers of students that tend to be too large in the context of these smaller schools. The school system has been proactive in working to eliminate barriers to special-education students' attending small schools. We worked with board of education specialists to get a system-wide waiver from the New York State Education Department that has allowed the merger of dollars targeted for special-education and mainstream students and the individualized placement of children with special needs in regular classroom settings. This is the norm in most states, and we hope it will be so in New York as well.

Instead, for the most part, what needs changing is much of the prac-tice and perspective of those inside the system but outside the schools who supervise, rate, and regulate day-to-day school life. School professionals need to know that, as long as they demonstrate they are working effectively to increase student achievement, they will have the authority to make key decisions about personnel, scheduling, budget, curriculum, instruction, and assessment within the framework of city and state guidelines. Virtually all of this could happen without legislative change if those in power want it.

Recent changes in New York education law mandate that all schools have school-based budgets within 2 years. When other changes will occur is less clear. And, even then, the granting of such authority does not eliminate the need for the system to provide leadership, instructional expertise, and other kinds of supports. Indeed, most important is the need for supervisory personnel to support the efforts of these pioneers to bring lasting change for the better. When we issued the second invitation to start or restructure small schools, we specifically asked the applicants what rules and regulations they wanted relief from. Almost no one pointed to a law, a regulation, a written standard operating procedure. Most responses, instead, reflected the following concerns of a project director who wanted his school separated into two smaller entities:

> The authority to make our own decisions about budget, personnel and programming are crucial. . . . On a building level, our school still falls under the supervision of the Principal. Although our Principal is very supportive of our efforts, we do not know if a future Principal will be equally encouraging. Our school may not fit in with our District's overall strategy. Many current policies run counter to our goals.

As this director implies, superintendents and principals change frequently not only in New York City but throughout the country. This lack of stability has many negative consequences for school systems. Whenever there is a change, we worry whether the new leaders will approve of and support the small, distinctive schools in their domain.

What form does this support take? In our experience, these small-school communities want and need useful help and guidance, including professional and technical assistance covering the entire gamut of schooling. When they get it within the system, the role of a nonprofit organization such as New Visions is significantly diminished—a great thing in our view. But too often what these schools face is the absence of ongoing constructive supports and the presence of continual sea changes, mandates, protocols, and directives. The call for autonomy here and elsewhere and the popularity of charter legislation among many reformers reflect the legitimate desire of school communities to be able to work in an environment free of those continual sea changes.

Our fixation on size and autonomy is real. But we also struggle with inadequate resources and overcrowded, poorly maintained buildings. And those of us engaged in this work cannot ignore what may be the biggest issue facing us—the lack of capacity in the system to educate students at high standards. As I write, there is a desperate search throughout New York City to find stellar candidates for school leadership and teaching positions. In at least one instance, two of our schools were intensively wooing the same candidate. A number of community school district superintendents have called to see if we at New Visions know of any good candidates to lead schools, old ones and new ones. We need a pipeline within each school system to identify, develop, nurture, and reward top-quality school leaders—leaders who expect students to achieve at high levels; who can structure curriculum and pedagogy to help them get there; who have the knowledge and skills to work hand-in-hand with community partners; who respect and learn from students' families; who can assume responsibility with other members of their team for budget, assessment, scheduling, and so forth.

These issues, of course, affect all schools, big and small. Indeed, it is important not to label all issues as distinctively those of small schools. We need all the allies we can muster.

CONCLUSION

However tough the experience of creating and nurturing small schools has been, we believe more than ever in the potential of small learning communities. And, happily, so do growing numbers of people. The small schools are no longer, as they were in 1991, well-kept secrets. They are too numerous and too popular with students, families, community groups, and an increasing percentage of managers within the school system for them to disappear. I suspect, though, that intermediaries—nonprofits such as New Visions for Public Schools—will still be a necessary part of the landscape for some time to come.

REFERENCES

Fine, M. (1996). *Refusing to be deferred: An evaluation of the dream and practice of New Visions Schools.* New York: New Visions for Public Schools.

Rose, M. (1995). *Promised lives.* New York: Penguin.

CHAPTER 9

School Reform: A System's Approach

Judith A. Rizzo

In November 1995, at the beginning of Rudy Crew's tenure as chancellor of the New York City public schools, I joined his administration as deputy chancellor for instruction. A few months later, I participated in a meeting of four institutional partners, known collectively as the New York Network for School Renewal, which had lately secured an Annenberg grant to develop new small schools. This consortium was comprised of the Center for Collaborative Education, New Visions for Public Schools (formerly the Fund for New York City Public Education), ACORN (Association of Community Organizations for Reform Now), and the Center for Educational Innovation. I listened with great interest as they struggled to design an organizational and operational model to oversee the burgeoning number of these schools, to determine the eligibility and the soundness of newly proposed schools, and to ensure accountability. This struggle was natural, as concerned, responsible adults tried to come up with a workable management structure. The need to come up with an effective and efficient model, however, was in conflict with their commitment to autonomy. At one point, the design that was forwarded eerily resembled a school system, and the oversight group was beginning to resemble a school board. When one of the partners pointed out to the others that they were veering toward re-creating a bureaucracy, a collective shudder went through the room.

A century or so ago, those first designers of what we now know as public school systems must have had similar conversations. Our forebears were a fiercely independent group with strong personal ties to their local schools. The desire for efficiency and the nascent scientific management model, along with the rise in populations in our cities and the influx of immigrants, all influenced the move away from locally controlled schools to a corporate model. School systems, led by superintendents, evolved as a mechanism both to manage large numbers of schools and to vouchsafe to an entire community that one person could be held accountable for the quality of education received by all its youngsters.

The need to design organizational structures is innate. It was not out of any evil intent to stifle creativity or limit educational opportunities that school systems were first created. Along the way, some school systems, particularly larger ones, became so bureaucratic that their central administrators developed a management style that focused on command and control. Command and control is a military model that found its way into school organizations by way of corporations. Although this approach may be well suited to preparing and managing an army, it was questionable at best in the context of schools, and it is not, in its unreconstructed form, appropriate today. But neither is anarchy. A balance is required, and that is the essence of the work of the leaders in school organizations today—to build school systems that will support a variety of educational settings and provide needed school autonomy without compromising equity, efficiency, and standards of quality and accountability. In order to achieve this, a complex and integrated series of structural changes need to be introduced into school systems, and New York City poses unique challenges.

SYSTEMIC CHANGE

New York City has the largest and arguably the most complicated school system in the country. It encompasses about 1,100 schools, approximately 1.1 million students, almost 70,000 teachers, 32 community school superintendencies, 6 high school superintendencies, 1 special-education superintendency, and 1 chancellor district superintendency. Over 16% of the students speak a language other than English, and 140 languages are represented. The budget for the New York City schools is over $8 billion.

During our first months in New York, we evaluated the general condition of the organization by analyzing both hard data—such as test scores, finances, facilities, and internal systems—and anecdotal data—the many versions of the same essential complaint about bureaucratic obstacles, communication problems, lack of focus, and unclear accountability that influenced analysis of the organization's internal systems. It was obvious that in order to support any enterprise like small schools, we needed to attend to some of the health issues of the system as a whole. In fact, when we arrived, the New York City schools constituted a system in name only. There was little coherence among the school districts and between the districts and the central office. There were, however, a plethora of policies, procedures, regulations, and rules, all unevenly applied.

We began by putting in place an organizational model that would more efficient operationally and more effective instructionally, a system th: would ultimately be more responsive to and supportive of its constituer schools and districts, while being more accountable and "transparent" t(the general public. We strove to build a performance-driven learning system.

In this administration's vision, the development of a performance-driven learning system would allow both uniformity in high performance standards and diversity across schools. Such a system would have five key characteristics:

- It would clearly define standards for student learning;
- It would develop and articulate educational strategies for student learning;
- It would align resources and actions to carry out these strategies for student learning;
- It would evaluate the effectiveness of its educational strategies and their execution by measuring student learning with appropriate evaluation instruments;
- It would continually revise its educational strategies and/or their execution based on the performance outcomes achieved.

Although these seem straightforward and reasonable, reorienting a large school system to behave in a performance-driven mode is not an easy task. One of the more complicated issues in a system our size is to differentiate the roles and responsibilities of each of the segments of the system.

Fred Newman and Gary Wehlage (1995) provide some guidance in resolving this issue. Their report was the result of a multiyear study of successfully restructured schools from around the country, funded by the U.S. Department of Education and prepared at the Center on Organization and Restructuring Schools, whose advisory panel includes the American Federation of Teachers, the National Association of Elementary School Principals, the National Association of Secondary School Principals, and the Association for Supervision and Curriculum Development.

Successful schools are those that hold high expectations for student achievement and have structured themselves to attain that goal for all of their students. Newman and Wehlage (1995) point out that whereas these schools varied widely in how they achieved their goals—there was no one curriculum or standard pedagogy to which they all subscribed—they did share some common elements. All of these schools were relentlessly focused on high student achievement; all were engaged in "authentic pedagogy" specifically linked to their goals; and all had organized their school struc-

This is true for large and small schools alike. No one disputes the many benefits derived by students in small schools, but the primary emphasis in public education must be on consistently providing high-quality instruction in a school environment focused on student achievement. Graduates of small and large schools alike will need to be able to succeed in the same competitive marketplace. As Pat Wasley stated in her speech at a 1997 Bank Street College conference on small schools, "Smaller schools are not better if they don't do more for kids; [these schools] need to couple skill at innovation with rigor and show that kids are doing better."

We believe strongly that standards should not be developed locally. The global economy dictates that our students be able to compete on national and international levels as they enter the work force. Standards cannot be set at the school level; they need to be uniformly accessible to all students in a school system. In December 1996 we proposed to the central board of education that the New York City schools adopt the rigorous standards developed by the New Standards project. These reflect many years of work by teachers, administrators, parents, and academics from several states and school districts around the country including New York, both state and city. The standards are based on what we believe students will need to know and be able to do in order to be successful in the 21st century. The New Standards reflect the work and recommendations of internationally recognized organizations such as the National Council of Teachers of Mathematics, the National Science Foundation, and the International Reading Association.

In March 1997, we began a customization process to produce local standards documents in English language arts, Spanish language arts, and English as a second language. This document, which in fall 1997 was distributed throughout the system, contains samples of our own students' work as exemplars of the performance standards. These samples came from every borough and every district in New York City. It became clear through this process that many of our students were already producing high-quality work and that many of our teachers were practicing effective instructional strategies.

We conducted a similar process for calibrating the math standards, which we disseminated in fall 1998. The science standards and applied learning standards were released in 1999. However, our primary focus, especially at the elementary level, is on language arts.

EDUCATIONAL STRATEGIES

Clearly defined content and performance standards drive curriculum, instruction, assessment, and professional development. Although the standards must be set at the system level, we do not believe that curriculum and instruction should be dictated centrally. These need to be developed and managed at a level closer to schools, and by those schools that have the capacity and the desire to design their own. Many of our small schools are theme-driven and want their curriculum and instructional strategies to be aligned with those themes. They also want curriculua that both reflect the particular interests of their students and are interdisciplinary. They understand that the responsibility to set standards rests with the central board of education but do not want curriculum, instruction, professional development, or school organizational structure to be dictated by a central office. We respect and support the appropriateness and necessity for schools to design their own curriculum, instruction, professional-development, and school organizational structure so long as these are aligned with the standards. It is the role of our administration to ensure that districts and schools receive the necessary guidance and resources to engage in this work.

Key to all of our efforts is professional development. Educators at every level of our system need to develop the skills necessary to bring all students to higher levels of achievement. Many of our schools, including our new and small schools, have clear instructional goals and have engaged in school-based professional development that is closely aligned with those goals. Others have experienced professional development that is top-down, uneven, and unfocused.

As Newman and Wehlage (1995) have suggested, an appropriate role for a central or district office is to provide professional development to schools. This should be done either directly or indirectly as the situation warrants. A direct form of professional development is called for when a system-wide initiative is introduced and the information can be better and more cost-effectively delivered on a system-wide or district-wide basis. An example is the introduction of an early childhood assessment system, which I describe later in this chapter.

Although central delivery of professional development is sometimes appropriate, this administration is firmly committed to school-based models. Central's (or district's) role is to provide the resources that schools need to plan, design, implement, and evaluate professional development and to ensure that it is ongoing, focused on their individual needs, imbedded in their organizational goals, comprehensive, and high quality. To guide districts and schools in this effort, we have organized into one user-friendly document the several proven and research-based models of professional development already in use in our system, together with the funding available to support them. We are currently developing a consumer guide on effective programs and best practices to further assist our districts and schools to make informed choices about the content of their professional development. A group of community school district superintendents are working with us to identify and document these practices.

RESOURCE ALIGNMENT

To carry out the strategies that lead to high student achievement, superintendents and school-based staff need resources. In a performance-driven learning system, all resources—fiscal, human, time, materials—are focused on student learning. When this administration arrived, there was no reliable way of tracking or reporting how our operating budget of over $8 billion was spent. In our first year, we produced a series of comprehensive school-based budget reports that clearly tracked the dollars allocated from the central board through district offices to schools. We produce these each year in increasing detail and with enhanced clarity. We have begun and will continue to ensure that all of our constituents understand these reports and can use them to make informed local decisions about how funds should be spent.

As a natural corollary to knowing how money is allocated, we have begun empowering districts and schools to make more of the important decisions about the use of those dollars. We began a process called performance-driven budgeting in several community school districts and two high school superintendencies, a small-school network, and one school under the chancellor's jurisdiction. This initial group volunteered to participate in the first round of work so that we can learn together how to make the budget process more responsive to the needs of schools and districts. We plan to bring more districts and schools into the process each year so that, at the end of 3 years, the whole system will participate.

With the passage of the new governance legislation, discussed later in this chapter, came a commitment to school-level governance. We have designed a process for school decision making that involves the key constituents—school administrators, teachers, parents, community members—who will be engaged in assessing their school's needs, planning for improvement, and deciding on the allocation of resources. These school leadership teams will make decisions at the school level beginning with the 1999 school year.

To guide school leadership teams in their planning, we have designed a self-assessment system called the Performance Assessment in Schools Systemwide (PASS). The PASS system is based on those elements that have been confirmed by research and experience to be quality indicators of effective schools. These include an effective school organization, a climate of high expectations for students and staff, parent engagement and involvement, timely and ongoing assessment, focused professional development, consistent curriculum and authentic instruction, and appropriate instructional resources. Using PASS, schools can assess their strengths, identify areas that need improvement, and plan accordingly.

Many of the small schools are already well positioned to engage in performance-driven budgeting. Many of them have already established a shared decision-making model that includes administrators, teachers, staff, parents, students, and community and university representatives. A strong spirit of collaboration characterizes many of these schools. Performance-driven budgeting is another step toward autonomy at the school level. System-wide efforts like the school-based budget reports and performance-driven budget process empower schools to align resources with their own curriculum and professional-development needs.

ASSESSMENT

The fourth critical component of a performance-driven learning system requires evaluating the effectiveness of educational strategies by using appropriate instruments. To accomplish this, we have focused on aligning student assessment with our standards and providing districts and schools with timely and useful data about how well their students are progressing. We have begun by introducing more rigorous performance-based assessments in language arts and math and by providing professional development to teachers. So that we can have information about our students sooner, we have also developed the Early Childhood Language Assessment System. This system allows teachers, principals, and parents to assess and track the ongoing literacy development of our students in grades K–3. We know that the first years of literacy development are the most critical for children, yet this is an area in which solid assessments are sorely lacking. The intent is to provide teachers with a reliable and valid assessment tool for their on-demand use. Beginning in fall 1998, all early childhood teachers throughout the system began their training in using these performance-based assessments to inform their instructional practice.

Until 1999, we have had two separate testing programs in New York City: one imposed by the New York State Education Department and one used within the system to provide more performance-based data. We began early in our tenure to improve and streamline our testing program and have worked closely with the state's department to coordinate our joint efforts. Beginning in the 1998–99 school year, the state's department implemented a new testing program in grades 4 and 8 that more closely resembled the performance-based tests New York City adopted in spring 1996. This means we can eliminate duplication of testing at those grades and obtain better information about how well students are doing both within the city and in the city compared to the rest of the state.

At the same time the New York State Education Department has introduced more rigorous high-stakes Regents exams for high school students, beginning with a newly developed English Regents exam in the spring of 1999, and continuing in other content areas in succession over the next several years. At this point, Regents exams are no longer an option but a requirement for graduation from high school. Many practitioners at the high school level, particularly those in small schools, have strong reservations about the use of standardized proficiency tests that students have to pass in order to obtain a New York State Regents diploma. These educators prefer using more performance-based assessments, such as portfolios.

A representative group from some of our small high schools has been working internally to design alternative forms of assessment so that their students can demonstrate their proficiency through other means. Also, in the past, students had to take and pass prescribed Regents-level courses in order to be prepared for Regents exams; the content and sequence of these courses were determined by the New York State Education Department. New York City educators have been working with the state to obtain variances or waivers in the course work that students take so that individual schools can utilize their own locally developed curricula to cover the same content areas.

The issues of variances and alternative assessments are of particular importance to the proponents of small schools, because they desire both the flexibility and autonomy to create curricula that reflect their themes and instructional philosophy and the ability to design a variety of methods for assessing their students' proficiencies. Instead of struggling with these issues by themselves and having to contend with both the school system and the state, these schools have found an ally in this administration. My office has assumed a leadership role in this effort by convening the work groups on alternative assessments, by certifying variances and encouraging their use throughout the system, and by championing these issues with the New York State Education Department. We have added credibility to the ideas generated from many small schools and demonstrated our commitment through staff and resources. No longer are these issues the vital concern of a few schools; they have become an integral part of the city's educational agenda.

ACCOUNTABILITY

In a performance-driven learning system, changes in educational strategies or their management are made when high performance outcomes are not attained. The new governance legislation is one example of how this system has restructured itself to improve student outcomes and reestablish mechanisms of accountability within the system.

In 1968, the state legislature in New York, impatient with years of mismanagement and a mercilessly bureaucratic board of education, decentralized the New York City schools with the intention of creating more locally responsive leadership. It eventually carved out 32 community school districts within the five boroughs. Each community school district was governed by a locally elected school board of nine members, who hired and fired superintendents, principals, and other personnel. The local boards had power over budgets, programs, and policies for kindergarten through 8th grade.

The seven-member central board appointed by the five borough presidents and the mayor retained jurisdiction over the selection of the chancellor, the overall budget process, the city's 120 high schools, special education, facilities management, and the central data systems, including personnel. The central board also had policy-making authority. However, for the most part, the community school boards, and their superintendents, acted autonomously. The chancellor had little real authority over the K–8 system but, as the symbol of central authority, was nevertheless held accountable by the public for virtually everything.

By the time our administration came to New York, disenchantment with decentralization was already rampant. Although some community school boards conducted themselves with integrity and worked collaboratively with their superintendents to improve education in their districts, too many others acted negligently, even corruptly, and were failing their students. Soon after our arrival, we began lobbying for a change in the law. In order to be able to carry out the far-reaching changes we knew were necessary, we would need the authority to influence the actions of community district superintendents more directly. Within a little more than a year of our arrival, the state legislature modified its decentralization law and created a new governance structure for New York City's public schools that gave significantly greater authority to the chancellor for hiring, supervising, and evaluating community superintendents. Local boards no longer have jurisdiction over personnel or budget. They have assumed the appropriate role of a school board: selecting and evaluating the superintendent, setting goals and priorities, establishing educational policy, and facilitating the meaningful involvement of parents and community. They have become, in theory, policy-setting bodies. The administration of the district now is wholly the responsibility of the community superintendent.

Under the new structure, superintendents receive 3-year performance contracts, and the chancellor now shares the responsibility for evaluating the performance of the community superintendents with community school boards. Among the tools the chancellor will use to evaluate superintendents are the district comprehensive educational plans (CEPs), which must be approved and signed by the superintendent and the community school board after public presentation and comment. At the district level, the comprehensive education plan should reflect the needs identified by the schools through the PASS process.

Over the years, the story of decentralization has been well documented, and although the new governance structure is recent, much has been written about that as well. They are referenced here, along with strategies to ensure accountability, to provide context for this administration's current efforts. What is useful to note about the recent changes in governance law is that the New York-based proponents of small schools much prefer to work in the new environment created by the changes. They understand that accountability is a reasonable price for autonomy. They understand that a system that is out of control cannot support or sustain any kind of meaningful decision making at the school level. They further understand that the ultimate success of their schools depends in large measure on the health of the system as a whole.

In the previous section, I discussed the creation of a performance-driven learning system as an essential vehicle for ensuring that all students achieve high academic standards. Additionally, we have taken steps to facilitate the initiation of new schools and charter schools and to provide them and other high-performing schools with more school-based autonomy.

NEW-SCHOOL PROCESS

There is no dearth of good ideas in our school system. Many teachers, administrators, parents, community activists, and academics have a concept of schooling they would like to develop. In a system as large and diverse as ours, we should be constantly discovering and designing new and better ways of educating our students. We should be able to offer our students and their parents a wide variety of settings, curricula, and learning experiences. Large comprehensive high schools, for example, are suited to many of our students. Others need and want smaller, more personal settings. Some students desire a theme-oriented school in the sciences or the arts; others, a general education with a more traditional curriculum. Some students want to experience a variety of settings, taking advantage of the number and variety of cultural and educational opportunities in New York City. All want excellence—and there is no one single model that will meet all their needs.

We realized that the process of developing a new school in our system was ambiguous, even ad hoc. Although to be duly recognized as a new school has always by state law required the approval of the central board of education, there was much variability in the means by which such schools were formed and approved. In the early days of our administration, board members began to raise serious questions about the effectiveness of some schools that had been established over the preceding 5 or 6 years.

For many years, the creation of new schools favored politics over process. Information is power. People who know how to navigate a complicated bureaucracy like ours have an advantage. People with access to high-ranking policy or decision makers have an even greater advantage. School systems are intrinsically political, and there is a permanent government imbedded in their hierarchies that outlasts the changes at the top. These are the folks who keep the institutional traditions alive, the true bureaucrats who maintain standard operating procedures, who ensure that the bureaucracy does what it was intended to do—perpetuate itself. These people hold the keys to getting business done. The truly savvy know how to maneuver through both levels in order to get what they need. Until now, the bureaucracy worked only for those who knew how to work it; our goal is to demystify the workings of the system and to make it more accessible to those who bring forward ideas that increase the kinds and quality of educational options for our students, including new, small schools.

We have taken a step in that direction by recently developing a straightforward process for starting new schools and charter schools. The document that defines the process is called Learning Communities; it was issued in fall 1998. Among the developers of the process were educators in our current small, new schools. The document clearly outlines steps to follow that ensure all the necessary pieces are in place before the resolution to create a new school comes before the central board. It sets out guidelines for preparing a clear vision and mission, defining the organizational structure, and declaring the curriculum and instructional focus. It involves convening a representative group of parents, teachers, and community to plan for and commit to the new-school. The process provides guidance in the identification of space and other technical issues. The Learning Community document also designates the appropriate contact persons within the system to assist new-school developers along the various steps of the process. In addition, we have built start-up costs for new schools into the budget. By clarifying the process and providing technical assistance to those who undertake it, we hope to encourage an entrepreneurial spirit among our constituents and send a clear message that we value these efforts.

CHARTER SCHOOLS

The Learning Communities document anticipated the introduction of charter legislation in New York State in December 1998. Although we have grave concerns about the political impetus behind this legislation and some uneasiness about particular provisions in the law, we nonetheless regard it as an opportunity to provide more autonomy to some of our successful small schools as well as to establish some new, small charter schools.

New York State was the 38th state to enact charter-school legislation. This movement continues even though the jury is still out on how well charter schools actually perform both academically and operationally across the country. At a recent national charter-school conference in Denver, charter-school proponents reported that many promising charter schools were failing because of operational problems (U.S. Department of Education, 1999). Because they were distracted by budget, facility, and related issues, charter-school directors, staff, and boards were not able to focus on their educational mission.

But because this administration has predicated its reform efforts on the assumption that public school systems can learn to behave in ways that simultaneously promote both autonomy and accountability, what we have already established here has positioned us to fully commit and contribute to the success of these schools to an unprecedented extent—not just philosophically but also practically and operationally.

We have already begun working with several of our small high schools that have indicated their desire to convert to charter status. However, the school teams have indicated that they do not want to be completely disconnected from the school system precisely to avoid the operational issues that plague many charter schools around the country.

New York City public schools who choose to convert to charter status and new charter schools will have the option of entering into a memorandum of understanding with the school system wherein they will identify the goods and services they would like to "purchase" from the central office. Some of the services already identified include insurance, food services, payroll, facilities, and legal services. We are prepared to accommodate the needs of these schools and to adjust our operating practices as needed.

Indeed, we intend to use charters as a learning tool for this school system. We believe that through supporting converted and new charters we will learn to let go of unnecessary, burdensome, and bureaucratic practices that consume time and energy at the school level. We believe that a fair and competitive environment will nurture creativity and provoke a reexamination of the kinds of supports schools actually need to prosper.

As we remove the operational and procedural obstacles identified by these charter schools, we intend to remove them for all high-performing schools. We expect that ultimately all New York City public schools will benefit.

DIFFERENTIATED MANAGEMENT

Our data indicate that our schools perform along a continuum. Some are performing at very high levels; others are not producing acceptable student achievement. Most are somewhere between the two. We believe that schools and districts that are performing at the highest levels have earned the right to be more autonomous and our relationship with them should be more facilitative and empowering. Those schools and districts performing at the low end of the spectrum require intervention that is more directive and prescriptive. Small schools are subject to the same natural laws; although we have granted them some autonomy, they will keep it, lose it, or enhance it on the basis of whether they produce results.

We have established a differentiated management approach for those schools and districts that evidence the characteristics that entitle them to more autonomy. Besides looking at student achievement, we consider value-added indicators of school effectiveness: the presence of strong leadership; collaboration among administrators, teachers, and parents; a clear instructional focus and strategy; and an organization structured around student learning, integrated professional development, and the use of student-assessment data.

Those districts, schools, and small-school networks involved in the first phases of performance-driven budgeting have experienced more autonomy and discretion in the use of their money. They have been given much latitude in budget development and spending. We mean to increase the number of schools and districts that are given similar decision-making authority. Moreover, as schools and districts identify procedures and policies that constitute bureaucratic obstacles to decision making, we continue to review the feasibility of modifying or eliminating them. Many of our small schools are eager to be given more autonomy and authority.

One of the perennial challenges of systemic reform is the issue of scale. To confront this challenge we have identified two entire community school districts where we will scale up many of the reform efforts discussed in this chapter along with several innovative operational reforms that heretofore have been implemented primarily on a school-by-school basis.

In these two districts the entire school communities will redefine the relationships between their schools and the district offices and between the district offices and central administration. Each school in the districts will use a school-based decision model that will involve school administrators, teachers, parents, and community. Although these districts will not be able to take advantage of the charter legislation, which frees schools from state regulations but prohibits whole-district involvement, they can be relieved of systemic rules and regulations.

The changes that we have initiated in the New York City school system have been motivated by our commitment not only to supporting the creation of small schools but also to making the school system congenial to a variety of organizational structures. Small schools are not the only answer, but they are part of an answer to the challenge of meeting the educational needs of all our students.

Although our administration supports the concept of small schools, we recognize, as many of its proponents do, that in and of itself, small is not sufficient. All of us want many of the benefits small schools can offer students, and these have been amply described in preceding chapters, but we need to find some breakthrough answers for the issues that are particularly challenging in small-school settings: how to offer a full complement of courses to students; how to fully accommodate those students who are not proficient in English; how to make instruction fully accessible to students with specialized needs; how to develop reliable and rigorous student assessments aligned with the unique curricula and course sequences in some of these schools; how to balance the desire for autonomy with the need for accountability. Many of these challenges are not unique to small schools, and to the extent that we can combine forces with various partners throughout the system, we will be more able to find better solutions and innovations that work for all students in the system.

During the last 3 years, we have collaborated closely with small-school practitioners.

Leaders of the small-schools community have assisted in system-wide change in several important ways: participating in the early phases of performance-driven budgeting; assisting in the development of the Learning Communities process; designing and refining performance-based assessments; sharing best practices with other educators; and helping to train parents to participate in school-based decision making.

As we ask small-schools leaders to work with the system, we in the central office also expect to provide support to small schools by making the changes that will render the system more accommodating to them. As a result of our partnership, both the schools and the system as a whole have benefited.

The issue of "scaling up" is critical in New York City because of the sheer size of our school system. It is also an important issue for proponents of small schools and for systemic reform everywhere. As an industry, we can institute successful change on a small scale, at an individual school or within a small network of schools. Although this continues to be an important effort, the real question—and the one I believe the future of public education depends upon—is, can we do it on a larger scale? This does not mean that we should attempt to re-create a system in which all schools look alike, but we need to ask whether we can we engineer the kinds of structural and behavioral changes that are required on a system-wide basis so that individual schools can redesign themselves and prosper. Can we institutionalize the effective practices that are working in some schools so that students in all schools can benefit? I think that we have to, and thanks to the willingness of our partners to work together with us, we have made a good beginning in the New York City school system.

We are convinced that small schools cannot flourish on the margins of the system; they need to be an integral part of it. Nor can the system flourish if it can accommodate only one organizational model, if it discourages change, or if it inhibits innovation, whether by design or by a failure to adapt. Our work to restructure our system, to make it more flexible and responsive, will allow many of its best practitioners to refocus on student achievement.

What I think bodes well for the small-school movement in New York City today is that its supporters here seem more sophisticated and politically astute than many reformers of the past. To their credit, they are also committed to assisting with whole-system change and are not solely concerned with their own schools and programs. A 1997 *Education Week* article about the Annenberg grant recipients describes their journey from "grand rhetoric and euphoric visions" toward "more mature projects that seek to work with—not outside of—the existing system" (Olson, 1997, pp. 1, 30). This does not imply a return to the free-thinking days of 60s-style reform when much of the satisfaction came from challenging institutions and breaking them down without thinking about what to replace them with. Today's reformers accept the challenge of influencing the system as a whole and working within it to begin to institutionalize better, more responsive, and more responsible management systems. As Heather Lewis, co-director of the Center for Collaborative Education, commented, "We can't expect the system to change overnight. And we are not content, any longer, to sit in the cracks" (Olson, 1997).

Small-schools educators are critical partners for making New York City the best urban school system in America. By promoting diversity and excellence among our schools, their interconnectedness to the system will be a benefit to all our students. This administration welcomes their vision and leadership.

A special thanks to Lai-Wan Wong for her valuable assistance on this project.

REFERENCES

Newman, F., & Wehlage, G. (1995). *Successful school restructuring: A report to the public and educators.* Madison, WI: Center on Organization and Restructuring of Schools.

Olson, L. (1997, June 25). 'Annenberg Challenge' proves to be just that. *Education Week, 16* (39), 1, 30.

U.S. Department of Education. (1999, March 14–17). Charter Schools National Conference: Strengthening networks and student achievement. Denver, CO: Author.

CHAPTER 10

The Role of a Union in School-System Reform

David Sherman

In April 1983 American Federation of Teachers (AFT) President Albert Shanker astonished nearly 3,000 union delegates at a meeting of the New York State United Teachers in Albany when he asked them not to have a "knee-jerk response" to the calls for reforms in the educational system of the United States.[1] He acknowledged that many proposals and reports had, in the past, been attacks on teachers and teachers unions rather than calls for fundamental changes in the way students learn and teachers teach; however, he urged that the latest reports, most notably *A Nation at Risk*, issued just a few days before his address to the delegates, were different in that they offered constructive proposals for improving education. The studies contained, he continued, "some of the greatest opportunities we've ever had to improve education and our status as teachers." He reiterated this message to an audience of union activists at that summer's AFT convention in Los Angeles. The following year, addressing the same group of union delegates he had spoken to the previous April, he amplified his comments.

> Now there are a lot of things that we can't do; a lot of things are not in our control; quite a few things take money or they take legislation or they take a change in the way things are structured. But one of the things that our members must come to realize is that we have a stake in the quality of public education. If we have schools with a substantial number of teachers who really shouldn't be there, if we hire people who are illiterate . . . it will affect the public support for public education. Now that's a difficult reorientation for me, as it is for you or for anybody else. We're a union. What does a union do? (Oreskes, 1983, p. 1)

What so stunned many of those present in Albany on that day in 1983 and at subsequent meetings was that a union leader who had led the drive for union representation of teachers, fighting off charges that such representation was "unprofessional," and who had not hesitated to lead teachers in New York City on three major strikes, the second of which was the longest teacher walkout in the nation's history, and who had been called everything from a union militant to a wild man intent on destroying the world, should be asking such a seemingly basic question as, "What does a union do?" The answer seemed to be quite simple. Unions should increase their efforts to work collaboratively with others and at the same time begin to examine their roles and responsibilities in the area of school quality and reform. But this "new unionism" was a revolutionary idea. It would involve a delicate balancing act between traditional union areas of concern—raising teachers' salaries, improving working conditions, protecting teachers against unfair treatment, enhancing pension and health benefits—and the need for changes and flexibility in the way teaching and learning are conducted in the schools, changes that would involve new roles not only for unions but for teachers. It would mean working closely with parents, the community, business groups, government leaders, and higher education. It would mean reexamining the goals of collective bargaining and union work rules. It would mean making decisions based primarily on educational rationales.

The first local unions in the country to answer Al Shanker's question, "What does a union do?", were Hammond, Indiana, and Toledo, Ohio, where peer intervention and review methods for determining teacher competency, an area previously under the purview of administration, were instituted in collaboration with the local unions. In Dade County, Florida, the school district and the United Teachers of Dade developed a policy of school-based management and shared decision making that allowed teachers and administrators in schools to make decisions involving scheduling, staffing, instructional programs, and budgeting at the school level—decisions that had previously been made at the district level.

In New York City the reaction to Al Shanker's call to teachers to "do everything we can to improve public education" was muted. Many teachers, still overwhelmed by the drastic cutbacks in the city's educational spending due to the fiscal crisis of the late 1970s felt too overwhelmed and unsupported to take on new responsibilities. City leaders, including the administrators at 110 Livingston Street, headquarters of the New York City Board of Education, were wary of anything proposed by Shanker, the skillful union negotiator. Community leaders in some parts of the city, still rankled over the racially charged strikes of the late 1960s, were cautious, at best, in dealing with a teachers union.

Shanker resigned from his position as president of the United Federation of Teachers (UFT), in December 1985. He continued as president of the AFT until his death in 1997. Despite scattered efforts around the country, little had changed in traditional labor–management relationships. Shanker's message had given impetus to a movement for "professionalizing teaching"—teachers would have a greater voice in decisions made at both the school and district level and would be compensated at a level that respected their professional status. In return, they and the schools in which they taught would be held to higher levels of accountability.

Sandra Feldman, the new president of the New York City UFT, began to put her ideas and Shanker's message into practice by reexamining the role of collective bargaining and expanding the definition of those who should be "represented" by the union. In her first address to the union membership at the UFT Spring Conference in 1986, she declared, "As the demography of this city has changed, and as children become more and more a forgotten minority, our role as a teachers' union more and more becomes that of a children's' lobby as well." It was a duty for the teachers union to fight for improved educational programs, lower class sizes, more classroom supplies, new school construction, repairs for crumbling schools, and increased parental involvement. Some of these objectives could be accomplished through traditional negotiations with the employer, others would take lobbying in City Hall and the state capital. Fifteen months later she reported on some of the union's accomplishments in the area of school reform: a mentor-teacher program designed to help new teachers in their classrooms in a supportive, nonjudgmental environment; a "Teacher's Choice" program that gave teachers an allocation to purchase instructional materials based on students' needs according to their professional judgment, and a pledge to repair schools.

Beginning in the 1985–86 school year and continuing throughout this period, the New York City Council, as a result of the lobbying efforts of the UFT, allocated funds specifically for the reduction of class size in grades 1, 2, and 3 to a maximum of 28 in any classroom and an average of 25 within a school. Increased state aid for education, secured through the lobbying efforts of the UFT's statewide affiliate, New York State United Teachers (NYSUT), enabled the city council in subsequent years to allocate funds to cap most high school classes at 34, kindergarten at 25, and grades 7 and 8 at 28. Compared with class sizes in surrounding school districts, even these numbers were on average 8 to 10 students higher. Yet, unfortunately, some of these class-size improvements were wiped out by major budget cuts in the early 1990s. These early gains did not come out of collective bargaining, where management would probably have looked for a quid pro quo— most likely in the area of teacher salaries—to pay for these items but rather through lobbying city and state lawmakers for funding. (Unfortunately, the strongest opposition to some of these improvements came from the organization representing supervisors and administrators.) The union knew that relying on city and state monies, year after year, to ensure the continuance of school-improvement efforts should not be their only strategy. Therefore, a strategy to expand the use of collective bargaining was instituted. The contract could be used to provide flexibility to foster far-reaching reforms as well as improvements in teacher salaries and working conditions. Nevertheless, the leadership of the UFT knew that for many of its members, especially those who had come of age during the early years of the struggle for union recognition and teachers' rights, and for those who worked in the majority of schools where top-down management was still the style, the entire issue of "teacher professionalism" was still unclear. They had always thought of themselves as professionals in a tradition-bound, unresponsive system that did not recognize their professional status. Their response to the question Al Shanker had asked at the beginning of the decade was still: Protect the rights of members against an autocratic, often uncaring board bureaucracy through enforcement of the contract, an understandable answer given their experience or current situation, or both. The union leadership knew that as leaders and as a powerful voice in the New York City educational community, they could neither live in the past nor fail to represent the interests of their members. Prior to the start of negotiations in 1987, the UFT sent out a survey to nearly 70,000 active UFT members, asking them to prioritize areas for the upcoming negotiations. In addition to questions in traditional areas such as salary, health benefits, and changes in the grievance process, the survey included items asking teachers for their opinions on increased participation in decision making at the school level, involvment of peers in a teacher evaluation process, and changes in the transfer plan. Many of the professional items that the union put on the negotiating table in 1987 were the result of this survey. As expected, salary, benefits, and reduced class size were the top priorities, but members also asked for a greater say in education decisions made at the school and felt that the union should play a role in helping or, if necessary, removing teachers whose professional competence was in question. The so-called professionalism items that were put on the table in 1987 were a direct result of this survey. In addition, during the term of the contract that was subsequently negotiated, union representatives visited schools to speak directly to members to gauge their feelings about the implementation of the professional items and their impact upon teaching and learning. This emerging "labor-education" focus of the UFT was also a topic of articles in the union newspaper, discussions at meetings of union delegates, workshops and conferences, and informational updates set directly to the homes of members both during the negotiations and over the 3-year period of the contract. In this way the union leadership set the pace for its role in school reform, but did it with the encouragement and input of members along with the knowledge and confidence that these same members were informed and supportive.

In the 1987–90 Agreement between the Board of Education and the United Federation of Teachers, both parties recognized:

> that a sound educational program requires not only the efficient use of existing resources but also constant experimentation with new methods and organization. The Union agrees that experimentation presupposes flexibility in assigning and programming pedagogical and other professional personnel. Hence, the Union will facilitate its members' voluntary participation in new ventures that may depart from usual procedures. The Board agrees that educational experimentation will be consistent with the standards of working conditions prescribed in this agreement.

The UFT negotiated some of these items in the 1987 contract. The Peer Intervention Program (PIP), designed to provide peer assistance on a voluntary, confidential basis to staff "who believe that their teaching competence will benefit from that assistance" was established. A staff development program for new teachers, the content of which was to be jointly developed by the board and the union, was negotiated. New teachers, according to their professional needs, would be able to choose from a variety of workshops, conferences, and seminars that would enhance their professional competence and recognize the different educational backgrounds. This was a major departure from the top-down, one-size-fits-all, mandated series of after-school workshops that lumped all elementary school teachers together, for example, regardless of their experience, the grades they taught, or the special needs of their students. During their first year, new teachers were also relieved of administrative assignments such as lunch duty and bathroom patrol. A clause, known as "professional conciliation," set up the framework for a process whereby teachers and supervisors could resolve differences in professional judgment in the areas of curriculum mandates, textbook selection, program offerings, and student testing procedures. Probably most important, the contract included a clause known as school-based options (SBOs), the first major "waiver" provision of the contract. This item stated:

> The union chapter in the school and the principal may agree to modify the existing provisions of this Agreement or Board regulations concerning class size, rotation of assignments/classes, teacher schedules and/or rotation of paid coverages

Modifications would require approval of 75% of the teachers, the principal, the district union representative, the community superintendent, and the chancellor of the school system as well as the president of the union. The UFT adopted a policy that approval on the presidential level of these SBOs would be contingent upon a sound educational rationale for the modifications.

Feldman, in a letter to the chapter leaders, stated

> We know that this program [School Based Options] must begin slowly and be handled carefully, but if you have a principal and faculty—or even a few teachers—really interested, this can be an exciting and fruitful road to education improvement.

Most teachers, because of the clear focus of the SBO provision, viewed this contractual item as an opportunity to modify the instructional program in order to improve teaching and learning rather than as a management inroad into traditional union rights. One elementary school set up an ungraded primary unit for 5- to 9-year-olds based on the recognition that young children develop and learn at different rates. Several high school science departments modified the class-size provisions of the contract in order to program several larger classes for lectures with smaller groups for labs and seminar-style classes. The SBO clause was the first time the UFT and the board of education agreed to "waivers" of contractual provisions on a school-by-school basis. The clear focus on educational improvement and the protections provided by the contract combined to make this waiver provision the most used "educational reform" clause of the 1987 contract.

What also made this contract highly acceptable to the membership were the enhancements in teacher salaries over the 3-year-term of the agreement. The $20,000-to-$35,619 range of salaries in the 1986–87 school year would increase to a range of $25,000 to $50,000 in the 1989–90 school year, the last year of the contract. Although this left the salary of New York City's teachers significantly lower than the salaries of teachers in surrounding areas, the salary package showed members who might have been leery of the union's new use of collective bargaining that their representatives could successfully and simultaneously negotiate improvements in fundamental bread-and-butter areas while taking on a leadership role in instructional areas. It was these professional items that laid the groundwork for greater teacher and union participation in school reform efforts. The 1987 contract proved that a union could negotiate both traditional bread-and-butter issues and professional enhancements. This new use of collective bargaining did not go unnoticed. The *New York Times*, in a front-page article, noted,

"The contract . . . attempts for the time to address professional questions. Previously, contract negotiations have centered solely on pay" (Perlez, 1987, p. A1). *The Daily News*, the city's tabloid newspaper with the largest circulation, editorialized, "A major effort to revive and reform the schools is overdue—and now underway . . . the new teachers contract has the potential to contribute to that vital—historic effort . . . the contract's real benefits go far beyond money. . . ." ("Teachers contract!," 1987, p. 32)

As teachers were given the opportunity to effect educational changes in their schools, they began to look at the entire "culture of schools." For example, the requirement that teachers "clock in" was a not-so-subtle, daily reinforcement of the factory model of education. A tentative step was taken in 1986 by then Chancellor Nathan Quiñones when he asked any principals who were interested to submit proposals for a pilot project on alternatives to the use of time clocks. However, when Richard Green, the former superintendent in Minneapolis, became chancellor in 1988, he viewed New York City's clocking-in requirement as antithetical to the whole idea of teacher professionalism. His first official action was to end the use of time clocks in all schools. The concern of some experienced administrators that the schools would cease to function effectively without time clocks proved unfounded.

The UFT continued its fight to improve the schools. Having successfully used collective bargaining as a tool for educational reform in its 1987 contract, the UFT concurrently adopted a lobbying strategy to provide funds in the budget for lower class sizes in the early grades, instructional supplies, and a variety of other improvements that would create a better learning environment. New York City is a dependent school district, with most public school funds coming through the City of New York. The union did not feel that teachers should pay for lower class sizes and other improvements in the schools out of their salary package. In a city where average teacher salaries are $10,000 to $20,000 lower than those in surrounding school districts, the UFT felt that asking teachers to accept even larger discrepancies in salary between themselves and neighboring colleagues to pay for items that are clearly the responsibility of a school system was an unacceptable option. Besides bringing needed funds for educational improvements into the schools, the lobbying strategy, which over the past 11 years has become an integral part of the UFT's efforts to support educational reform, has also served to focus the city's lawmakers on the condition of the city's public schools and their role in their improvement. This strategy has had broad influence, most visibly in California, when in 1996 the governor and legislature allocated $800 million to reduce class sizes in the early grades statewide.

With the selection in 1989 of Chancellor Joseph Fernandez, discussions began between the UFT and the school system during the 1990–91 school year on implementation of a policy called School-based Management/ Shared Decision-making (SBM/SDM). The UFT and the new chancellor were quick to take advantage of changes in the Chapter I legislation, known as Schoolwide Projects (SWP), that had been made in the spring of 1989. The original legislation, variously known as Chapter I and Title I, was developed to provide extra support for schools with large numbers of students from low socioeconomic areas but had targeted specific children and often led to the growth of pullout programs and fragmented instruction. In New York City, SWP allowed SBM teams of parents, teachers, administrators, and others to upgrade the entire educational program in schools where at least 75% of students were from low-income families by commingling federal funds with other resources for instructional planning. The legislation's mandate for school-based teams fit in perfectly with the chancellor's and union's philosophy of school-based management and, in January 1990, it became New York City's first SBM/SDM initiative. Over the course of 3 years, the original cohort of 37 schools volunteering to use this form of school-based management to start SWP grew to more than 300 schools. Teams were able to make use of the funds collaboratively to lower class size, hire staff that would help the school implement its educational plan, or devise innovative programs. The old pullout model was replaced in most of these SWP sites by a coordinated, collaborative approach. As with other reform efforts, the rationale for implementation had to be educational. Profiting from the mistakes made by school-based management initiatives in Dade County and elsewhere, the UFT directed attention to professional development and facilitation in order to focus school teams on instruction rather than governance, administration, or personalities. In order to help school teams develop sound instructional models for implementation, the union's educational programs, the Teacher Centers Consortium (TCC) and the Special Educator Support Program (SESP), took the lead in staff development. These educational programs had come into existence in 1978 and 1979, respectively, and were funded with a combination of federal, state, city, and union monies. They had concentrated on providing low-cost graduate-level college courses as well as professional workshops and conferences and in-school support for teachers. As programs with more than a decade of school-based professional development experience, they were uniquely equipped to work with teachers, administrators, and parents. The teachers who worked in these programs and staffed the programs' school-based resource centers were well aware of the day-to-day issues that concerned schools. At the request of, and with support from, the school system, several specialists from UFT educational programs formed a core of facilitators who went to Title I SWP schools and worked with teams, helping constituencies that had rarely, if ever, worked together to focus on team collaboration, to develop instructional practices based on the needs of their students, to reach consensus on school plans, and to implement their plans with appropriate professional development and parent training. The facilitators also brought team members information about budgeting (the most requested item), scheduling, assessment, and the use of data to inform instruction. In addition they were able to cut through the board bureaucracy to get answers and access resources for the schools. In a survey of teams taken a year after the start of the initiative, most ranked the support of a facilitator as the most necessary item for success.

On March 26, 1990, the chancellor, following intensive collaboration with the UFT, followed up the first school-based management initiative with a request for proposals from any school that wished to

> try something new; to redefine roles, relationships and responsibili-
> ties; to share in decision-making; and, to experiment with a wide
> variety of curricula, instructional strategies, staff development
> models, and organizational approaches which will result in
> strengthening the quality of instruction.

New York City's version of SBM/SDM was different in that it was not mandated. The decision to participate would have to be made at the building level by educators and parents who knew the day-to-day realities in that school. The union was up-front in telling its members that if they had a good working relationship with their administration and if they worked closely with parents who were willing and ready to participate, this was the way to go. If these situations did not exist, then the school was not ready and no school staff should be pressured to participate. In June 1990, a committee of union and board representatives selected 80 schools, from nearly 125 that had submitted proposals, for participation in the SBM/SDM initiative. For choosing schools, there were two basic criteria: (a) an educationally sound rationale for the changes proposed and (b) evidence of a willingness on the part of teachers, parents, and administration to work together to improve instruction and learning. Schools selected were able to seek waivers of contract provisions and board regulations, and in subsequent years waivers of certain funded state requirements were added. The only hard and fast rule was that laws protecting students' civil rights, their health and safety, and their access to a free and appropriate public education would not be abridged. As with the SWP initiative, instructional specialists from UFT educational programs went to schools as facilitators in order to help teams to come together and form a common educational vision for the school. One school revised the class hours in order to meet the needs of the large number of latchkey students who attended the school. Another school decided to revise its curriculum to reflect more fully the large number of newly arrived immigrants in the school. Probably the most ambitious reforms instituted by an SBM team were the peer-evaluation and staffing procedures set up at International High School with the full cooperation of the staff, the administration, the union, and the board of education. (These experiments in peer evaluation and school-based staffing had been in operation, with union and board year-to-year approval, in the school for several years, but it was only with the advent of SBM/SDM that they could be legitimized and their continuance assured. The procedures used for staffing in this one high school would become the basis of the model used when the union decided to push this change in reform in the city's schools.)

In the early 1990s perhaps the most controversial area of school reform had to be addressed: staffing. A transfer plan based on seniority had been negotiated in the 1960s. An objective criterion such as years of service would allow all teachers to transfer into any school where a vacancy existed, regardless of patronage, race, or politics.

Staffing of schools was done centrally based on certification and the needs of the school system, although the 32 decentralized school districts had much leeway in the hiring process and a subterranean system of hiring existed in many schools and districts. Many teachers secured positions through relying on personal relationships with a school's teachers or principal rather than dealing with the central board of education bureaucracy. Community school districts were able to "hide" positions and in many places seemed always one step ahead of the central board's inefficient computerized tracking systems. As most critics agreed, the teacher hiring process was relatively free of the political deal-making and favoritism that characterized the hiring of supervisory staff and school aides in many community school districts. However, as large numbers of nontraditional schools began to spring up, the union realized it would have to take a hard look at staffing and transfer practices. In the spring of 1993 Chancellor Fernandez announced the opening of 50 small (no more than 500 students each), theme-based schools. In addition, many of them would be organized with grade levels that would cross the traditional elementary, middle, and high school lines. These schools had been developed collaboratively among the public school system, universities, cultural organizations, unions, and nonprofit organizations, most notably the Fund for New York City Public Education (now the New Visions for Public Schools Fund) and the Center for Collaborative Education, the New York City branch of the Coalition of Essential Schools. Prior to this announcement, there had been no coordinated effort to open new schools of this type.

As new schools were being created, the UFT and the board had to look at the other end of the educational spectrum: What was to be done with schools that were unsuccessful? This question had come up early in 1993 when the UFT, parents, the local superintendent, local politicians, community leaders, and businesses entered into discussions about the future of Andrew Jackson High School, a 2,300-student school with a history of academic failure, racial strife, and violence. It was agreed that rather than creating "programs" or "houses," a complete restructuring of the utilization of the Andrew Jackson school building was necessary. No new students, beginning with the 1994–95 school year, would be admitted to Andrew Jackson. Four smaller magnet "campus" schools, each with its own theme, principal, budget, and staff, would share space in the Andrew Jackson High School building.

Over the course of 3 years, the remaining Andrew Jackson students would graduate and the four small, autonomous schools would replace it. On prior occasions when schools had been closed or reorganized, 30% of the new staff would be selected by the principal or central board and the remaining positions would be filled by the UFT transfer plan strictly on the basis of seniority. This agreement dated back to 1970. An agreement was worked out in which teachers could volunteer to transfer and would be given the opportunity to list preferences for placement. Volunteers were grouped by license and given preferences by seniority. Staff members from Jackson were also given, if they so desired, the opportunity to apply to any or all of the new schools. Priority for a position in one of the new schools would be based on educational qualifications; seniority would be a factor only if two candidates were equally qualified. The application process would consist of an interview by a personnel committee composed of board and union representatives and members of the Campus Magnet Schools' planning committees. Union officers and representatives held several stormy meetings with the staff of Andrew Jackson to explain their options as union members. The staff voiced some amazement that the union, their protector, would actually be involved in the closing of a school, no matter what its failures. Yet the union leadership knew that even though it could not defend the existence of failing schools, this did not mean that members' rights would be trampled by management. The issue was brought to the floor of the Delegate Assembly of the UFT by union representatives from Andrew Jackson, and the issue suddenly was no longer the fate of a single high school but rather seniority and member rights. As with other matters involving the union's role in school reform, the membership was given the opportunity to debate the issues, receive and disseminate information, question leadership, offer suggestions, and ultimately decide upon the issue through a democratic procedure. All staff members of the now former Andrew Jackson High School were ultimately placed in one of their preferences.

As the UFT continues to reflect on its role as a member of the educational community, it realizes that the answer to Al Shanker's question "What does a union do?" has to be ongoing. Many of the reforms that we have fought for over the past 17 years have been for changes in the administrative structure so that the needs of students take priority over any bureaucratic or political agenda. We have initiated and fought for programs that support teachers and the students in their classes. We have not been shy about protecting our members from arbitrary, unfair, or unprofessional treatment. Nor have we stopped fighting for enhanced salaries or improved working conditions, for that's also a big part of what a union must do, and we make no apologies for that. The process has been evolutionary rather than revolutionary. Now we are working to support improvements in instruction. We are prepared to do this in partnership with the board of education, parents, business leaders, lawmakers, and others. The most recent contract between the UFT and the Board of Education (1995–2000), entitled Joint Intentions and Commitments, includes a preamble, which states:

> Enhanced student achievement based upon high standards and expectations must be the driving force behind every activity of New York City public schools. To accomplish this, we must reinvent schools so that decision making is shared by those closest to students, including parents, teachers, administrators and other stakeholders. Layers of bureaucratic impediments must be peeled away so that flexibility, creativity, entrepreneurship, trust and risk-taking become the new reality of our schools. Before the millennium, the factory model of the 1900s must make way for the child-centered schools of the next century. To this end, the Union and the Board mutually agree to join together with other partners in the redesign and improvement of our schools, including closing those that have failed and supporting their restructuring. We must challenge ourselves each day to improve student learning, based upon academic rigor, newfound flexibility, meaningful assessments and true accountability. Roles and responsibilities of parents, staff and other partners must be defined. The standards to which we hold our students must never be lower than those we hold for our own children. To accomplish this, we must focus on both the depth and

breadth of each proposed instructional and operational change, each designed to support the children and their teachers, whom we expect to meet these rigorous standards.

Change must be service-oriented, supportive and sufficiently flexible so that each school's educational vision can become a reality. It must be practical, possible, efficient and timely. Respect for each other and for every student must be unconditional if we are to accomplish what we must.

This preamble also lists issues for immediate attention, areas in which discussion has already begun. They include school-based budgeting, parent outreach and support, professional development, and early intervention and prevention of inappropriate referrals to special education. The preamble to our union contract is unique in that it charges us and the board to make policies and decisions on the basis of student need above all else.

We are already putting this rhetoric into practice. Failure here is not an option if a reformed and improved public education system is to serve the leaders of the next century.

NOTE

1. This chapter is a condensed version of a longer paper prepared by Dr. Sherman, which is available from the United Federation of Teachers, 250 Park Ave., New York, NY 10010.

REFERENCES

Oreskes, M. (1983, May 1). Shanker urges teachers to aid school reforms. *New York Times*. p. 1.

Perlez, J. (1987, September 1). Teacher pay raise won in New York. *New York Times*. p. A1.

Teachers contract: A step in the crusade. (1987, September 2). *The Daily News*. p. 32.

CHAPTER 11

Inching Toward Reform in New York City: The Coalition Campus Schools Project

Linda Darling-Hammond, Jacqueline Ancess, Kemly McGregor, and David Zuckerman

The act of reinventing an institution as familiar and universal as the American high school involves reexamining old structures and decisions in light of new demands.[1] A long history of high school reform efforts demonstrates that, although the expectations for school outcomes have changed dramatically since the turn of the last century, the structures and tools used to meet those demands have changed very little. Educators are striving to teach the most diverse group of high school students in our nation's history to meet challenging academic standards traditionally applied only to a tiny few. Yet teachers are working in highly fragmented, stratified institutions created to batch-process the masses of students for routine, nonintellectual work and structured to minimize both intensive, long-term relationships and opportunities for serious in-depth learning. To those who have worked in such institutions, it is clear that the expectations suggested by new standards for all students cannot be achieved within the constraints that currently exist.

John Goodlad (1984) has noted that "the schools we need now are not necessarily the schools we have known" (p. 2). We cannot rely on the past as a guide to the choices we must make for the future. Before educators can reinvent high schools, however, they must first reimagine them, allowing new forms to follow new functions rather than letting habits and traditions determine what is possible. This, of course, requires a willingness to depart from what Sarason has called the "regularities of schooling" (1982)—those forms and procedures schools adhere to because they are predictable, safe, and familiar, if not always effective—and some ideas about what strategies might prove more successful.

A STRATEGY FOR CREATING NEW SCHOOLS

For the last 5 years, the Coalition Campus Schools Project (CCSP) has been reimagining and reinventing high schools. Its mission has been to phase out some of New York City's large, unsuccessful high schools, designed at the turn of the last century, and to replace them with smaller, more intimate and academically demanding learning environments—places where young people can form relationships with the adults who teach them and where they will do work that enables them to think critically, solve problems, communicate well, and master challenging material. The project was born in 1992, when the Coalition of Essential Schools (CES), the Center for Collaborative Education (CCE, the New York City affiliate of the coalition), and the New York City Board of Education launched an urban high school reform initiative to create new schools where existing large comprehensive schools had failed.

The CCE is a network of 40 New York City public elementary and secondary schools that are members of the nationwide CES. Together, the CCE, the CES, and the board of education secured $3 million from private foundations to start 11 new small schools to replace 2 large high schools that would be closed down and their buildings reconfigured.

This collaboration was part of the board of education's broader school-restructuring initiative, which in that year launched more than 40 new schools through the CCSP, a foundation-funded New Visions project that invited new-schools proposals from city educators as well as schools launched by the board of education and local community school districts directly. With the recent addition of the Annenberg initiative, New York has by now created more than 100 new-model schools since the early 1990s. Many of these new schools move into wings of existing large buildings; others find homes in smaller sites that belong to the board of education or are leased. The CCSP strategy, which replaced entire large schools, was to hothouse the new, small schools for their first few years at sites other than the big school building. Later, some would move into the building, and the others would continue to serve students in the original catchment area, thus expanding the schooling opportunities to children in the community.

In the first 2 years of its implementation, CCSP began the phaseout of two of the city's more troubled high schools—Julia Richman High School in Manhattan and James Monroe High School in the Bronx. Typical of many other neighborhood comprehensive high schools, these large warehouse institutions were constructed to manage 3,000 students apiece. In the selective schooling system that evolved over many decades, they were schools of last resort for students not selected into any others, but few students successfully negotiated them. In 1992 Julia Richman had a 4-year graduation rate of 36.9%; the comparable rate for James Monroe was only 26.9%. There were about 20 such high schools throughout the city enrolling approximately 65,000 students. Known for their high rates of academic failure as well as social discord reflected in squadrons of security guards manning metal detectors at their doors, these schools seemed to entrap the most vulnerable students in an inextricable web of failure. (See Chapter 7 for a detailed description of the Richman reform project.)

This report describes what we learned from our research on the launching of the project and of the first six CCSP schools in Manhattan. Occasional reference is made to the CCSP experience in planning for the second cohort of schools in the Bronx. This report examines the achievements and problems the project encountered in its initial years, assesses outcomes for students in the third year of operation, and discusses the implications of the change strategy for the continuation of this and similar reforms in large urban school systems. We pay particular attention to the system issues attending this kind of reform initiative.

Although elements of the "birthing" process are common to the start-up of any school, the context of this effort makes it unique. The CCSP allowed existing highly successful alternative schools to help mentor new schools into existence by partnering the new schools with more established schools that could help them design programs and provide professional development. The project also links clusters of small schools in educational networks that help to protect them and their campuses from the vulnerability of isolated reform while offering shared supports and learning opportunities. Although this strategy proposes to change one school at a time, its potential for replication over time challenges education leaders to envision how they might support and manage system-wide school reform.

SYSTEMIC CONCERNS

In committing itself to support such broad-scale reform, the board of education has been confronted with the exciting and daunting challenge of rethinking and redesigning its own core operations and procedures, perhaps even relinquishing some centralized approaches that it cannot manage as well as the schools themselves can. Like other large bureaucracies that are engaged in restructuring, the board is currently working through the dilemmas of fundamental change, whereas previously most innovations at the edges of the system encroached only on standard operating procedures. The problems that emerge juxtapose issues of high standards and standardization, of flexibility and proceduralization, and of centralization and decentralization of various functions.

The board must decide whether to support new schools by allowing exceptions to standard operating procedures (maintaining a policy of innovation at the edges) or to transform fundamentally its ways of doing business so as to undertake widespread systemic change by creating what Deputy Chancellor Harry Spence has called a differentiated system. Such a system would be structured by a set of policies flexible enough to acknowledge the diversity and range of school-level need and capacity. It would encourage school-initiated, customized innovation to help schools become more successful and accountable. It would provide support where needed and work with districts and schools to ensure equity and access.

The board has, in addition, a third choice, one that also has historical precedent—killing innovation by emphasizing procedures over purpose. As in previous reform eras, that, too, is a possible outcome of an inability to rethink cumbersome, often unnecessarily standardized operations so that they can be focused on supporting school and student success. (For a view from the top of the NYC hierarchy, see Judith Rizzo's Chapter 9. For a detailed description of the change process at one high school, Julia Richman, see Ann Cook's Chapter 7).

SCHOOL OUTCOMES: THE FIRST 3 YEARS

Despite the many barriers to success, all of the schools demonstrated from their first year that they could provide an environment more supportive of student success than that provided by Julia Richman. Among them the six schools registered an average attendance rate for their 9th graders of 88.5% by December 1993 as compared with Julia Richman's 66% the year before (NYC Board of Education, 1993).

By the end of the first year, the schools had each created thoughtful programs of study and a variety of innovative measures to support the educationally needy students they were serving. The Coalition School for Social Change was organized to ensure that teachers would work for extended periods of time with small groups of students whom they could come to know well. The faculty divided the 93 students into two groups, each working with four staff members during 2-hour blocks of course time, four times a week. During this time, math/science, history/social studies, and literature were taught, chiefly through students' working on projects either individually or in teams. In addition, the students from each block were separated into three advisory groups run by individual staff members who were on their teaching teams. These groups met for 5 hours a week, working on academic skills in reading and mathematics as well as on personal concerns. The advisor kept track of each student's overall performance and contacted the family whenever necessary, for example, when the student was absent for more than a day or two, when academic or social problems emerged, or when progress updates were due. Individual parent conferences were held three times a year. A portfolio system was developed to guide student work and evaluation. As one teacher remarked of the results of all these efforts by the end of the first year, "Eighty-five to ninety percent of our students have a real sense of belonging to something."

At Landmark High School, the 90 students in grade 9, many of whom had experienced almost no prior school success, were assigned to pairs of teachers who each took responsibility for 30 students for about 20 hours a week. One handled math and science, the other humanities. In addition, each ran an advisory group for about 45 minutes a day. Later a group tutorial session was added. The goal was to maximize the amount of time spent with students and to minimize the number of changes in adults, teaching styles, and subjects so as to enable more intensive study and more concentration on skills development. Cooperative learning, discussions, and project work could all be accommodated within the generous class time. One of the students commented: "I really like that it's only four classes that we take; in the old school you had to study a little on each subject and keep eight subjects in your head at once." Students also participated in service learning and electives or extracurricular activities called options, including art, musical theater, journalism, basketball, martial arts, video, and environmental action. Extensive narrative evaluation accompanied by a rubric shared with parents in conferences three times a year was the core of first-year assessment, which eventually grew into a portfolio system. At the end of the first year, the director summarized the widely shared view of faculty and students: "The tone is good. Morale is high. The kids are happy. They chose to be here. There's teamwork on the part of the faculty. There's growing pride in Landmark by the students."

The Legacy School for Integrated Studies served one hundred fifty 7th and 9th graders in its first year. Headed by a director who had taught at Central Park East Secondary School (CPESS) for 5 years and created its Senior Institute, the school borrowed many of CPESS's practices and created some new ones. To ensure small pupil loads and substantial personalization, each teacher taught two subjects and an advisory. Classes were offered in math, science, humanities, art, gym, and reading. (Reading was created as a separate class to help bolster students' skills in this area.) Clubs were offered in areas like arts and crafts, analytical thinking, and social issues. Essential questions guiding the first year were: How can everyone live the good life? and What is the relationship of order and chaos to life? These shaped studies in science on "What is life?" and "How do living things respond to changes in their surroundings?" In mathematics, topics included the study of chaos and order, sequences and patterns, classification of numbers, and laws governing operations. Studies of the quality of life included economic, environmental, and sociological research and statistical analyses. Among students' projects were neighborhood studies in Harlem and the Lower East Side featuring surveys, architectural inventories, interviews of residents, environmental studies of pollution and water quality, photos and artwork, and written reports. Students could articulate the effects of both the intellectual work and the school's caring. As one noted: "You can't just spend 5 minutes on homework. You must explain; that helps you build a strong mind." Another said: "They care for you. They tell your mother and father when you're late. They want explanations." As the director observed, "Parents are more sure we want their kids to succeed. They don't have to come in to advocate for their child."

Manhattan Village Academy started with only 60 students because of space limitations. A strong emphasis on collaborative group work and interdisciplinary, thematic instruction resulted in considerable team teaching among the faculty, each of whom taught one subject (math, science, English, and social studies) in hour-long classes that met four times a week. Students grouped in cohorts traveled together to all their core teachers, making separate choices for foreign language and "options" classes. A commitment to hands-on instruction was manifested in project-based learning featuring required exhibitions of mastery, community service a half-day each week, and frequent field trips. Advisories were, again, at the core of personalization, and parent conferences four times a year ensured close connections to families. At the end of the year the director noted:

> We've gone from daily crises to being a very good little school. The kids like it here. It's individualized. There is no fighting. The word is out; this really is a safe place, but that took a heck of a lot of work. Things have changed very drastically from the beginning. . . . The recruitment meetings for next year's students were great for us. All of us preaching to the unconverted gave us a chance to listen to each other, to testify. In a way, the staff did their own exhibition.

Manhattan International High School, like its parent school International High School, is reserved for recently arrived immigrants with limited English proficiency. Its nearly 90 students in the first year were from 22 countries and spoke 18 different languages. They were divided into four strands for hour-long blocks of math, science, English, and social studies. Family groups and community service are features shared with other schools. Many students also had internships in local businesses as part of a course called Personal and Career Development. Project-based assessment provided students many opportunities to explain their thinking orally and in writing as they developed English language skills. With the help of International High School staff, Manhattan International made large strides quickly. By April of 1994, students were presenting the first exhibitions of their work to committees of faculty and peers.

Vanguard High School's 80 students had to begin their year in an auditorium, having been evicted from the classrooms they were to have occupied because of dangers posed by asbestos. After weeks of negotiating for space and bouncing from the Boys Club to various field-trip sites, they finally found a building with several classrooms where they could remain for the year, albeit with few materials or supplies. As one Vanguard student put it: "When school first started, it was like we were homeless. . . . We kept bouncing from place to place." Finally, the school settled into a regular schedule in which two teams of teachers from math/science and the humanities took charge of two groups of students. All teachers helped out in Project Adventure classes and worked with advisories. Music and community service rounded out the curriculum, which sought to create interdisciplinary connections. Staff developed projects, portfolios, and other strategies for documenting student learning. Despite substantial student and teacher turnover that resulted from the stresses of the moves and other startup problems, progress was evident by the end of the second semester. As one of the humanities teachers noted:

> This semester we had something that much more closely resembled a genuine portfolio in that the work was all around a common theme. The quality of the work was really very striking. The kids went from not being able to write more than a couple of sentences in the fall to being able to write pages. And in every kid's portfolio, there was at least one piece which was good, which really embodied thought and self-reflection and analysis and insight. They took it seriously. And that, I think, is an improvement.

With all of the challenges, all six schools managed to create personalized learning environments in which adults could create strong relationships with students and families, extended time was available for instruction, and teachers had time to plan and work together. All used the concepts of advisory groups and a lean, core curriculum with long blocks of learning time toward this end. Most organized staff and students into houses, clusters, or teams that planned and worked together throughout the year. In addition to creating peaceful, caring environments, the schools increasingly made use of interdisciplinary studies, projects, and portfolios to create connections and applications that would deepen students' understanding and help them develop more proficiency in thinking and communicating.

The end result was that virtually all of the students we interviewed were impressed by the nuturing they had experienced in these schools, in contrast to their previous school experiences, and teachers described the satisfactions of succeeding with their students. According to much other research (for a summary, see Darling-Hammond, 1997), these two factors together—students who feel cared for and well taught and teachers who feel that their efforts are successful—are mutually reinforcing, leading to stronger educational communities and higher achievement.

With steady, intensive work by all concerned, the situation 3 years later is remarkable, given where the project started. Despite student bodies even more "at risk" than the student body of Julia Richman had been, by 1995–96 the six CCSP schools had surpassed the attendance rate of the old Julia Richman by 14.2% (see Figure 11.1), and their average rates of student suspension, disciplinary incidents, and dropping out were far below the citywide and Julia Richman averages. These differences are both educationally and statistically significant. The difference in annual dropout rates is especially notable: At only 1.2% annually, the average rate for the six CCSP schools is 80% lower than that of Julia Richman in 1992–93.

Figure 11.1. Student Outcomes at CCSP Schools

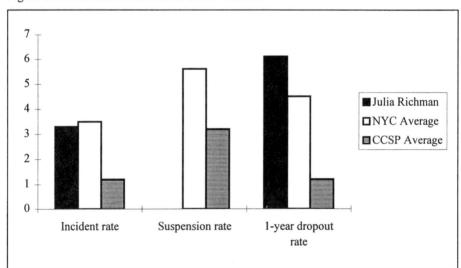

Source: Data are from the New York City Public Schools Reports "School Profile and Performance in relation to Minimum Standards" for Julia Richman for 1989–90 to 1992–93 and for each of the Coalition Campus Schools for 1993–94 to 1995–96.

Furthermore, students are registering substantial progress on measures of academic achievement, even though the traditional, generally multiple-choice, test measures are not designed to evaluate the kinds of learning the schools are seeking to cultivate. Average student gains in reading as measured by the Degrees of Reading Power tests and gains in language skills for Limited English Proficient (LEP) students as measured by the Language Assessment Battery are significantly higher than citywide averages. LEP students' progress was significantly greater than that of students at the old Julia Richman. Among CCSP schools, fully 91 % of LEP students annually gained at least 3 normal curve equivalents on the city's test, as compared with only 53 % of such students in Julia Richman.

Despite having students who are economically poorer, more linguistically diverse, and initially lower achieving than citywide or Julia Richman averages; despite keeping low-achieving students in school rather than encouraging or allowing them to drop out as is the case in large, traditional schools; and despite not organizing their course work around state tests, which they find poor measures of important knowledge and skills, the CCSP schools have produced a class of 11th graders who are doing as well as Richman students and students citywide on the Regents Competency Tests in reading, writing, and mathematics (see Table 11.1). When compared with students in schools that are demographically similar to the CCSP schools (for the three CCSP schools for which state report cards include "similar schools"), CCSP students achieve at significantly higher levels in reading and writing, and comparably in mathematics.

When measures are available that evaluate the critical-thinking skills, research and problem-solving abilities, and social outcomes the schools focus on—perseverance, determination, responsibility, and respect for others—the differences between their outcomes and those of traditional schools are likely to be even more pronounced.

CREATING SUPPORTS FOR INNOVATION: PROBLEMS AND PROSPECTS

Although fraught with problems, the new-schools development process also triggered important system reforms. The selection and hiring of directors and teachers for the CCSP schools showed the board of education's capacity to support innovation when it responds creatively, flexibly, and collaboratively to the need for new mechanisms. The success of new schools committed to a common set of educational principles is heavily dependent upon the ability of schools to hire faculty who believe in those principles and have the will and capacity to enact them. Because the board of edu-

Table 11.1. Student Outcome Data for Julia Richman High School, New York City, and the CCSP Schools

	Julia Richman HS	NYC Average	CCSP Average
Average daily attendance	72***	85	86.2
% of students making reading gains (3+ NCEs in one year)	52.4	43.6	56.9
% of 11th graders passing RCT or Regents test in:			
Reading	77.4	79.9	80.7
Writing	71.3	71.3	71.4
Mathematics	78.6	74.9	76.6
% of LEP students making adequate language gains	53**	65.4*	91.2

Source: Data are from the New York City Public Schools Reports "School Profile and School Performance in Relation to Minimum Standards" for Julia Richman for 1989–90 to 1992–93 and for each of the Coalition Campus Schools for 1993–94 to 1995–96. T-Tests of Group Means, one-tailed probability: *p<.10, **p<.05, ***p<.01

cation's traditional procedures for faculty selection and hiring have assumed that teachers are interchangeable, and because the assignment of teachers is centralized, a new policy and mechanism had to be developed to meet the needs of the new-model schools.

With the cooperation of the board of education, the United Federation of Teachers (UFT)—the teachers union in New York City—and the CCSP negotiated a process for selecting staff based on a model developed earlier by International High School. This model was later incorporated into the UFT–Board of Education collective bargaining agreement for all innovative schools. (See David Sherman's Chapter 10.)

Budgeting is another area in which the board of education demonstrated impressive capacity for core systemic change. The CCSP schools were provided with an adequate staffing allocation because of the small-schools funding formula developed in 1991 by the board of education in collaboration with a committee of principals. The collaboration and creativity used by the Board of Education to respond equitably to variation is an exemplar of how the board of education can profitably manage other aspects of innovation.

The purpose of the CCSP is not only to create new-model high schools but also to develop a sensible process for creating new schools that will pave the way for others. The use of networks to support change has enhanced the probabilities for new-school success. Within the CCSP, networking occurred on several levels, and the directors tapped into each of these to varying degrees. On the national level, the Coalition of Essential Schools (CES) led by Ted Sizer provided the philosophical underpinnings for the new schools. Coalition meetings attended by directors provided intellectual resources for their work and reminded each school of its connection with schools across the nation. Sizer has also lent his support to the board of education/CCE collaboration by participating in early and ongoing meetings with Chancellors Fernandez and Cortines.

On the local level, the CCE provided more immediate support. Each CCSP school director was partnered with an experienced CCE high school. CCE partner schools supported the new schools by volunteering to staff their personnel committees, inviting new directors and faculty to observe classes and attend faculty meetings, providing schedules and organization schemes for review, and sometimes providing peer assistance for curriculum development. CCE partner-school directors were accessible to provide the new directors with advice and support on an as-needed basis. CCE acted as a buffer for the new schools by negotiating for them with the many divisions of the board of education. CCE Co-director Heather Lewis and CCSP Co-directors Marcia Brevot and Deborah Meier were instrumental in navigating the project through the bureaucracy and the crises that occurred at various junctures. For example, whereas directors individually could do little about the space problems, as members of a network they were able to relegate this issue to the project's co-directors, who acted as point persons in addressing these issues at the system level. And though no individual new director would have been able to effect system innovations in staffing and student recruitment, their membership within a network and their relationship to the Alternative High School Superintendency allowed individual directors to focus their energies more on the business of their own schools than on system reforms.

In addition, since the schools functioned as a group, many more creative and systemic responses by the board of education were made possible. In at least some areas, the board could create policy for innovation for a group of schools rather than handle each one independently on a case-by-case basis. As in the case of hiring procedures, this advanced the schools' practices and the board's policies in tandem. The knowledge and expertise of the CCE/CCSP leadership, along with the hard work of many at the board of education, were drawn upon to find favorable resolutions to many of the other issues that arose as the project unfolded.

CHALLENGES FOR SYSTEM REDESIGN

The level of innovation generated by the creation of 32 new-model secondary schools over the last 2 years has intensified the tensions between the
diversity required by innovative schools and the board of education's standard operating procedures. As the former Alternative High Schools Superintendent Steve Phillips explained, it was possible to make exceptions for
one or two schools, such as finding alternate sites or waiving hiring procedures, when the impact on the system and personnel time were minimal.
The broad scale of the current high school reform initiative has made it organizationally impossible for the board of education to rely on its current
strategy of policy-by-exception to support innovation. As Lynn Savage,
senior advisor to former Deputy Chancellor Stan Litow, explained:

> Like it or not, an institution like the Board of Education with
> responsibility for over 1100 schools and a million kids is designed to
> meet the needs of the norm. Therefore it is also continuously in a
> position of having to be responsive to all sorts of regulatory, legal,
> and contractual stuff; it is geared to be responsive to these ex-
> tremely directive and limiting demands. A project such as this (e.g.
> one seeking non-traditional arrangements for teacher selection,
> student admission, space allocation) inevitably wants to do some-
> thing other than the current rules and regulations allow. Therefore
> for every aspect of this someone has to spend time and energy
> finding a way through the regulations, to let whatever happens
> happen without being entirely out of compliance.

As Savage's statement implies, a continuance of policy-by-exception
on a broad scale becomes organizationally impossible because sufficient
personnel are not available to find ways around traditional regulations. The
highly unusual demands of school start-ups also extend to the core issues
of student admission and teacher hiring that go to the heart of bureaucratic
assumptions about standardization and centralized management. The new
schools are based on personal, meaningful choices and commitments made
by students, parents, and faculty rather than on centralized assignment.
In contrast to the historical bureaucratic management of traditional schools,
none of these parties is viewed as an interchangeable part.

Savage's comment also illuminates how the hierarchical organization
exacerbates rigidity, making broad-scale innovation overwhelming to board
of education personnel while simultaneously blocking the creation of new
structures. When early on the reformers suggested creating a separate organization to respond to the new-schools initiative, Chancellor Fernandez

and Deputy Chancellor Litow rejected it, arguing that the board of education had to develop the capacity to respond in order to safeguard support for the initiative beyond Fernandez's tenure. Considering the turnover in chancellors in the years before and since that decision, the concern appears warranted.

Nonetheless, trying to launch innovation within the regular apparatus of the board has illuminated the shortcomings of bureaucratic management and placed in relief the need for internal redesign of the central organization, including delegation of critical responsibilities to those in the field who are trying to get the work done. In the CCSP, for example, Co-directors Meier and Brevot had hoped to have considerable authority to act, which never fully materialized. Where they were able to intervene, they located space, bargained for workable procedures, and broke logjams in the chain of bureaucratic decision making. However, the continued centralization of all functions large and small, even where it does not advance the completion of important tasks, is a questionable strategy for managing any organization. It is especially questionable when the need for change is so pressing and the failings of centralized procedures are so evident. The multilayered hierarchical system of management, which is simultaneously centralized and fragmented, creates unending complexities.

The board of education's dilemma is intensified by the knowledge that managing innovation through the regular channels is a much higher risk strategy for reform if the board of education cannot manage itself differently. Systemic organizational change would mean a redefinition of turf, which, as Chancellor Fernandez explained, triggers "fears. It all boils down to turf. It always does. . . . [It's] a fight [with] the established bureaucracy and the status quo." Fernandez's strategy for getting things done was personal intervention, which reinforced the culture of hierarchy. But even personal intervention required a continuous flow of information to him in a timely manner, not a realistic expectation in a system the size of the board of education.

Board of education officials charged with implementing the project also indicated the need for new organizational structures that cut across divisions. Phillips commented on the need for a system that would assign lawyers and architects to the Office of School Facilities in order to unify efforts to identify and renovate space. The director of that office confirmed this need:

> It [is] irresponsible to commit to something that could stall at any stage. I have no control over the attorneys. People held me accountable, as though I could deliver, and I couldn't. I wish I did have the control.

If bold innovations such as the current high school restructuring initiative are to have a chance, the board of education will need to configure teams that include in positions of equality those individuals closest to the level of implementation; develop new models for accountability that hold team members responsible for accomplishing the goals of the project, not just for the functions of their divisions; and provide a scope of authority broad enough for teams to take the initiative necessary to make things happen. Without the authority to do what needs to be done to make projects succeed, school-based practitioners willing to take up the challenge of reforming New York City's public schools will continue to face obstacles that limit their efforts to provide New York City's children with a better education.

CONCLUSION

What has the board of education's collaboration with the CCSP illuminated about high school innovation initiatives that aim to put teaching and learning at the center of educational reform? First, it is important to recognize the inherent challenge to "the system" that a change effort of this scope entails. Changes in all manner of standard procedures are demanded when effective schools are redefined in terms of size, curriculum, methods of student assessment, means for hiring staff, and strategies for recruiting students. It is rare that a system readily accepts such fundamental challenges. A system may respond by actively resisting, placing obstacles in the path of those seeking change. Or it may attempt to respond positively to the requirements for change, but because it is large, multifaceted, and highly specialized in its division of labor, it may not be able to do so in an efficient and timely manner on all fronts.

In the case of the CCSP, the New York City school system has responded creatively at some times and ineptly at others. For instance, the hiring process worked out with the assistance of UFT, the board, and the CCSP created a fair and useful strategy for staffing the new Manhattan schools while opening up new opportunities for professional involvement for teachers. However, this successful process gave way in its second year to a more "standardized" process less attuned to the ideas and influence of the schools themselves. The agreement in the most recent contract to allow this negotiated process to be used more widely in New York City schools is a good example of using change levers from innovative work to begin to transform the core operating procedures of the system. Even with its limitations, this is a big step forward.

Similarly, the budgeting process for new schools worked out among the board and school principals in 1991 was creatively and appropriately applied to this initiative, building on and extending a collaboratively designed policy that works to support innovation. However, confusion in implementing the agreement left the schools more hampered than necessary in acquiring needed resources. The question of greater financial autonomy for such things as ordering supplies and making minor repairs has yet to be tackled.

As the CCSP recognized, an informed-consent admission policy is needed for new-model schools if the schools and the school system are to be respectful of parents' and students' experiences and expectations. Instructional programs that substantively depart from the norm—that don't appear familiar to parents and students—must be actively chosen. Prospective parents and students ought to have opportunities to be convinced that new-model schools will offer significant improvements over their other options, that the risk involved in trying something new is worthwhile. An admissions process that cannot encourage and enable parents to see themselves as powerful actors on behalf of their children will compromise the effectiveness of the new schools as well as the success of their students. If the goal is to encourage parents to participate more effectively in the education of their children, then the means will have to be available for them to make knowledgeable decisions about that education.

The CCSP illuminates the areas where the board of education is still struggling to restructure its core operations, to create new structures and mechanisms so that it can develop organizational capacity to respond to and support school-level innovation and systemic change. There are too many innovative schools for them to be peripheral any longer, and holding these schools accountable for standardized procedures would defeat the purpose of having created them.

Under Chancellor Rudy Crew, the board of education is making further attempts to recognize and legitimate the innovations—and move them into the mainstream. Although a plan to eliminate the Alternative High Schools Superintendency and move the new schools into the central bureaucracy was considered, it was finally abandoned, given these schools' need to maintain their diversity and the system's commitment to nurturing the ongoing process of creating additional schools. Instead, new leadership of the alternative schools division is seeking to standardize procedures for managing the change process and the schools themselves. An effort was made to increase all school sizes to 600, both to deal with increasing enrollments and to give more students access to the education they provide. However, with much support from research on school size and culture, the schools balked at this proposal on the basis that a size increase would under-mine what they had already accomplished, so the plan is currently post-poned. There are other efforts to standardize procedures for matters ranging from staffing and budgeting to securing space and supplies. A critical ques-tion is whether these well-intentioned efforts can bring the schools in from the margins without eliminating the practices that define the schools as innovative and enable them to be so extraordinarily effective. The board is managing competing ideas about how to ensure equity and access and how to institutionalize innovation while keeping it innovative.

It is clear that educational reform for New York City schools will re-quire the simultaneous restructuring of the board of education itself. Cur-rent reformers in both the schools and the board will need to invent a governance structure and management process that replace hierarchical habits and standardized procedures with means for co-constructing with schools the new strategies and structures that will enable them to develop diverse ways of achieving higher standards.

There is a fundamental reality the New York City Board of Education, like most large urban school systems, has not yet fully confronted: In order for schools to be effective, they must be able to respond to the diverse needs, interests, talents, language backgrounds, and experiences students bring to schools—and they must be able to do so in a way that both personalizes the educational experience and spurs a drive toward high standards and levels of learning. The traditional methods for enforcing standards— through standardized curriculum and testing procedures, linked to speci-fied course and credit requirements—have failed to allow for responsive teaching. They have also failed to create intellectually challenging standards related to real-world performance demands. In fact, current curriculum and testing guidance, especially at the high school level, undermines serious inquiry and performance in many fields by its focus on superficial coverage and rote learning rather than deep understanding and by its emphasis on factual recall rather than high levels of skill and application of knowledge.

This problem was acknowledged by the reforms under way in New York State's New Compact for Learning and the related work of the state Curriculum and Assessment Council to develop new curriculum frame-works and assessments that would replace the older Regents exams. That hierarchical control aimed at standardization does not produce high qual-ity is evident in the striking failures of New York's large comprehensive high schools as well as in the mediocre results produced by New York State's top-down testing reforms of the 1980s, which have led to decreases in the state's graduation rate and little improvement in overall achievement. For these reasons New York's state university system argued for efforts to develop portfolio and performance assessments for high school graduation and college admission to replace the former Regents exams. The new assessments proposed by the council and university system are intended to allow more diverse approaches to curriculum that meets more intellectually rigorous core standards.

However, this approach to supporting school innovation—enabling diverse approaches aimed at common learning goals—collides with the traditional top-down management of school operations historically used in New York City and State. The state has created a single-assessment system less ambitious than the portfolio assessments used by the new schools and threatens to eliminate the waivers that have allowed students to replace multiple-choice tests with research papers, scientific experiments, and mathematical models. Battles about the nature of the new testing system have not yet been resolved, as the state bureaucracy insists on maintaining traditional tests largely measuring rote skills, whereas educators in higher education and extraordinarily successful secondary schools argue for performances of understanding. Alongside these battles a number of questions emerge:

- How can the state and the city boards of education develop the capacity to provide top-down support for bottom-up reform?
- How can state and local agencies support and be responsive to broad-based, school-initiated change initiatives?
- How can the board of education, the CCPS network, and other new-school initiatives encourage school-level commitment to high standards while also supporting school-level autonomy to develop the diverse means for achieving those standards?
- How can the board ensure that individuals charged with doing the work of school change have the authority and capacity to get the work done?

As corporations and other large-scale organizations have learned, innovation generally requires a reduction in hierarchical layers, delegation of authority, and placement of resources at the front lines where the work must get done. Supporting and strengthening the authority of school networks like CCE—creating new forms of negotiated accountability and supports for local schools—could become a means for safely delegating responsibility. The precise nature of the changes needed is just beginning to be understood. What is clear is that as New York City continues the process of reinventing the American high school, it must be equally visionary in reinventing the system itself.

APPENDIX

Additional information on these schools, including research results, can be found in the following publications:

Ancess, J. (1995). *An inquiry high school: Learner-centered accountability at the Urban Academy*. New York: National Center for Restructuring Education, Schools, and Teaching.

Center for Collaborative Education. (1993). *Coalition Campus Schools Project brochure*. New York: Author.

Center for Collaborative Education. (1993). *Member schools brochure*. New York: Author.

Darling-Hammond, L. (1997). *The right to learn: A blueprint for creating schools that work*. San Francisco: Jossey Bass.

Darling-Hammond, L., Ancess, J., & Falk, B. (1995*). Authentic assessment in action: Studies of schools and students at work*. New York: Teachers College Press.

Darling-Hammond, L., Snyder, J., Ancess, J., Einbender, L., Goodwin, A. L., Macdonald, M. B. (1993). *Creating learner-centered accountability*. New York: National Center for Restructuring Education, Schools, and Teaching.

New York Council on Curriculum and Assessment. (1994). *Learning-centered curriculum and assessment for New York State*. Albany: New York State Education Department: Author.

NOTE

1. This chapter is a condensed version of a larger report of the same title that is available from NCREST. The data for this report are drawn from New York City school record data; observations and interviews within CCSP schools; observations of meetings involving CCSP members, CCE directors, board of education officials; documents from the board of education and CCSP; and interviews with the directors of the new CCSP, the co-directors of the CCSP, directors of the CCE partner schools, and board of education officials.

REFERENCES

Goodlad, J. (1984). *A place called school: Prospects for the future*. New York: McGraw-Hill.

NYC Board of Education. (1993). *New schools, Fall, 1993, preliminary report*. New York: NYC Board of Education, Student Information Services: Author.

Sarason, S. (1982). *The culture of school and the problem of change* (2nd ed.). Boston: Allyn & Bacon.

PART III

The Shape of Things to Come

CHAPTER 12

Can the Odds Be Changed? What It Will Take to Make Small Schools Ordinary Practice

Deborah Meier

There are numerous stories of schools that have been successful with students who would otherwise count among society's failures. However, such school successes rarely set the stage for Big Reform agendas. These one-of-a-kind schools flicker brightly, a few manage to survive by avoiding the public's attention or by serving powerful constituents, the rest gradually burn out.

THE SEARCH FOR SILVER BULLETS

To the vast majority of serious policymakers, the existing exemplary schools offer no important lessons. Most policymakers define "systemic" change so that it applies only to the kinds of solutions that can be more or less simultaneously applied to all students irrespective of particulars; solutions, in short, that seek to improve schooling by taking away the already too limited formal powers of those closest to the students. Examples range from more proscriptive curriculum, new, more centralized testing systems, fiscal rewards and penalties, or changed school-governance bodies.

School-level folk are as skeptical about the capacity of any of these top-down recipes to impact deeply on the minds of teachers or children as policy-level folks are of the idiosyncratic bottom-up ones. Practitioners—in classrooms and central offices—know at heart of the top-down reforms that "this too shall pass," that is, they can be either skirted or overcome. They wait out the innovators. Policymakers work overtime to come up with ways to circumvent such resistance. The more things change, the more they stay the same.

This is a climate that encourages impatience: Enough's enough! If we can't marry top-down and bottom-up reform better, we're probably in for big trouble. Giving up on the new thought that all children can learn to use their minds well is hard, especially for those of us who know firsthand that schools as designed are hardly suitable for the job, and that vastly more children can be well-educated if we designed schools differently. We've "tasted" it. It seems both near and so far. Perhaps if we posed the problem differently, such odd-ball schools might offer us systemic answers. The NYC Network project, like similar projects cropping up around the country fueled by the growing interest in vouchers and charters, has posed the problem from the bottom up: Seek a solution to the systemic by looking at the particular. By posing problems differently, different solutions become possible.

A good school is filled with particulars—including particular human beings; it is these that lie at their heart, that explain their surprising successes. In fact, it is these particulars that inspire the passions of those involved and draw upon the best in each. Maybe what these "special" schools demonstrate is that every school must have the power and the responsibility to select and design its own particulars and thus surround all children with powerful adults in a position to act on their behalf in open and publicly responsible ways. That may be the "silver bullet."

Will grown-ups all jump at the chance to be such responsible adults? Of course not. Most have never been asked to have their own wonderful ideas much less take responsibility for them. Many will be leery because with the freedom to design their own particulars must come new responsibilities for defending results. But the resultant practice, responsible citizenship, is not only a good means for running a good school; it's also the central aim of public schooling. How convenient.

In designing a way to make it easier to invent powerful and responsible schools, we can stack the deck in favor of good schooling, so that great schools are more likely, good schools become ordinary practice, and poor schools get dealt with more quickly. It will require us to learn how to make judgments about schools with standards in mind but not with a standardized ruler in hand. We've too long acted as though, in the name of standards, we had to treat students and teachers like interchangeable parts. Nothing could be worse for standards and nothing could be more unnecessary.

We already know some of the common features of exemplary schools—public or private—that serve ordinary and extraordinary children well. For example:

• *Small*. It helps if a school is of reasonable size, small enough for its faculty to sit around a table and iron things—like standards—out, for everyone to be known by everyone else, and for the school and its families to collaborate face to face over time. Small enough so that children belong to the same community as adults, not abandoned in adultless subcultures. Small enough to both feel and be safe. Small enough so that phony data can be easily detected by any interested participant. Small enough so that the people most involved can never say they weren't consulted.

• *Self-governing.* It helps if those most directly involved have autonomy over critical decisions. Only then will it be fair to hold people accountable for the impact of their decisions. This will entail creating democratic adult communities that have the power to decide on staffing, leadership, and the full use of their budget, as well as particulars of scheduling, curriculum, pedagogy, and assessment.

• *Choice.* It helps if there are sufficient available choices for parents, children, and teachers so that schools can be different from each other, have a definite character, special emphases and styles of operating that appeal to some but not all. Responsibility flows more naturally from willing and informed parties. (If schools are small, they can share big, old buildings and choices can be easily available).

These three qualities—schools that are small enough in size, sufficiently self-governing, and self-chosen—offer a good beginning. They won't in themselves solve anything, although together they could help solve everything.

Two different historic developments in New York City—Community School District Four's 22-year experiment with schools of choice and the city's Alternative High School division's 12-year history creating dozens of small-school alternatives, came together in the 1990s to create a potential alternative to business as usual; they challenge "business as usual." These developments caught the public's fancy, creating a movement on behalf of small schools of choice for all ages and types of students. The genie was out of the bottle and hard to put back. The idea attracted the attention of families who did not see themselves as "at risk." Word of mouth suggested that students in these schools matched their counterparts academically and surpassed them on many critical dimensions: college attendance, work preparedness, ability to perform socially valued tasks, and improved scores on typical academic assessments. The research community gradually confirmed such impressions. The studies suggest such schools provide for the possibility of a community powerful enough to be compelling to young people, a club worth "enlisting" in.

The skeptics say: It can't work en masse. Whether we create another 100 or 200, some starting from scratch, others carved out of existing schools, it can't be built to last. All agree that under present circumstances such schools have a limited future. The reformers argue, however, that "present circumstances" are not writ in stone.

WHY EXCEPTIONS CAN'T BECOME THE NORM (UNDER PRESENT CIRCUMSTANCES)

Without deep-seated changes in the system that surrounds these small schools of choice, history suggests that the critics will be right: Most will water down their innovations or give up. As their numbers increase so, oddly enough, does their vulnerability. This is one case in which there may not be more safety in numbers. For one thing, they tax the capacities of the existing institutions—both the formal system and the godfatherly individuals and organizations that spring up to provide nurturance and cover. Second, as their numbers increase they're more noticeable. This, in turn, created new demands to bring them into compliance. Why are they allowed to "get away" with this or that? mainstream colleagues ask. Who do they think they are? Third, as new roadblocks appear requiring Herculean responses, school folks begin to complain of weariness; the original fire in the belly that fueled the pioneering spirit begins to wane. Doing the new and the old at the same time seems more and more unfair, an imposition rather than an opportunity. (Critics call this the loss of the charismatic leader or the loss of the "Hawthorne" effect that surrounds innovative enterprises.)

The existing system is simply not designed to support such oddball entities. It believes in its mission of control and orderliness. The people who man the present systems do not see themselves in the business of trying to best match teacher to job, child to school. Nor could they do so if they wanted. Instead, whenever they look at a problem, they've been trained to seek, first and foremost, ways to solve it by rule. If it's not good for everyone, it's not good for anyone. To make exceptions smacks of favoritism and inefficiency. Each exception thus must be defended over and over again. How else can we hold them accountable?

The results of such rule-boundedness are well documented, above all by the critics of public education like Chubb and Moe (1990) in their thoughtful book on the limits of public education. (We all know that the expression "work to the rule," for example, describes a form of job sabotage.) Except for small enclaves in the large institution, where special constituencies carve out their own intimate sub-schools (those little sub-schools designed for the top students or for the most vulnerable), the school as a whole remains remarkably anonymous and unchangeable, the model for a nonlearning institution. But there is an alternative. It means changing the "circumstances" so that those three magic bullets—small, self-governing, self-choice schools described earlier—can be at the mainstream, not the sidelines, of the system.

If good schools in the private sector nearly all share these three characteristics, why can't we do it publicly for all students? Because, it's said, it's politically not feasible where public monies are at stake. If that's the rub of the argument, then we should either roll over and admit defeat or make it politically feasible. That means inventing a system of accountability for public monies and educational results that doesn't require bad educational practice. It's as simple as that—and as hard as that.

CHANGING THE "PRESENT CIRCUMSTANCES"

Small, self-governing schools of choice could be encouraged to flourish, grow like Topsy, spread like weeds if we built our system for them, not them for our system. To create highly personalized schools we have to be willing, however, to shift both our practices and our mind-set cautiously and relentlessly over many years. Present practice isn't inevitable. What we have, after all, is a human invention that's only 100 years old. But just because it's one of those new-fangled ideas that doesn't work doesn't mean it will fade away naturally. In fact, it's got a tenacious hold. But what it's not is the inevitable product of our human nature. In fact, its particularly in conflict with our humanity and everything we know about the rearing of the young.

Until the relationships between all people—parents and teachers— responsible for raising our children are changed—which is what the magic three are all about—changing the parts (curriculum, pedagogy, assessment) won't matter very much. But it's precisely because, in the long run, these professional "details" matter a great deal that we need to create a system of schooling that allows us to spend our time and energy honing them, close to home. As Ted Sizer wisely said when Central Park East Secondary School was started, "Keep it simple, so that you can focus on what will always remain complex—the mind of each individual learner and the subject matter we're trying to help her master." We've done the reverse far too long.

We shouldn't declare all schools independent tomorrow. We shouldn't remove all rules and regulations by fiat. We shouldn't even downsize all schools by fiat. Until we have more parents clamoring for change, teachers with the skill and confidence to try them out, and living examples of how we'd make schools that opt for greater independence also more accountable, we need to keep our ambitions in check. We're aiming at change that sticks, not another fad.

On the immediate agenda, for example, is creating a series of large-scale pilot "laboratories" to see how it might work if we let the existing idiosyncratic schools, with their already eager stalwarts, officially break loose and be different. Add to them all those interested in staffing new schools to replace the worst of our current enterprises. Then we'll need a lean master contract between these schools, the union, the city, and the state, covering the most basic contractual obligations as well as those unwaivable local, state, and federal rules pertaining to health, safety, and equity. If those on the sidelines can sit back and watch, not rush in as the pioneers develop their own answers, including mistaken ones, we'll learn something. The present system of schooling and accountability is chock full of mistakes, after all, not to mention disasters that are perpetuated year after year. Of course, we're accustomed to them, so we barely notice. This time, let's notice both—with equal clarity. As a way of noticing, let's honor forms of accountability that support rather than sabotage the very qualities such independence is trying to achieve: accountability through the responsible exercise of collective human judgment.

The magic three—smallness, self-governance, and choice—provide some of the necessary basic ingredients for more responsible individual schools and thus for more accountability. Smallness creates self-knowledge, self-governance allows for a range of voices now often missing, and choice permits disgruntled parents and teachers to vote with their feet. But while these three qualities appear to undercut some of the pressure for ever more external accountability, there's a strong argument for adding several other ingredients that will support the development of a more responsible community of schools. And not just because it's politically smart, but because without a powerful system of public accountability, good individual schools can too easily become stuck in routines, parochial, smug, and secretive—even tyrannical. Smallness, for example, makes it harder to hide from the impact of bad leadership as well as good leadership.

There are several forms of public accountability that are not only compatible but actually supportive of school-based initiative. One way to improve the odds, compatible with good schooling, is to increase constituent voices about the work not only of their own school but also of other people's schools in terms of student outcomes, equity, and fiscal integrity. Experience suggests that networks of schools can offer us an opportunity to have the best of both worlds: individuality and close external accountability. We need ways to hold schools up to a mirror, to ask "Is this what you meant to be doing?" We need to tackle professional myopia and defensiveness. We assume that school children learn by being exposed to criticism, but we have not transferred that to the way teachers and schools learn. For this to happen, we need to create instruments that are consistent with the very qualities that led us originally to propose small schools: instruments responsive to often nonstandard ways to maintain high standards. What strong democratic schooling needs are new forms of horizontal accountability—focused on the collective work of the school.

The first step involves creating stronger internal accountability systems, such as those pioneered in places like Central Park East Secondary School, Urban Academy, and International High School, which use both peers and external critics—college faculty, parents, community members, and other high school teachers—to examine their students' work. It's the job of the faculty, for instance, to grade its own students and determine when they meet its school-wide standards, a task too few schools take seriously today. But the faculty, in turn, needs to be publicly accountable for such judgments—to both its internal constituents and the larger public as well.

At the next step, schools must answer formally to each other for the quality of their work. Through the creation of networks of sister schools, not uncommon in private schooling, we can learn how to look at each other's work as critical friends—with the accent on both criticism and friendship. (Such networks can also serve to make up for any problems of scale, if schools choose to use them that way.) Schools that provide feedback on the work of sister schools are creating built-in professional-development tools as well as a powerful form of parent and community education. There is nothing better for one's own learning curve than having formally to observe and provide support to others.

Thus networks in addition need "cooler" non-collegial audiences to answer to. For this we need formal review panels—public auditors—composed of both critical friends and more distanced and skeptical publics to attest to the credibility of networks and the work of their schools. It is such bodies that must demand convincing evidence that the network of schools under review is doing its job, is on the right track, is acting responsibly. Such review panels must ultimately be responsible to the larger, democratically chosen public authorities.

And finally, all of the above—teachers, parents, assessors, legislators, and the public—need a shared body of credible information, actual student work as well as statistical data, as evidence upon which to build their reflections and judgments.

These are the essentials for creating public credibility, but they are also the essentials for producing good schools. The task of these varied groups of observers—the school's immediate community, the networkers, and the external review panels—is not to find the one "right answer" but to push those closest to the action to act with greater enlightenment.

It's no idle dream. In New York City alone, with the support of funds from the Annenberg Challenge, nearly 100 small schools have broken down into 20 such self-chosen networks and begun the work of shared support and accountability to each other. Nearly 100 more are in planning stages. Simultaneously a review-panel system to accredit such networks and to maintain audits of their work is in formation. Also under way is the creation of a system for collecting credible and accessible data. Meanwhile, the kinds of freedoms and financial flexibility schools will obtain in return for heightened accountability are being examined, as the system explores ways to reinvent its operations. The largest city in the land may end up with the biggest experiment on the potential of smallness.

CONCLUSION

We periodically imagine that we can avoid the messiness of human judgments and create a foolproof "automatic" system to make everyone good or smart or intelligent—or at least, pretend to. Then we get upset at the bureaucracy it inevitably spawns. But if juries of our peers will do for deciding life-and-death matters of law, why not juries of our peers to decide life-and-death matters of education? As Winston Churchill once said about democracy itself, nothing could be more flawed, except for all of the alternatives. Of course, juries need guidelines, a body of precedents, rules of procedure, evidence, and the requirement to reach a publicly shared decision. This will not come easily or overnight; and like democracy itself it rests on restoring levels of mutual trust we seem inclined to abandon altogether. To our peril.

The principle we need to keep forefront in our minds is clear: How will this or that policy impact upon the intelligent and responsible behavior of the people closest to the students (as well as the students themselves). That's the litmus test. Creating forms of governance and accountability that are mindful first and foremost of their impact upon effective relationships between teachers, children, and families will not be an easy task; it may not even show a blip on next year's test scores, but shortcuts that bypass such relationships are inefficient.

If we do it right, we might in the process help create responsible and caring communities that are more powerful than those adultless subcultures that dominate far too many of our children's lives and that endanger our larger common community. The problem we face is, after all, more than "academic."

REFERENCE

Chubb, J., & Moe, T. (1990). *Politics, markets, and America's schools*. Washington, D.C.: Brookings Institution.

CHAPTER 13

Contexts of Productive Learning, Governance, Charter Schools, Pilot Schools, the Creation of Settings, and the Wailing Wall

Seymour Sarason

In a paper I wrote in 1965, I said that if the educational-reform movement continued as it was in terms of substantive focus and style of intervention, I held out no hope for its success, even partial success.[1] With each of my subsequent publications, my prediction became more explicit. *The Culture of the School and the Problem of Change* (1971) and *The Predictable Failure of Educational Reform* (1990) are but two examples of the course of my thinking. Back in the 1960s and 70s most people willingly approved dramatically increased expenditures for school reform. They did not expect immediate improvement, but they certainly did not expect that by the end of the millennium their expectations would confirm the adage that the more things change, the more they remain the same.

Indeed, today many people no longer believe that increased expenditures will accomplish anything, and among these "many people" I include a far from minuscule number in the educational community who will not say publicly what they say privately (to me, at least). That is especially true in regard to our urban schools, which they regard as lost causes.

A number of questions have to be asked and answered (however provisional and incomplete the answers) if one seeks to judge and redirect reform efforts. The three important questions are:

1. Why is it that despite the billions and billions of dollars expended in the post–World War II era, the results have been so meager or, some would say, nonexistent?
2. You can always find a classroom here and a classroom there, a school here and a school there (almost always an elementary school), the

191

features and accomplishments of which are exemplary. Why is it that these isolated instances remain isolated, that is, they do not spread or diffuse to other classrooms, or to other schools in the system?

3. Why is it that as students go from the elementary to the middle and high school their level of boredom and disinterest discernibly increases?

I regard the second question as the important one, because how you answer it speaks volumes about the other two questions. The brief answer to the second question is that our educational system has all of the features of a nonlearning system: It learns nothing from its failures, and it is incapable of learning from and then spreading a "success." This is not explainable on the basis of individual psychology, there are no villains who have willed this state of affairs. It is a system of parts that are not coordinated in a structural sense and among which there is little agreement about the purposes of schooling; indeed, the parts are frequently in an adversarial relationship.

What are the parts of the system? Teachers, school administrators, boards of education, the state department of education, colleges and universities, the state legislature and executive branches, the federal government, parents—these are the parts that make up the system. In one way or another, directly or indirectly, with varying degrees of formal power, each of these parts plays some role in determining what goes on in a classroom. Despite the fact that there are hundreds of thousands of classrooms, the behavioral and programmatic regularities in these classrooms is highly similar (Goodlad, 1984; Sarason, 1971, 1996). How the classrooms are organized, the role of teachers and students, the content of the books, and the allocation of time to this or that activity are some of the similarities. (Teachers ask questions, students answer them; each student works alone, teachers teach a whole class, not individuals; the teacher is the classroom's legislature, executive, and judiciary).

It is understandable if you observe a classroom that you will "explain" what you see in terms of a teacher and a group of students heterogeneous in numerous ways. There is a truth to that explanation, but it is a partial truth because the major regularities you observe bear to some degree, large or small, the imprimaturs of other parts of the larger system. So, for example, how teachers teach is incomprehensible apart from how they were taught to teach in colleges and universities.

Sitting in classrooms you see teachers and students. You cannot see a system. A system is literally a creation, a conception, intended (a) to help us identify parts, (b) to flesh out their interactions, and (c) to give us direction for how to go about improving the system. For all practical purposes the educational reform movement has not been informed or guided by a systems way of thinking, which in large measure explains why we have learned so little from the far more frequent failures.

Let me illustrate the point by reference to the tragedy of the *Challenger* spaceship. Very quickly after the spaceship exploded and an investigation committee was appointed, attention riveted on failure of the O-rings to function because of the relatively cold outside temperature. The problematic relationship between temperature and the O-rings had been recognized and discussed *before* takeoff. Why was the takeoff not postponed? The long and short of the answer was that the agendas of representatives of private contractors and diverse parts of the NASA bureaucracy were conflicting. The launching of a spaceship is the end result of a very complicated system of parts very deliberately organized to avoid decisions that in any way to any degree might be a threat to safety. What the investigative committee determined was that, yes, the O-rings were the immediate "cause," but that "cause" was the end result of a system of adversarial parts marked by concerns about publicity, politics, money, status, and adherence to predetermined schedules. From the outset the investigating committee assumed that their task was not only to determine the immediate cause but also to determine if and how that cause was embedded in a system conducive to producing it and, therefore, requiring a change in the system. The decision to launch the *Challenger* was preceded by many other decisions by representatives of different parts of the system, not all of which were at Cape Canaveral. You can see a launch on TV, but you cannot see the system that makes it possible. In some vague way we know that a launch is the end result of the workings of a system, but it takes a tragedy for us to recognize that how a system is supposed to work is not the way it does work. We are far from recognizing that in regard to our educational system.

The concept of a system is bedrock to the sciences. In the post–World War II era, there have been more than a few scientists who have indulged their rescue fantasy to improve schooling. Back in the 1950s and 60s, we had the new math, new physics, new biology, new social studies. In no way do I suggest that these scientists were dealing with unimportant problems. But I do contend that in regard to these problems they sought, or at least assumed, that their accomplishments would spread, that is, their demonstrations would generalize far beyond the sites of their demonstrations. The spread was minimal if not nonexistent. It is ironic that none of these scientists transferred their system's way of thinking to education. Each identified a "cause" of poor school performance and sought to repair it. They did not ask: What is there about the system that produces the cause I seek to repair? They failed for a number of reasons (Sarason, 1971, 1996), but certainly among the most important is their failure to think in system terms.

Kenneth Wilson (Wilson & Daviss, 1996), a physicist, is the first scientist to deal forthrightly with education as a system. Aside from his emphasis on the present system as a nonlearning one, he directs our attention to the role of the continuous improvement or self-correcting features of a successful system. Needless to say, in the most unvarnished way, he says that our existing system is notable for its inability for self-correction. Indeed, he asserts that the present system is literally incapable of assimilating the self-correction process; it is unrescuable.

I agree. Beginning in 1965, orally and in print, I predicted that the reform movement would go nowhere. I elaborated on that prediction in *The Culture of the School and the Problem of Change* (Sarason, 1971). The limitations of that book are revealed in its title in that my focus was on one part of the educational system. I was and am gratified by the reception of that book. But soon after its publication I began, albeit slowly, to confront the system qua system, but resisted coming to the conclusion that however cogent my analysis of the school was, that school was embedded in a system that would continue to defeat its efforts to improve features in the culture of the school I had critically described. That explains my enthusiasm for Wilson's book. Wilson has not (yet) given us a blueprint of what it means to deal with the system qua system, although aspects of a blueprint are given in his book. I shall return to this point at the end of this chapter.

Let me turn to a reform that is getting a good deal of play and allows me to elaborate on some of the points I have made above. It is a reform that is heartening and disheartening, although I predict that the disheartening aspects will prevail.

I refer to charter schools sanctioned by state legislatures, allowing a small number of schools to go their own way, so to speak, schools that are not subject to the rules, regulations, and practices of the local or state board of education.[2] In the presidential campaign of 1996, both Dole and Clinton supported charter schools; indeed, Clinton said he was increasing the budget item to support such state programs, that is, there would be support for 3,000 charter schools.

What is heartening about the concept of the charter school is that it is the first "official" recognition that the present system is unrescuable; that is, it is a system inimical to change. The system is antichange, it is an obstacle to innovation, it is incapable of self-correction or self-improvement. A school has to depart from the system if it is to achieve its purposes. Neither Dole nor Clinton saw or made that point. In addition, Dole promised to eliminate the U.S. Department of Education on the assumption that by eliminating or mammothly reducing the federal government as a part of the system, the states would be unleashed from the bureaucratic intrusions of distant Washington. For Dole there was nothing wrong with the existing system that eliminating the federal part of it would not cure. Historically, that is nonsense; to voice such an opinion indicates ignorance of why and how the states pleaded for federal intervention (Sarason, 1998). To suggest that before the federal government became a part (a stakeholder) in the educational system, state control and supervision of schools had *any* of the features of a self-correcting system is truly to play loose with history. In any event, the implicit significance of charter schools cannot be overestimated.

There are several disheartening aspects of the charter-school movement. The first is that the charter school is being proclaimed as a kind of solution to the national problem of improving educational outcomes (witness President Clinton's intention to dramatically increase the number of such schools). The fact is that in the enabling legislation, state and federal, for these schools, there are no funds provided to describe, study, and evaluate the complicated process by which such a school is created, actualized, and develops, that is, the problems encountered, the modes of dealing with those problems, and the basis they provide for judging partial or complete success or failure. Even ahead of time, we know that these schools will vary in accomplishing their stated goals; we can say that with certainty. But we can also say with certainty that in the absence of dispassionate description and analysis, we will not know how to explain success or failure. The concept of a charter school is too important in its policy implications to depend on anecdotal evidence or personal opinion; in matters of educational reform, we have been down that road far too many times. Consistent with Wilson's (Wilson & Daviss, 1996) position, the charter schools now being created have to be considered as Model A, to be superseded by Model B (and then C), on the basis of carefully obtained evidence. Increasing the number of such schools does not mean their quality improves. Put in another way, unless the charter-school movement is informed by self-correcting, self-improving processes, we will get action uninformed by wisdom, and unreliable opinion, not the learning we need. Generally speaking, words like *research* and *evaluation* have far more odious implications in state governments than in the federal government. I am not talking about so-called basic research but research-evaluation applied to an important practical problem, the answers to which have important practical consequences.

With regard to the second disheartening factor about charter schools, refer to *The Creation of Settings and the Future Societies* (Sarason, 1972). That book addressed a problem that previously had not been formulated: Why do so many settings fail or fall far short of their mark? I defined a setting as one where two or more people get together over a sustained period of time to achieve agreed-upon goals. Marriage is the smallest instance, and a national revolution (e.g., American, French, Russian) is the largest, and certainly most ambitious, instance. Why I got interested in that problem and what I did to experience it are beyond the confines of this chapter, but several ideas nevertheless apply here. The first is that there are *predictable* problems encountered in the creation of a new setting. Especially important are the definition of resources and their limitation; intergroup dynamics that gloss over or ignore signs of disjunction between means and ends; and insensitivity to the reactions and perceptions of existing settings. A new setting is best described and studied concurrently, not retrospectively, because the seeds of failure or success sprout early. (Either way is methodologically daunting).

The charter school is an instance of the creation of a new setting. As I said earlier, as far as I can determine, neither the states nor the federal government have budgeted for careful studies of these schools. I would be surprised if no foundation seeks to support such a study, although my opinion of the track record of foundations supporting research-evaluation of educational policies—especially if such studies require a longitudinal methodology—is a dismal one. My age and health have prevented me from experiencing the creation of these new schools directly (I offer this as a disclaimer of sorts), but I have been able to talk with people who have direct knowledge about some of them. The information I have obtained confirms what I privately had predicted: These start-up schools are ignorant of the predictable problems I discuss in my book and, therefore, make almost all the predictable mistakes. These are not the words of someone who believes he has cornered the market on the truth about the problematics of creating a setting. But in more than 25 years that book has been in print, I have been sent at least a score of manuscripts (mostly book size) from individuals who wanted me to know that what I had written was largely correct. None of these authors could find a publisher.

I am plugging neither my book nor my ideas. I am trying to make the point that precisely because charter schools represent the most forthright critique of and challenge to the existing educational system and are being applauded as the best thing since sliced bread, charter schools' advocates should feel the deepest obligation to study them in as careful and diverse ways as possible so that subsequent generations of charter schools can benefit from the successes and failures of earlier models. Absent such studies of a sample of Model A charter schools, there may well be no Model B or C. That would add another chapter in the unpleasant history of educational reform. The existing system is a nonlearning and non-self-correcting one. The same appears to be characteristic of the way in which charter schools are being conceived and implemented. I hope I am proved wrong, even though I do not relish the possibility of having to engage in the process of self-correction.

Charter schools represent an alternative to how a single school can be governed. This gives rise to the more general question, How might a new educational *system* be governed? I began to ask that question the more I read about the Constitutional Convention of 1787. That convention was called to repair the inadequacies and dangers of the Articles of Confederation. It became evident, especially to James Madison, that the articles were unrescuable; and, rather than engage in an effort of repair, the assembled group started, so to speak, from scratch. Over several hot, steamy months in Philadelphia, they fashioned a historically momentous document. (Slavery was the fateful blind spot, of course.) It was not easy. The issues—historical, moral, political, organizational, economic, geographic, racial (slavery), and the variations in the size of the colonies—were complex indeed, and the framers had the wisdom to include a self-correcting mechanism, that is, the amending process.

I refer here to the 1787 convention for two reasons, one is a glimpse of the obvious, the other somewhat less so. Both have direct bearing on my conviction that in regard to a new governance system for education, nothing will ever happen unless and until national political leadership convenes the equivalent of a constitutional convention—in size comparable to that of 1787—to critique our existing educational system and to outline changes or propose a new system. Let me just add at this point that in recent years I have asked scores of individuals and groups this question: If you were starting from scratch, would you come up with the existing system? No one ever said yes (Sarason, 1998).

The most striking feature of the 1787 convention is that its participants may well be the most mature, intelligent, probing, dedicated group that has ever been assigned a crucial public task. The related but less obvious feature is that they did not want or need a staff of experts to help them analyze and define the issues. By virtue of direct experience, they knew the issues, which is not to say that they did not, initially at least, have dramatically different views about how to deal with those issues. And by virtue of education and an unexcelled interest in and grasp of moral-religious, political history, they were the experts. They were not chosen for purposes of window dressing, that is, putting their imprimatur on a final report written by others. For them the convention was not a part-time activity. At great personal cost to themselves and their families (given what transportation was like in those days), they gave their all. And they had the courage to depart from what was and sail on truly uncharted seas. They did not do this with complete confidence; they knew the risks and uncertainties of what they were proposing. But they also knew that what was could never be the basis for forging a nation.

My call for a commission on the governance of education, to be appointed by both the President and the Congress, will understandably generate sardonic laughter among those who are familiar with the history of such commissions. For example, those who are familiar with President Reagan's commission that gave us *A Nation at Risk* may claim, as I do, that with friends like that, education need never worry about having enemies. It is a report containing pallid generalities, and a sense of urgency and crisis followed by nothing resembling a concrete idea or proposal—in short, a pretentious sermon. But then again, it is par for the course for politicians (and other well-meaning individuals) to talk about educational reform in ways that confirm Mencken's maxim that for every important public problem there is a simple answer that is wrong. But in expressing their various opinions, they also confirm the adage that it is hard to be completely wrong.

Although it is true that on an actuarial basis, one should not expect federally sponsored commissions or groups to issue reports that clearly have their intended consequences, there are two instructive exceptions (Sarason, 1998). The first is the group that during World War II had the task of planning for services to and care of what would be an unprecedented number of battle casualties. Neither past performance, location, or quality of its facilities, nor the structure and ethos of its organization enabled the then Veterans Administration (VA) to discharge its obligation to World War II veterans. The long and short of it is that a planning group came up with concrete proposals that essentially created a new VA and also changed medical education in general. The second exception is the federally sponsored Joint Commission on Mental Health, which dramatically changed states' approaches to mental health problems, especially in relation to state mental hospitals which were essentially poor-quality, overpopulated warehouses that, like VA hospitals, were in the middle of nowhere and unrelated to communities and centers of training and research.

Why did the plans of these two groups break new ground?

1. There was a recognition that drastic changes were in order, not only in the professional communities but, crucially, *at the highest layers of political authority and leadership* (that, of course, was also the case in 1787).
2. The groups were comprised of people with long, *direct* experience with the problems with which they had to deal (again, as in 1787). Few, if any, of the participants were selected in terms of window dressing. It is obvious, at least to me, that most were chosen because of their dissatisfaction with the past system and its practices.

3. They did not focus on considerations of cost but rather on the over-arching question: What needs to be done to improve the quality of care? (In the case of the 1787 convention, the question front and center was how to harmonize central power and authority, on the one hand, with individual liberty, on the other hand). They did not need to do extensive studies to demonstrate what was obvious: The existing system was dramatically costly, those costs would escalate, quality would not improve.

4. Precisely because of the level of political sponsorship of the groups and of the social and economic climate of the early postwar years, the groups had reason to believe that their proposals would be widely diffused.

In regard to education, the first feature above is simply not in the picture; that is, political leaders show no understanding that the governance of the educational system is a major cause of the system's inability to engage in self-correction. It would be relevent here to refer to Dr. Linda Darling-Hammond's report on preparatory programs for educators, a report reflecting the views of a group whose members (with two or three exceptions) had had long and direct experience with these programs. I have to assume that the participants were not chosen because they were content with things the way they were, although they by no means held identical viewpoints.

I hope I am wrong in predicting that her report will go nowhere, have no impact, and will be said again by another group 10 or 20 years from now. In the months since that report appeared, I am amazed (I should not be, but hope does spring eternal) how many people in and out of the educational and political communities have not heard of it, even though its contents are compelling, disturbing, and call for action long overdue. It has received no play in the mass media. Just as there are "nonpersons," this will be a "nonreport."

Why is it that no president or others in high elective office have ever commissioned that kind of report by that kind of group? One does not have to be an expert or a savant to conclude that, given the inadequacies of our schools, *maybe* the preparation of educators is *one* (not the only) of the major problems we need to understand and seek to change. Nevertheless, the more general point is that at whatever point you start, the governance of the system—if ignored, glossed over, or shortsightedly bypassed—will be the greatest, most resistant obstacle to your efforts. And it is the governance issue that requires political leadership to take the initial step to get it clarified. Absent that step, we will continue to prove that the more things change, the more they stay the same.

Governance is a can of worms, as I indicate in *How Schools Might Be Governed and Why* (1997), in which I sketch a new form of governance. That book contains my provisional ruminations. Clarification of the governance issue is beyond the capabilities of one person. The end result of the 1787 convention could not have been achieved by one person. The ratification of the Constitution was possible largely because of political initiatives and leadership; even so, final satisfaction required the addition of the Bill of Rights.

What are the major purposes of educational governance? Not all major purposes are of equal value. Is there one overarching purpose, which, if not achieved, makes the achievement of other purposes unlikely? In all of my writings, my answer has been that the overarching purpose is promoting and sustaining contexts of productive learning. The single best *visual* example of what I mean is the movie *Mr. Holland's Opus*. In the first half of the film, Mr. Holland's approach to and practices with his high school students illustrate a context of *unproductive* learning with which we are all too familiar. His students are bored, hostile, semisomnolent. In the second half of the film, Mr. Holland has his epiphany: He is forced to recognize that he had been totally insensitive to "where the learners were and had started." Armed with his predetermined, calendar-driven curriculum and assuming that his knowledge and love of music could be poured into and assimilated by his students, he had produced the opposite of what he had intended. He did not know—he had never been taught to know—that the artistry of teaching inheres in the ability to start where the learner is and to use that starting point to build bridges to new knowledge and outlooks heretofore not in the student's ken. William James and John Dewey discussed this a century ago in regard to the classroom.

There is another way of making the point. What if you asked university professors this question: How do you justify the existence of a university? In one or another way, the answer would be that the obligation of the university is to create and sustain contexts in which its faculty learns, changes, and grows in relation to the responding professor's interests. You can have a university with no or very few students. The assumption is that the faculty will create a similar context for their students. What if you ask school teachers this question: How do you justify the existence of an elementary, middle, or high school? The clear answer would be that it is for students, period. *If contexts for productive learning do not exist for teachers, they cannot create and sustain that context for students.* And that is precisely the dilemma of students and teachers in the model American classroom, and that is most glaringly true in our urban schools. The present system of governance cannot rectify this state of affairs because that very system is its major bulwark. As I said earlier, the founding fathers were crystal clear about the overarching purposes of governing, and this knowledge informed everything they taught and did. All things considered, they did a pretty good job.

You can talk about and legislate for high standards, you can change curricula, resort to block scheduling, advocate for vouchers and charter schools, require teachers to take more courses, lengthen the school year, involve parents, support site-based management. You can do all these and kindred more, but if the governance system is not explicitly designed for and obligated to creating and sustaining contexts of productive learning, what we have now will continue to disappoint and, by any cost-benefit analysis, remain wasteful in the extreme.

By temperament I do not suffer from dysphoria. The one exception is when I look back over my decades of experience in and writings about educational reform. In that regard my frustration is best conveyed by my favorite Jewish joke. A journalist was assigned to the Jerusalem bureau of his newspaper. He got an apartment overlooking the wailing wall. After several weeks he realized that whenever he looked at the wall, he saw the same old Jew praying there. The journalist wondered whether there was a publishable story here. He went down to the wall, introduced himself, and said, "You come every day to the wall. What are you praying for?" The old Jew replied, "What am I praying for? In the morning I pray for world peace, then I pray for the brotherhood of man. I go home, have a glass of tea, and I come back to the wall to pray for the eradication of illness and disease from the earth." The journalist was captivated by the old Jew's sincerity and persistence. "You mean you have been coming to the wall every day to pray for these things?" The old Jew nodded. "How long have you been coming to the wall to pray for these things?" The old Jew became reflective and then replied, "How long? Maybe 20, 25 years." The journalist was flabbergasted. "You mean you have been coming to the wall every day for all those years to pray for all these things?" The old Jew nodded. "How does it feel to come to the wall to pray every day over so many years for these things?"

The old Jew replied, "How does it feel? It's like talking to a wall."

NOTES

1. A different version of this chapter appeared in *Daedalus* as "Some Features of a Flawed Educational System."

2. The degree of autonomy varies from one state to another. In Connecticut half of the 24 charter schools would be the responsibility of that state's department of education, although the degree of responsibility is unclear. Because *any*

charter school has to gain approval from the local board before its application can be studied and approved by the state department of education, that school must explain why "leaving" the local school district would be necessary for it to improve educational outcomes. That the local system may not look kindly on the implicit or explicit criticism of its workings, and that such criticism may result in compromises in the substance of the application, is not an indulgence in fantasy. For reasons I have stated, we will never know what (if any) consequences flow from such potential dynamics.

REFERENCES

Goodlad, J. (1984). *A place called school.* New York: McGraw-Hill.

Sarason, S. (1971). *The culture of the school and the problem of change.* New York: Teachers College Press.

Sarason, S. (1972). *The creation of settings and the future societies.* San Francisco: Jossey-Bass.

Sarason, S. (1990). *The predictable failure of educational reform.* San Francisco: Jossey-Bass.

Sarason, S. (1996). *Revisiting "The culture of the school and the problem of change."* New York: Teachers College Press.

Sarason, S. (1997). *How schools might be governed and why.* New York: Teachers College Press.

Sarason, S. (1998). *Charter Schools: Another flawed educational reform?* New York: Teachers College Press.

Wilson, K. & Daviss, B. (1996). *Redesigning education.* New York: Teachers College Press.

CHAPTER 14

The New American School District

Evans Clinchy

As Seymour Sarason eloquently points out (and all of our authors seem to agree with him), the primary obstacle to a radically transformed and much more productive system of American public education is not any one part of our existing system but *the unrescuable system itself.*

Our failure to educate all of our children and young people well cannot be accounted for simply by saying that our schools lack high academic standards, or that we do not have a strong enough system of testing and accountability, or that the teachers and administrators in our public schools are incapable of doing the job well, or that parents are insufficiently involved, or that our colleges and universities remain aloof and unconcerned about the public schools.

Nor, as Deborah Meier and our charter- and pilot-school people all point out, is it that we lack knowledge about what ought to be done, about what works. There is impressive evidence supporting the idea that schools based on Meier's "magic three" of smallness, self-governance, and choice and Sarason's "principles of productive learning environments" can be created and can succeed in providing outstanding educational experiences for their students. We know what such schools look like, what they need in order to be created in the first place, and what they then need in order to survive and prosper.

This doesn't mean that "we" have all the answers. But as Meier and our other authors put it, we do now know enough about what actually works in real schools with real children and young people of all shapes, sizes, and colors to understand what needs to be done in order to begin to allow those environments to become the Meierian/Sarasonian norm rather than the exotic exception. That is, we know how a "rescued" system *should* work, and we even know many of the new rules and regulations that must be the backbone of any such new design if it is going to succeed.

In short, we do have enough of the answers to warrant large-scale, carefully planned and executed experiments to test these ideas in a broader—indeed, a system-wide—arena. It should also be stressed here that although most of the action along these lines is currently taking place in our large urban systems, *everything said about the unrescuability of those city systems is fully and equally applicable to our suburban and rural systems, that is, to all schools and all school systems throughout the land.*

But we also know that changes of this magnitude are not going to be accomplished by any one part of the system all by itself—not by the teachers in individual schools, not by teachers and administrators unions, not by the central administrators in our school districts, not by outside community groups, and not by local school boards or state boards and departments of education or by the U.S. Department of Education.

It will take the *collaborative* efforts of all these people and all these institutions to create such a new system, very much including our institutions of higher education—the colleges and universities that control much of what goes on in our elementary and secondary schools.

The ideal beginning of such a national collaboration would be, of course, Sarason's educational version of a national constitutional convention, but even he admits that such a miracle is unlikely to happen. In its stead, we can only look to a greatly expanded series of local, state, and national networks that share the aims and convictions of the people speaking in this book.

ONE SUCH NETWORK

In 1993, school-reform leaders in Chicago, Denver, New York, Seattle, and Philadelphia met to create a network to promote the decentralized reform of their educational systems. They called themselves the Cross City Campaign for Urban School Reform.

The credo of this collective of reformers was succinctly summed up in the campaign's seminal document, *Reinventing the Central Office, A Primer for Successful Schools*,[1] in these words:

> Students succeed in schools that have high standards, that are small
> enough so that students and teachers know each other well, that
> have authority and resources for teaching and learning, and that are
> accountable for results. But for schools to be accountable for results,
> schools and their communities need authority. They need to be able
> to decide what and how they will teach to meet high district stan-

dards, who will be hired, and how they will spend their funds and use their buildings.

The reformers went on to advocate "a fundamental revision of urban public school systems, one that shifts all funds and most authority to the schools and dismantles centralized bureaucratic structures." They then described in considerable detail "what a model decentralized system would look like." The model covers six areas: governance, budgets, curriculum and instruction, personnel, facilities, and accountability.

In each of these areas the campaigners spelled out how responsibility and authority for the basic functions in each of these areas should be distributed—what authority and responsibilities should be lodged at the level of the individual school, what authority and responsibility should remain with the central district, and what role external organizations can and should play.

They also listed some of the ways in which these decentralization plans can "go astray" and be done in by recalcitrant bureaucracies and politicians.

The one area in which the campaign does not take a strong and clear stand is the necessity for public school choice, one of Meier's "magic three" requirements. The reformers do stress the necessity for the "sharing of a school's mission" on the part of everyone in a school (staff, students, and parents). They also give a passing endorsement to charter schools, thus implying that a system of public school choice (and only *public* school choice) should exist on the part of not only all parents and older students but all school staff. But they do not explicitly include such choice as one of the primary requirements for any radically decentralized school system.

It is therefore of great importance to reiterate the arguments set forth in this book's introductory chapter. *We need to make it clear that in any truly democratic school system based upon decentralization and parent and professional choice, it cannot be the task of the people running the system to advocate and impose any one true and only way of educating children and young people on all parents and all schools. No federal, state, or local education authority can or should impose on everyone any single set of academic standards, any single curriculum, any single way of organizing and running a school, or any single set of assessment methods.*

What is needed here is a genuine diversity of educational approaches requested by every school system's parents and professional staff. As we have already noted in the discussion of magnet schools, this diversity will run the gamut from traditional to very untraditional, progressive schools.

Those of us who strongly advocate the creation of new, small, autonomous, and very progressive schools can both hope and expect that many of the schools in such a system of diversity and choice can and will be the kind of schools we believe are best for children and young people. But just as we do not believe that the traditional, nonprogressive model should be undemocratically imposed on everyone, we do not believe that our model should be so imposed.

What we are arguing for is a genuinely and democratically free marketplace of educational ideas and approaches within our public school systems. If, in the natural course of the cultural evolution of such school systems, new, small, autonomous, progressive schools prove to be the most successful and therefore the most desired approach to schooling, then more such schools can and will be selected. As they are increasingly requested by parents and teachers, more such schools will be created, and in this process, unwanted schools will not be chosen and will gradually die out.

If, on the other hand, the reverse occurs and it is the new, small, autonomous, and progressive schools that are not chosen and thus die out, well, so be it. It will not be the first time that a good idea has gone down to historical defeat.

ONE POSSIBLE WAY OF GETTING TO DECENTRALIZATION, DIVERSITY, AND CHOICE WHILE MAINTAINING DEMOCRATIC EQUITY

If we decide that what we want is decentralized local systems in which not only small, autonomous schools but parent and professional choice are integral parts, we will have to revise our current conception and operation of those systems. Foremost in this revision must be the process by which we gradually replace educationally antiquated schools with new ones.

The pilot schools in Boston and the new, small schools created in New York and elsewhere certainly give us some vital information about how this can be accomplished. But in both those cases, the schools were created largely by inspired educators who, if not always eager, were at least willing to take on the entrenched bureaucracies of their school systems and create the new schools.

But in neither of these systems is there yet a comprehensive, permanent transformation of system structure, making such schools the norm. And in particular, as we saw in the Pearlman, French, Rizzo, and Sherman chapters here, neither of these systems (nor any of the systems described in the Cross City Campaign documents) has yet created and permanently installed a carefully designed, system-wide process for creating new schools that includes not only school people but all parents, all teachers and principals, all older students, a broad spectrum of community groups including the business community, and, one can sincerely hope, the higher education establishment, without which little is going to happen.

Such a process has been embryonically explored over the past 20 or so years in two Massachusetts communities, the cities of Lowell and Worcester. When faced in the late 1970s and early 1980s with the state-mandated necessity to desegregate their school systems, each of these cities set up a comprehensive citywide planning process as the first and most crucial step in its desegregation and system-redesign plans.

To begin the process, the local school board and central administration in each of the systems created a Citywide Parent Planning Council made up of two elected parent representatives from each school in the city (and because many of the elected parents happened to be teachers in the system, the councils ended up being parent/teacher councils). Although the councils were operationally supported by the central administration (and were financially supported by the state and federal governments) and each had members of the teachers and administrators unions as ex-officio participants, only the elected school representatives had voting power.

The councils then conducted extensive studies of the possible range of educational approaches the members of the council thought their school systems might wish to create in the form of magnet schools. Indeed, the ultimate aim of the entire process was that eventually *every* school in each of the systems would become a voluntarily integrated magnet school that could be chosen by both parents and teachers, the only restriction on such choice being that all schools must end up having desegregated student bodies.

In order to determine that full range of educational possibilities, the council members (with the assistance of the central administration, outside consultants, and local higher education institutions) examined the burgeoning magnet-school movement, consulted the historical record, and sought out every other possible source of relevant and useful information. As often as possible, teams of parents, teachers, and administrators visited examples of that full range, including not only very traditional models (among them Mortimer Adler's Paideia schools) but also very untraditional, progressive schools such as Montessori, "open," integrated-day, and "micro-society" models. Many of these schools also featured curricular specialties, such as the fine and performing arts, science and technology, the humanities, global studies, and so forth. In Lowell, federal desegregation magnet-school assistance funding enabled those teams to visit such potential models all over the country.

Once the councils in Lowell and Worcester finished this preliminary information-gathering part of the process, they sat down to the arduous task of deciding upon the eight to ten models they thought would be best suited to their particular school system and most desired by the system's parents and teachers. On the basis of the models selected, they designed surveys that were distributed in all appropriate languages to all parents in the city (and in Worcester, to all teachers as well). The surveys were aimed at discovering (a) whether parents really wanted to be able to choose the kind of schooling their children received and whether teachers really wanted to be able to choose the kind of schooling they practiced, and (b) whether parents would be willing to abandon their neighborhood schools and put their children on buses in order to get them to the school of their choice (if such proved necessary). In the Worcester case, the council also wanted to know whether teachers would be willing to transfer voluntarily from their present school to a school employing the kind of schooling they wished to practice.[2]

When these surveys were conducted back in the 1980s, many observers inside and outside the systems (but not those of us outsiders who were helping to design and conduct the surveys) expected that many parents might feel insufficiently informed to make such choices or even unable to really know and decide about the kind of schooling that would best benefit their children. Indeed, some school system people predicted that the return rate would be as low as 10% of the city's public school parent population (an attempt was made to reach parents of nonpublic schoolers as well, but the nonpublic schools were not eager to cooperate by providing parent names and addresses).

We were also told that if parents did choose, they would most often select the good, old-fashioned, highly academic, back-to-basics schools with which they were most familiar (and which most of them had gone to), and that it would be the teachers and principals who would choose the more innovative models. There was a further prediction that not only would parents select the traditional-model schools but poor and minority parents would be even *more* likely than the presumably better educated and therefore "more enlightened" middle-class majority parents to do so.

When the actual survey results came in, not a single one of those expectations was met. In the several Worcester surveys, for instance, the parent return rates never dropped below 50% when the returns were properly analyzed and at times ran as high as 80%, with poor and minority parents responding at a rate slightly higher than that of the majority parents. Further, the models most requested by all parents were *not* good, old-fashioned, back-to-basics schools. In Lowell, for instance, the two most popular models were the fine and performing arts and "micro-society" models, whereas in Worcester one of the most requested models was a Montessori school.

Moreover, the poor and minority parents, *not* the majority middle-class parents, more often selected the less traditional models. And further, it was the *parents* in both cities who wanted the more adventurous schools, whereas the teachers and principals more often selected the traditional models.

Over the following 16 years—and against considerable bureaucratic odds—each of these systems made essentially every school in the city an integrated school of both parent and professional choice. This is not to say that every different kind of school the parents wanted was created or that all existing schools were replaced by new, small, autonomous schools on the Meierian model. (Although in Lowell, the fine and performing arts and "micro-society" models *were* instituted as such schools; and as old schools have been replaced by new facilities, the city has developed a range of different kinds of schools.) And, of course, parental choice is not total and unconstrained, because all such choices are controlled by the necessity to guarantee that every school has a racially and ethnically integrated student body.

But now the educational diversity created in these two cities (and throughout the country where magnet schools exist) is being threatened and will be destroyed by the *Nation at Risk*/Goals 2000 "world-class" academic standards, standardized curricula, and high-stakes-testing juggernaut if that regressive movement is allowed to become the standard, uniform American educational model.

However, let us assume for a moment that such an educational and social disaster can somehow be avoided. In that case, school systems seeking educational diversity and both parent and professional choice will have created and conducted their system-wide survey process and will have discovered the full range of diverse educational approaches that parents and professional staff want the system to create. Now the system must redesign itself along the lines suggested in the previous chapters. The system should ideally have the following characteristics:

• The district must have a *permanent*, well-publicized process for creating new, small, autonomous schools, a process that continues the democratic practices embodied in the survey process itself. Such a process would enable interested principals, teachers, parents, older students, outside community organizations, artistic and cultural institutions, and even suitably reformed institutions of higher education to join together first to plan and then to create and operate not only the full range of schools requested by the surveys but all such schools as needed in the future. This process would also, of course, include the possibility of following the Richman/Monroe example of breaking large schools down into complexes of new, small schools and services.

- As the results of the survey process become known and the creation of specific new schools is approved by the local school board, the now transformed central-office structure must make this new-school planning process a reality by providing the necessary technical assistance and a budget to cover the planning and start-up costs for each new school. This would eventually include providing adequate facilities and all necessary equipment and supplies as well as assistance in the staff and student recruitment and assignment process.

- A major part of the new-school planning process would require that the planners of each new, small, autonomous school spell out in clear, nontechnical language the school's educational philosophy and pedagogical approach; a description of the school's educational mission that will be shared by all staff members, all parents, and all older students. This needs to be followed by a general outline of the school's curriculum, organizational and operational structure, disciplinary procedures, parental involvement proposals, staff-development activities, and so on. All of this planning should be done cooperatively with the revamped central administration and subject to school board approval.

- Such planning must also include a carefully designed assessment and accountability plan tailored to the specific philosophical and pedagogical mission of that particular school, a plan that may or may not include the use of standardized achievement tests, portfolios, and other means of "authentic" assessment. Again, all such assessment plans must be developed cooperatively with the central administration and subject to school board approval.

- The new-school creation process must also ensure that all such schools, and indeed all schools in the system, have the philosophical, pedagogical, curricular, organizational, staffing, and fiscal autonomy to carry out their educational missions.

- The staff and student assignment processes must be designed so that the principal, all staff members, and all students in each school are in by choice, because they all share and believe in the school's philosophical and pedagogical mission. The district's student admissions policy must also control all such admissions by parental and student choice in order to guarantee that all poor, minority, female, and special-needs students have fair and equal access to all schools and that therefore the student bodies of all schools reflect the racial, ethnic, sexual, and socioeconomic makeup of the district's student population.

- All new schools should be small enough so that everyone can know everyone else and no student can ever get lost. Small size is defined roughly as 200 for an elementary school, 300 for a middle school, and 400 for a high school. These sizes can be obtained, of course, by breaking down large schools into these smaller, autonomous units. Each school must also limit class size—no more than 20 students in a class—to enable the school to carry out its mission.

WHAT IT'S ALL ABOUT

The Cross City Campaign concludes its *Reinventing* document with a stirring declaration of what it sees as the challenge not only for their own organization but for all public schools (slightly edited here to include *all* schools everywhere):

[We] have come together motivated by crisis and hope. The current conditions in which far too many of our . . . children live, especially children of color and those whose families are poor, are intolerable. Economic injustice and lack of work have forced families to live in poverty, in settings filled with violence and drugs. Yet all communities have assets and strengths—intellectual, spiritual, cultural, and physical—that provide the essential building blocks for raising children and revitalizing community life.

Public schools are central to this hope as the institution that carries forward a vision of democracy, justice, and inclusion— grounded in community and invested in young people. We all have a stake in the millions of young people growing up . . . and attending public schools. The work over the next decade is to make the visions described in this paper a reality.

The people who have written for this book couldn't agree more.

NOTES

1. This document can be obtained from the Cross City Campaign for Urban School Reform, 407 South Dearborn St., Suite 1725, Chicago, IL 60605, Anne C. Hallett, Executive Director (312-322-4880), Fax (312-322-4885).

2. For a detailed description of these surveys and the survey process, see *Choice in Public Education* by Timothy W. Young and Evans Clinchy, New York, Teachers College Press, 1992.

Appendix:
Sources of Further Information, Networking, and Technical Assistance

The following are sources of further information on the small, autonomous school movement and the new, democratic system of public education.

Institute for Responsive Education
50 Nightingale Hall,
Northeastern University
Boston, MA 02115

Karen Mapp, President
(617-373-2595)
Fax (617-373-8924)

The Center for Collaborative Education–Metro Boston
Dan French, Executive Director
Jennifer London, Coordinator
(617-242-7730)
Fax (617-242-7723)

Dr. Thomas W. Payzant
Superintendent of Schools
Boston School Committee
26 Court St.
Boston, MA 02108

(617-635-9000)

Center for Collaborative Education
1575 Madison Ave, Room 201
New York, NY 10029

Heather Lewis, Director
(212-348-7821)

New York City Board of Education
Dr. Judith Rizzo
Deputy Chancellor
Room 1022
110 Livingston St.
New York, NY 11201

(718-935-5660)
Fax (718-935-4238)

New Visions Schools
96 Morton St., 6th Floor
New York, NY 10014

Beth Lief, President
(212-645-5110)

NCREST (National Center for Restructuring Education, Schools and Teaching)
Box 110
Teachers College,
Columbia University
New York, NY 10027

Jacqueline Ancess, Director
(212-678-4193)

The Dewey Project,
University of Vermont
Burlington, VT
Kathleen Kesson, Director

Index

About the Editor and Contributors

Jacqueline Ancess is Associate Director of the National Center for Restructuring Education, Schools, and Teaching (NCREST) at Teachers College, Columbia University, in New York. For over twenty years she has worked in the New York City school system as a teacher, school director, and district administrator.

Ann Cook is co-director of the Urban Academy, one of the schools in the Julia Richman Education Center in New York City.

Linda Darling-Hammond is Charles E. Ducommun Professor of Education at Stanford University where she heads the teacher education program. She is also Executive Director of the National Commission on Teaching and America's Future and author of *The Right To Learn*, recipient of the AERA Outstanding Book Award in 1998.

Dan French is Executive Director of the Center for Collaborative Education, Metro-Boston, in Boston, Massachusetts.

Meredith Gavrin, formerly a teacher at the Institute for Collaborative Education in New York City, is now setting up a charter school in New Haven, Connecticut called the New Haven Academy.

Beth J. Lief is Executive Director of New Visions for Public Schools in New York City.

Kemly McGregor is a doctoral candidate at Teachers College, Columbia University, and a Research Assistant at NCREST.

Deborah Meier, formerly Principal of the Central Park East Schools in New York City, a MacArthur Fellow and author of *The Power of Their Ideas*, is now Principal of the Mission Hill Pilot Elementary School in Boston, Massachussets.

Larry Myatt is Director of the Fenway Middle College Pilot High School in Boston, Massachusetts.

Linda Nathan, formerly co-director of Fenway Middle College Pilot High School in Boston, is now Headmaster of the Boston Arts Academy, a pilot school in Boston, Massachussets.

Robert Pearlman, formerly Director of Research for the Boston Teachers Union, is President of the AutoDesk Foundation in San Mateo, California.

Judith Rizzo is Deputy Chancellor for Curriculum in the New York City Public Schools.

Ellalinda Rustique-Forrester, formerly a Research Associate at the National Commission on Teaching in America's Future at Teachers College, Columbia University, is currently studying British education at London University.

Seymour Sarason is Professor Emeritus of Psychology at Yale University and author of many books on education and education reform.

David Sherman is Vice President of the United Federation of Teachers, the New York City teachers union.

David W. Zuckerman has been a school teacher, school administrator, an organizational consultant and a staff developer. He was a Senior Research Associate at NCREST and a graduate student at Teachers College, Columbia University.

Evans Clinchy, the editor, is Senior Consultant at the Institute for Responsive Education at Northeastern University in Boston, Massachusetts. He is co-author with Timothy W. Young of *Choice in Public Education,* editor of *Transforming Public Education: A New Course for America's Future* and editor of *Reforming American Education from the Bottom to the Top.*

LOGANVILLE HIGH SCHOOL